Mandy van der Velde
Paul Jansen and Neil Anderson

GUIDE TO MANAGEMENT RESEARCH METHODS

Blackwell
Publishing

© 2004 by Mandy van der Velde, Paul Jansen and Neil Anderson

BLACKWELL PUBLISHING
350 Main Street, Malden, MA 02148–5020, USA
9600 Garsington Road, Oxford OX4 2DQ, UK
550 Swanston Street, Carlton, Victoria 3053, Australia

First published 2004 by Blackwell Publishing Ltd

4   2008

Library of Congress Cataloging-in-Publication Data
Velde, Mandy van der.
  Guide to management research methods / Mandy van der Velde, Paul
Jansen, Neil Anderson.
     p. cm.
Includes bibliographical references and index.
ISBN 978-1-4051-1512-4 (pbk.: alk. paper)
1. Business–Research. 2. Management– Research. I. Jansen, Paulus Gerardus
Wilhelmus, 1954-II. Anderson, Neil, 1961-III. Title.

HD30.4.V44 2004
650′.07′2-dc21

                                            2003010086

A catalogue record for this title is available from the British Library.

Set in 10pt on 12.5pt Meridien
by Kolam Information Services Pvt. Ltd, Pondicherry, India
Printed and bound in Singapore
by Markono Print Media Pte Ltd

For further information on
Blackwell Publishing, visit our website:
http://www.blackwellpublishing.com

Guide ınagement Research Methods

CONTENTS

LIST OF FIGURES

Part I

PLANNING THE RESEARCH PROJECT

Chapter 1

INTRODUCTION

▌ 1.1 WHAT IS THE NATURE OF FUNDAMENTAL ORGANIZATIONAL RESEARCH?

The aim of fundamental organizational research is to gain insight into certain events, processes and phenomena. In this respect, fundamental organizational research is no different from any other scientific research. Fundamental organizational research, however, specifically refers to phenomena about and within organizations (for example, causes of absenteeism, effects of a particular management style, or the consequences of a particular financial reporting method).

Researchers want to describe, explain, predict and affect these phenomena. These phenomena may concern different aspects of an organization: the external environment such as suppliers, investors and clients; or the internal environment, such as personnel. The phenomena under investigation can be found at different levels: at an individual, group, organizational level; or at a societal level. All these aspects and levels are linked.

▌ 1.2 WHAT DISTINGUISHES FUNDAMENTAL ORGANIZATIONAL RESEARCH FROM APPLIED ORGANIZATIONAL RESEARCH?

In studying an organization, a researcher may have two objectives in mind:

1. To make a contribution to scientific knowledge by gaining a better understanding and explanation of organizations (*fundamental research*).

2. To make a contribution to a real-world situation by solving problems (*practical* or *applied research*).

A researcher may thus conduct research out of pure scientific interest in order to acquire general knowledge (the researcher's major aim is *to understand*) or may investigate a certain problem situation in order to solve this specific problem (the researcher's major aim is *to interfere*).

Although there are similarities between pure or fundamental, and practical or applied research, there are also clear differences. The main difference is that fundamental research primarily focuses on acquiring scientific knowledge, mostly in the form of explanations formulated in *theories*. Applied research primarily concerns real-world problems that must be solved, the focus is on *practical actions*.

To a certain extent, the difference between fundamental and applied research is artificial. Fundamental organizational research may lead to – intended or unintended – important adoptions or even a change in management. In addition, theories of a organizational scientist practically always concern issues that are relevant in real-life situations. No scientist will come up with a theory on a random issue. The occasion is usually a practical event.

Conversely, applied research may give rise to theory formulation. In solving problems, practice-oriented organizational researchers encounter new questions and problems, and find ways to solve them. By a systematic classification and analysis of their experiences, practice-oriented researchers can make a contribution to a scientific organizational theory.

Fundamental research is based on theories and abstract concepts. Therefore, in going from fundamental to applied research, concepts and their interrelationships must be operationalized. That is, they must be made concrete, specific and quantifiable. Vice versa, in going from applied to fundamental research, concrete and specific phenomena must be generalized.

An important difference between fundamental and applied research is related to the origin of the research questions. In fundamental organizational research, research questions arise from theory or scientific literature, and are therefore *created* by the researcher. In applied organizational research, research questions often stem from a particular client in an organization and are thus *presented* to the researcher. Therefore, applied organizational research often has a different *starting point*. For example, researcher and client have to exchange information or reach an agreement on the exact nature of the research question before the start of the research project.

Furthermore, fundamental organizational research and applied organizational research have different *end points*, the latter paying more attention to questions such as: What is the use of the study? For whom is this study interesting? In other words, the emphasis in applied organizational research is on usability and practical relevance.

It is important to note that – despite its focus on usability – applied organizational research is based on scientific methods. Applied research is just as scientific as fundamental research. Whether research can be qualified as scientific or not, depends on the research method – not on the research objective.

▌ 1.3 METHODOLOGICAL REQUIREMENTS AND RULES OF FUNDAMENTAL RESEARCH IN GENERAL

Fundamental research must meet a number of requirements. First, researchers must have a good knowledge of what already has been found out with respect to the research topic and should base their research questions on previous findings in the literature. A researcher cannot therefore just come up with a research question, but has to take into account all the findings from previous research.

Furthermore, researchers must stick to a number of methodological rules, reflect on them explicitly and answer for their use. Scientific research:

- is objective, reliable and precise;
- can be replicated;
- is public;
- is ethically well considered;
- presents simple answers to research questions ('parsimonious'); and
- presents general or generalized answers to research questions.

Objective means that research data are collected independently of the personal values of the researcher. *Replication* means that other researchers should be able to repeat the study. This leads us to another requirement: research must be *public*. In principle, the findings of research should be accessible for other researchers, so that they are able to repeat the research. Publicity also refers to the research design. Therefore, research reports pay a great deal of attention to the design and conduct of the research. *Ethically well considered* means that the conduct of research and its findings may not cause any harm – directly or indirectly – to all parties involved in the research. *Simple* means that the research is conducted by using a minimum number of concepts and hypotheses on the relationships between them. Generally speaking, a theory that explains a phenomenon in a simple way is preferred to a more complex theory explaining the same phenomenon. Finding answers that can be *generalized* means that the research findings should be generally valid. That is, a researcher must produce findings that can be applied to other settings.

It is important to note that one cannot meet all requirements at the same time. It may be possible to combine two requirements, for example, to seek for answers that are simple and can be generalized. However, meeting two requirements at the same time will practically always be at the expense of a third requirement. This is further illustrated in Figure 1.1.

In Figure 1.1, general research is opposed to specific research and simple research is opposed to complex research. The opposite of precise research is global research. The diagram shows that simple and precise research will typically be specific, and thus less general. Conversely, general and precise research is often complex. This illustrates that it is practically impossible to meet the three requirements of general, simple and precise research at the same time.

Most of the time, general and simple statements are not precise, but global. For example: 'Organizations that do not become more flexible and customer-oriented will not survive'. We can easily think of organizations for which this statement does not apply. Besides that, this statement leaves us with questions: flexible in what; customer-oriented to whom? General and precise statements are often not simple, but as complex as reality itself.

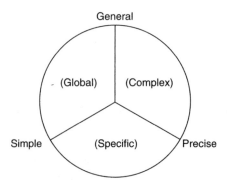

Figure 1.1 Research results: different quality criteria (from Weick, K.E. 1979. *The Social Psychology of Organizing*, 2nd ed. Reading, MA: Addison-Wesley).

For example:
'Socially supportive leadership affects the organizational commitment of independent task units, if dependent task characteristics, self-management, group cohesion and a high level of self-efficacy are observed for the group members involved'.

Often statements can be simple and precise only at the expense of generality.

For example:
'On Wednesday 15 April, 1998, the railroad traffic at Amsterdam Central Station was blocked from 16.14 for 43 minutes as a result of a power failure'.

A researcher should therefore – depending on the situation and nature of the problem – select two out of the three requirements. Meeting all three requirements at the same time is a mission impossible.

It is important to note here that a number of the requirements of objectivity, reliability, preciseness, replicability, publicity, ethics, simplicity and generalizability in conducting fundamental organizational research are harder to meet than in any other research. For example, the results of fundamental organizational research that was based on a specific organizational situation may be in conflict with the desired generalizability of the results. Replicability may also form a problem: it is not always possible to study the same phenomena in the same company in the same way. A study of organizational change is a good example: this type of research cannot be repeated under the same circumstances.

Finally, the desired publicity may be at stake because organizations are – because of competitors – not always keen on releasing information.

Meeting the requirements of scientific research is more difficult for an organizational researcher than for any other researcher. However, this does not mean that less effort is allowed: organizational researchers must take an objective, neutral and independent position at all times. They must respect all the different theories, facts, argumentation and logic in their line of reasoning. Clear and simple concepts must be defined to the maximum possible extent; and operationalized as well. Choices concerning the research method must be made explicit and answered for. Also, researchers must be aware of the ethical consequences of their actions for (persons within) the organization, during and after the research.

▋ 1.4 CLIENTS

Organizational research mostly involves clients. A client may take many forms. A client may be external, for example, a company hiring a student for doing research – or internal, for example, the HR department of the company you work for asking you to study absenteeism. You can also think of a researcher at a university conducting research for an external client, a government department for instance.

The frequency of contact between researcher and client may vary. Sometimes the parties involved prefer to have no contact at all in order to safeguard the objectivity of the research. At other times, the only function of contact is the exchange of information. The researcher is then usually the one who takes steps towards contact. He or she decides when and what information is given to whom. In this situation, the researcher is the only one responsible for the research.

Contact is more frequent and intense when the client makes decisions about the individuals and issues that will be involved in the research, the interpretation of the results, or the content of the final research report. This influence may lead to very careful and delicate negotiations between the researcher and the client. For example, the client wants particular results. By narrowing down the research design, research method and sample size, it may be possible to obtain such results. Thus, indirectly, the client manipulates data. The research may be intended to maintain an existing situation, or to justify or postpone a decision. It is important to be aware of this influence. An organizational researcher must always watch out for possible hidden intentions of a client.

The conduct of research may lead to unconscious or unintended changes. For example, some groups of people receive certain relevant information – and other groups do not. It is also possible that the research brings up issues that have never received any attention within the organization. One of the issues playing a role here is the time frame between the research and the feedback on the results. Quick availability of results is the best starting point for a more detailed discussion on the causes (of the results) and any possible changes.

ORGANIZATIONAL DIAGNOSIS

The procedures in *organizational diagnosis* provide a clear example of cooperation between a researcher and client. Organizational diagnosis centres on a preventive study of the current organizational situation aimed at a timely identification of chances and threats. First, the internal and external functioning of an organization is mapped out in order to determine which situations are considered problematic. Second, an analysis is made of the exact nature of the problem and the fields of force of the different parties. Not all the parties experience problems in the same way. An insight into these differing views is gained by looking at the differences and similarities between, for example, the functional areas in an organization, the divisions, departments, regions and hierarchic levels. The information used for this investigation may (partly) be provided by the client. In addition, the researcher determines whether the problem is an individual, group, organizational or social problem. In this way, the problems are classified, key persons are identified, and priorities – according to these key persons – priorities are listed. Finally, consent on the steps to be taken must be reached, and formal arrangements on this matter must be made.

ACTION RESEARCH

Another example is *action research*. This type of research is often used in organizations with the aim of positively affecting cooperation problems, organizational change, organizational culture, and other situations in which more persons are involved.

In action research, the researcher makes an inventory of the problem field and – together with the persons involved in the organization – gains insight into the relationship between subfields. There are two reasons for actively involving these persons in such an organizational diagnosis:

1. The research provides a shared insight for all parties involved into their own situation, enabling them to suggest solutions based on their experiences.

(Continues)

Action Research (*Continued*)
2. The research convinces parties involved of the necessity to change, and motivates them hereby.

One important function of action research is thus to reduce the resistance to change. Often, workshops (work conferences) are organized to reach explicit commitment and agreement on a change. In addition, so-called *change agents* can be employed to facilitate changes.

The report of action research mostly takes the form of an intervention that is subject to evaluation, comments and adjustments.

Summarizing, action research adds to the implementation of change. This experience also generates knowledge. In such cases, it can be qualified as scientific research that can contribute to the development of a theory, and researchers must be able to explain to fellow researchers why they used certain scientific rules.

■ 1.5 OTHER PARTIES INVOLVED IN THE RESEARCH PROJECT

Besides the client, there are other parties involved, who have their own interests and who may try to exert influence on the research. Colleagues, for example, are often concerned with evaluating the scientific relevance of research. They check whether research has been conducted according to the rules of science. Colleagues may be 'immediate' colleagues, working at the same university or research institute. They may also be professional colleagues: working on the same research topic, all over the world. Often, colleagues form groups, each of which represents a theoretic mainstream. On congresses, colloquia and in scientific journals, a forum of fellow scientists decides on the value of each individual research. In this way, the quality of the building blocks of scientific knowledge is being watched. Respondents may also have an interest in the results of the research. For example, a study is conducted into the amount of time (the number of hours) that a student spends on a specific subject. Students do not want their course to be worth fewer credits.

In general, personal influence from researchers in scientific research is reduced to the maximum possible extent. For example, the statement 'the aim of research is to extend the general body of scientific knowledge' eliminates the client as a source of influence. The methodological rules that a researcher must follow in conducting research are directed at the principle of all researchers being exchangeable.

1.6 OVERVIEW OF THE STEPS IN THE RESEARCH PROCESS

The first step in scientific (or, more specifically, fundamental organizational) research is to define the subject of research: what is the research about? Then formulate a problem definition – that is, the key question you want to address in your research. As mentioned earlier, a problem definition may originate in a scientific interest, or stem from a real-life question, for example a client in an organization.

The second step is to gather all the relevant information that can be found on the subject: reading the literature and having exploratory talks with *experts* or so-called *key persons* of the organization involved is necessary to specify the problem explicitly.

Next, the problem definition, design and planning of the research are prepared in further detail. For fine-tuning in this matter, the client may be contacted. On the basis of specific literature reviews, formulate your expectations ('hypotheses') with regard to the practical part of the research. For example: 'Individuals with a low level of job satisfaction will call in sick more often than individuals with a high level of job satisfaction'. To test these expectations, design an empirical research. Look for or create *measurement tools* and select *research units* or *research objects*, for example, individuals, organizations or annual reports.

Next, the research is conducted. Collect the data. Process, prepare, analyse and interpret them. The final steps are the report and presentation of the research project.

Figure 1.2 gives a description of all the successive and interrelated steps. Each chapter in this book corresponds with a step in scientific research.

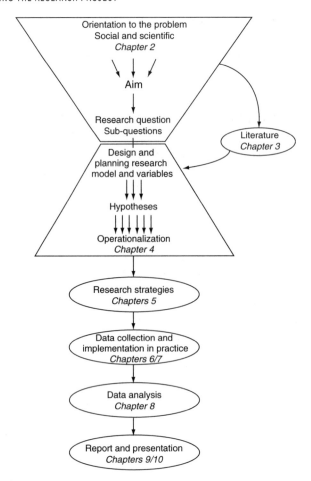

Figure 1.2   Overview of research steps.

Chapter 2

PROBLEM ORIENTATION

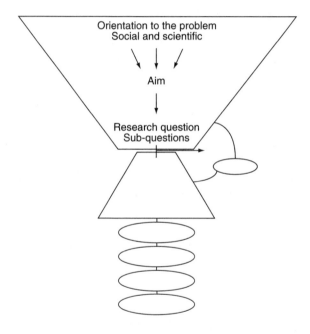

▌ 2.1 INTRODUCTION

The first step to take when conducting scientific research is to establish
the aim of the research and formulate the main research question. In
most cases, however, you must do some essential work before this
point. For example, you should determine what is already known
about the topic by studying the published literature. After this you

must determine what type of research (or supplementary research) you should conduct in order to formulate your research question and answer it.

Research entails making choices. This is because the area to be studied is almost always too expansive. You must make *explicit* choices: the question must not be allowed to remain vague. You must be clear about the exact problem for which you want to arrive at a solution, what you want to achieve, why the problem is important or interesting, what knowledge will be required to find the solution and how you can arrive at the solution.

Answers to all these questions are usually not immediately available. It is a long road from a global description of a topic to an exact formulation of the specific problem. For example, the clear formulation of the research question may take months for a Masters thesis and perhaps a year for a PhD dissertation.

However, the road you take with this preliminary work is crucial to the success of the research. When conducting research, the following rule applies: a well-formulated question is already a half-answered question. An explicitly formulated research aim and research question establish a guiding principle for the entire research project because they clearly indicate what you can and cannot involve in the study. They serve primarily to delineate and focus your area of research to prevent you from getting lost. If you forget to include relevant issues, there is a danger that you will be unable to answer the research question. This is obviously disastrous, because you usually cannot conduct the research over again. On the other hand, if you include too many issues in the research, this requires not only time and money, but there is also the danger that you will be unable to answer the research question in the time allowed or that you may end up answering a different question than the one you initially formulated.

■ 2.2 ESTABLISHING THE AIM OF THE RESEARCH

When establishing the aim of the research, you must make clear *why* you are doing the research, *what* you want to achieve and *for whom* you want to achieve this: what is the desired final product? As shown in Chapter 1, a distinction can be made between a *theoretical* aim, which usually involves a contribution to scientific knowledge (for example, developing or testing a specific theory about absenteeism), and a *practical* aim (for example, helping to solve a problem from the daily practice of controlling absenteeism or developing an instrument to measure the tendency of employees to be absent). As discussed briefly in the previous chapter, the distinction between a theoretical and a practical aim within scientific organizational research is somewhat artificial because both can be present at the same time. In that case, the results of the research not only contribute to theoretical knowledge, but are also applicable to practice (for example, a theory that can be used to design a measurement instrument with which absenteeism frequency and duration can be predicted).

When formulating a research aim, you must not lose sight of the feasibility of the research in terms of time, money, and whether or not the 'research units' are prepared and available to participate. *Research units* are the objects on which the research is conducted; they must be defined in your research aim. Such units can be individuals (called respondents or subjects), departments, companies or annual reports. These units or objects have certain attributes that are variable. For example, individuals call in sick or do not call in sick, departments differ in their percentage of absenteeism, companies differ according to the degree with which they take absenteeism-limiting measures, absenteeism can be reported in different ways in annual reports. Such attributes of objects are the *variables* in the research. When conducting research, we attempt to establish *relationships* between variables.

As previously stated, it is also important to consider who ultimately benefits from the research: the managers, the employees, yourself as a researcher or the government? This is important because it relates to your choice of the variables in the research. In applied research, you must choose variables that can be manipulated or influenced by the individual or organization that ultimately uses the research results. For example, it is useful for the management to measure employees' satisfaction with wages only if they are capable of actually doing something about the ascertained dissatisfaction.

EXAMPLES OF RESEARCH OBJECTIVES

- Acquiring more insight into the causes of absenteeism within the company.
- Investigating the nature of the differences in culture between organizations and developing a classification system for these differences.
- Developing an accurate performance measurement for departments in an organization.
- Developing and testing a method with which administrative procedures can be described and classified.

▌ 2.3 FORMULATING THE RESEARCH QUESTION

The second step is the formulation of the research question. The research question is the central, briefly worded question that you are going to answer in your research: what exactly are you going to study? When formulating this question, you must define the *domain*, that is, the set of all objects to be studied (for example, individual employees of an organization), the attributes of the objects (for example, the tendency to be absent or job satisfaction) and preferably the expected relationship between the attributes of the objects (for example, low satisfaction is related to a high tendency towards absenteeism). Note that it is not the objects themselves that vary (for example, individuals or annual reports), but the attributes of these objects (for example, the tendency to call in sick or the information density of the annual report). This is why the attributes of the objects that you are interested in were defined as the variables in the research. In the research question you relate the variables from a specific domain (the set of research units or objects) to each other. An example of such a relationship is that dissatisfaction leads to more absenteeism.

Sometimes the research question is called a problem *statement* to avoid confusion with the questions that may appear at a later stage (in a questionnaire, for example). Nevertheless, a problem statement is always a question!

A distinction can be made between various types of research questions. The most important types are discussed below. These differ primarily in their depth. The type of question you choose depends especially on the quantity of pre-existing knowledge about the research topic. Generally speaking, an empirical testing question delves more deeply than an explorative one, while an explorative question delves more deeply than a descriptive one, since more is known about the underlying theory and the results from other research. After all, the aim is to arrive at general and generalizable knowledge.

1. If you are exclusively interested in the occurrence (or the frequency of occurrence) of objects (or characteristics/ attributes thereof), then this would be defined as *descriptive* research. You provide a precise inventory of the attributes of phenomena (for example, the percentage of women who call in sick for a long period) without indicating the relationships between them or providing an explanation for them. No theory is present nor is any required. Often you present these frequencies as tables and figures accompanied with

simple data summaries such as the mean and the variance of variables (see Chapter 8).

> For example:
> 'What is (...)?'; 'What does (...) look like?'; 'Which (...) are present?'

2. If you suspect that there are possible causes or influencing factors for attributes of objects, this is defined as *explorative* research. This is concerned with the tentative formulation of relationships between phenomena and explanations of them. There is still no theory and/or hypothesis present: the aim is to develop these.

> For example:
> 'What is the link/relationship between (...) and (...)?'; 'Why is (...)?'; 'How is it possible that (...)?'

3. If you want to explicitly evaluate a relation or a difference based on a number of criteria, this is defined as *empirical testing* research. You statistically test whether certain explicitly formulated relationships or correlations between phenomena exist and whether specific explanations indeed apply. You investigate concrete expectations (hypotheses, see Section 4.3) or a coherent set of ideas (a theory) to see if they stand up to analysis.

> For example:
> 'Is there a significant positive correlation between (...)?'; 'Is it true that (...)?'

4. Finally, *advisory* and *prescriptive* research questions can occur especially with applied organizational research.

> For example:
> 'Is the implementation of (...) desirable? If yes, how can this best be done?'

The type of research question has consequences for the design and implementation of the research. This will be discussed in more depth beginning in Chapter 4.

When formulating the aim and research question for a study, you must focus on the following aspects:

- Answer the following questions:
  – What exactly is the research question with respect to the topic?
  – For which problem do you want to find a solution?
  – What is the actual problem?

  – Why is this question important?
  – Who is interested in an answer to this question?
  – What knowledge is required to answer this question/solve the
    problem?
  – How can this be achieved?

- Explain the underlying ideas: make the assumptions explicit and
  clarify the concepts.
- Delineate the research question adequately: describe the domain
  clearly and precisely (the set of objects); the variables (the attributes
  of the objects in which you are interested) and the relationships
  between them (for example, do you expect to find a causal relationship between variables)?
- Make it explicitly clear whether this is descriptive, explorative,
  empirical testing, advisory or prescriptive research.
- Check to see whether it is theoretically possible to research this
  question, that is, is it possible to collect the empirical *data* with
  which you can answer the research question? For example, as part
  of a study of absenteeism you must determine whether a system
  of absenteeism registration is present. Is the frequency and degree of
  absenteeism properly recorded? In addition, it must of course be
  possible to measure the variables (for example, tendency towards
  absenteeism and work satisfaction). Vague, incomplete, complex,
  excessively expansive and theoretically unanswerable questions,
  such as *ethical* questions, cannot be studied empirically. You must
  either reformulate these questions, so that they can be studied
  empirically, or answer them in a different way.

    For example:
    The question of whether people should be allowed to call in sick if
    they are dissatisfied with their work is difficult to answer in empirical
    research. However, you could, for instance, try to answer this ques-
    tion by organizing a discussion between various stakeholders such as
    trade unions, employers, the government and experts in labour law
    and ethics.

- Finally, you should make sure the research question is clearly
  recognizable in the document. You can do this by explicitly defining
  the research question and distinguishing it typographically from the
  other text, for example, by indenting it and printing it in italics.

    Example
    The global topic of a study is absenteeism. This is obviously a very broad
    research area. This topic could be approached, for example, from the

point of view of medical science or from that of organizational science or psychology. It is possible to investigate the causes as well as the consequences of absenteeism. A descriptive study of absenteeism can be conducted ('how high is the absenteeism within a company?'), an explorative study ('do two departments within a company differ in terms of their level of absenteeism?') or an empirical testing study ('is absenteeism caused by poor communication?').

Another limitation that can be imposed concerns the type of variables involved. For example, the literature study shows that it is not only the physical working conditions that play a role in absenteeism; the social norms and values of people at work may also have an effect. Less research has been conducted into the latter aspect. The research question, that is ultimately the focus of this study, is, 'Do social norms and values explain the differences in the level of absenteeism between two departments in the company?'

▌ 2.4 SUB-QUESTIONS

The third step is to draw up a number of *sub-questions*. These are short, clearly worded and independent subsidiary questions that are derived logically from the main research question. Answers to these sub-questions should contribute to the solution of the main research question. The sub-questions are independent, that is, one sub-question can be answered without knowing the answer to another sub-question. They often concern the distinct attributes of the main research question and the links between these attributes. Sub-questions should not enlarge the domain of the research topic, but should in fact make it more specific. They must also be based on proper assumptions.

> For example:
> Assume that the research question is 'What factors cause the high rate of absenteeism?'. In this question you imply the assumption that there is a high rate of absenteeism. But if you do not know that this is the case, you have got to include another question, 'Is there is in fact a high rate of absenteeism?'; 'What exactly is absenteeism?'; 'How do I determine whether the rate of absenteeism is "high", i.e., which figures from which companies do I use for comparison?'.

You often discuss the answers to these sub-questions in a step-by-step fashion in the report. Consequently, the sub-questions often define the structure of the report (see Chapter 9). Briefly summarized, you should 'translate' the initial problem (originating from theory or from the client) into the main research question of the scientific organizational research project and then break it down into the specific sub-questions for which you must find an answer. Later on in this book, another 'translation' will be made into the definitive questions that you will ask the respondents or experimental subjects from the company.

■ 2.5 THE EMPIRICAL CYCLE

In the previous section, four types of research questions were distinguished. The first three can be considered as parts of the total scientific research process during which one attempts to acquire more and more general and generalizable knowledge about organizational science phenomena. During this process, a number of phases are to be passed repeatedly. This is called the *empirical cycle* or the *regulative cycle*. Scientific organizational research takes place following this cycle, which is discussed below.

The fourth type of research question, which focuses on aspects that can be influenced or changed, is answered by the *design cycle*. This type of question is not concerned with arriving at general or generalizable knowledge, but instead aims at developing a concrete, specific application or intervention. Applied research makes use of the design cycle.

The empirical cycle comprises five phases, beginning with the phase where virtually nothing about the topic is known, and ending with the phase where a great deal of knowledge about the topic already exists. This empirical cycle, as the name indicates, can theoretically be repeated continually. As a result, one arrives at increasingly better (general, simple and precise) knowledge by repeatedly going through the cycle. Figure 2.1 provides an overview.

Phase 1: Description

By means of descriptive research you attempt to acquire an answer to a question of the type, 'What is (. . .)/ How much (. . .)?'. You notice something new and you record exactly what is happening. By conducting this type of research, you try to arrive at a description, or make an inventory or diagnosis of a scientific organizational phenomenon. To this end you establish a system of categories beforehand with which observations can be classified and with which you can attempt to

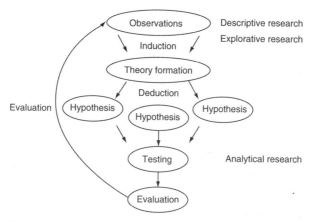

Figure 2.1 The empirical cycle according to De Groot (from de Groot, A.D. 1961, *Methodologie: Grondslagen van onderzoek en denken in de gedragswetenschappen* [*Methodology: Principles of Research and Thinking in the Behavioural Sciences*]). The Hague: Mouton.

describe the phenomenon. The *frequency* (how often does a specific phenomenon occur?), the *duration* (how long does the phenomenon last?) and the *intensity* (how strong is the phenomenon?) are examples of categories in which the phenomenon can be 'captured'.

Phase 2: Induction

By means of exploratory research you answer a research question of the type, 'What is the relationship between (...) and (...)?'. The first step in exploratory research is to determine whether two variables show a correlation or occur completely independently from each other. During this process, no immediately applicable theories and no clear expectations in the form of hypotheses are present. Based on specific, empirically observed correlations between attributes of objects (variables), you attempt to arrive at general and generalizable principles for a tentative, as yet untested, theory (induction) about these phenomena.

> For example:
> If it repeatedly turns out that the level of absenteeism in a certain company increases following the announcement of a reorganization, it could well be that, generally speaking, a specific method of announcing a reorganization is the cause of the increase of a specific type of absenteeism.

Phase 3: Deduction

If you derive specific, testable predictions (hypotheses) from an existing, general theory, this is defined as *deduction*.

> For example:
> 'According to theory, work pressure leads to higher employee turnover and more absenteeism. Therefore it is expected that because employees in the purchasing department experience more work pressure than sales employees, they will also be absent more frequently.'

Phase 4: Empirical testing

Empirical research answers a research question formulated as, 'Is there a relation between (. . .) and (. . .)?'. As stated previously, explorative research ends with formulating theories and hypotheses. By means of empirical research, you can determine the value of these theories and hypotheses, and therefore determine whether you have found support for them or not.

Phase 5: Evaluation

Finally, you evaluate this new theory regarding its tenability in various situations and at various times.

> For example:
> 'In another company, because work pressure has increased due to a reorganization, absenteeism has also increased.'

In summary: by means of descriptive research, you describe a specific organizational phenomenon: you map out the attributes of the objects in the domain. By means of exploratory research, you attempt to describe a relationship between a number of phenomena in the form of a theory and determine by means of empirical testing research whether or not the theory is tenable. A theory is never tested as a whole. This is impossible because a theory comprises a large number of statements, assertions, assumptions and conclusions. To test the theory you must therefore derive various hypotheses from the theory. *Hypotheses* are statements formulated on the basis of the theory about reality, or one aspect of reality. For example, during a reorganization, absenteeism increases as a result of increased work pressure. Because the hypothesis concerns reality (or a part of reality), it can also be determined whether support has been found for the hypothesis.

The theory is supported as long as no results emerge that falsify the theory or which cannot be explained by the theory as it is known at that time. This is the principle of *falsification* (as opposed to *verification*); you repeatedly attempt to disapprove the theory. After all, if it is demonstrated only once that a specific hypothesis derived from the theory appears to be correct, this does not mean that the entire theory has been proven. It can therefore be said that the theory has *not been rejected* or, even more strongly, is *supported*, but not that the theory *has been confirmed*.

There is always a possibility that you will encounter a phenomenon that has not yet been described in the theory or that is in conflict with current knowledge. The entire process then starts over; you first attempt to describe the phenomenon that deviates from the current theory, and you then try to discover relationships with other phenomena in the form of an improved theory. After this you test whether this new theory is tenable.

For example:
We go back in time to the point where the first thinking human emerged: Flint Stone. At a certain time, this individual becomes aware of the fact that grass is green and sometimes yellow. He notices that the colour of the grass varies throughout the year (phase 1: description). Flint decides to keep track of when the grass is green or yellow and to what degree the grass is green or yellow. At the time that Flint realizes there are differences in colour and starts to record these differences, descriptive research is already taking place.

Flint then takes up a new hobby: describing and recording. He records not only the colour of the grass, but also whether it is raining (phase 2: induction). When Flint begins to research whether there is a relationship between rainfall and the colour of the grass, explorative research is taking place.

The following step is that Flint looks at patterns (phase 2: induction). If it is raining, the grass is green. If it is dry for a long period, then the grass fades and becomes yellow. However, if a great deal of rain falls, then the grass also becomes yellow. The question is now whether these hypotheses are supported (phase 3: deduction). Is it the case that grass is normally green and that yellow grass is the result of too little or too much rain (hypothesis)? Flint decides to research this; at this point testing (phase 4: empirical research) is taking place. Flint then goes on a trip and determines whether the hypotheses are correct for all grasslands. As long as the colour of the grass varies between green and yellow depending on the quantity of precipitation, the theory appears to be supported.

Now assume that there is grassland, which turns blue after a rainfall. At that moment, Flint's theory is no longer supported. This means that Flint must modify the theory (phase 5: evaluation). A new theory must be developed which explains the occurrence of blue grass.

Chapter 3

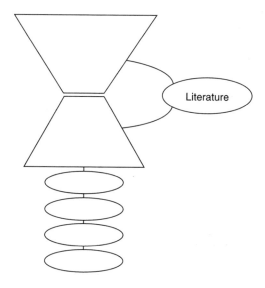

LITERATURE RESEARCH

■■ 3.1 INTRODUCTION

This chapter will go more deeply into the following research activity:
the collection of existing, relevant and recent information by means of
literature research.

Literature research is important because it is how you learn about
the current state of scientific knowledge in the domain of organizational studies with respect to a specific topic. By conducting literature
research, you can expand your own knowledge. This research activity
takes place in continuous interaction with the previous activity

(the formulation of the research question). You learn what is already known about the topic in the literature and what is not yet known. In this way you can determine what supplementary research you must conduct in order to formulate and answer your own research question in this area. After all, you don't want to reinvent the wheel or repeat the work of others. It is always preferable to answer the most specific questions and/or to solve the most specific problems.

▌ 3.2 TYPES OF LITERATURE

There are different types of literature. For example, there are newspapers and weekly magazines that contain *everyday knowledge*, where the authors are frequently journalists or public relations functionaries. In addition, there is *professional knowledge*. There is also *scientific knowledge*, which is published in scientific journals and books. The present book will focus primarily on collecting scientific literature.

Within the field of scientific literature, there are differences with respect to scientific quality. Journals vary in terms of rigidity of method and thoroughness of review procedures. Other journals have a more popular focus with particular attention to the practical application of results. For example, the *Academy of Management Review* contains primarily theoretical/conceptual articles and literature studies, while the *Academy of Management Journal* contains the results of empirical research. You can consult the *Harvard Organizational Review* to learn about trends in the practical application of organizational science.

Another type of classification for scientific literature is the following:

1. Primary publications (note that this does not concern primary and secondary *data*, the latter concept will be discussed later on in this book) concern original, theoretical, conceptual and/or empirical work, such as articles in scientific journals, books, theses/dissertations and internal reports; these are increasingly available electronically. You ultimately use these primary publications in the literature discussion. Publications of the following type are helpful for finding these primary publications.
2. Secondary publications include handbooks, bibliographies and review articles that provide introductions to, and summaries of, primary publications. *Review (summary) articles* provide summaries of developments within a specific sub-area and are often more up to

date than *handbooks*. *Bibliographies* systematically list (alphabetic-ally, chronologically, etc.) title descriptions of publications using an explicit criterion.

3. Tertiary publications are 'signposts' to secondary sources. These are journal publications that provide summaries of handbooks, bibliog-raphies and reviews.

A FEW SUGGESTIONS FOR MAKING A LITERATURE SEARCH:

- Begin with tertiary and secondary literature in order to acquire a broad overview of the research field and to ascertain the import-ant authors and historical controversies in this field. Keep track of which subtopics you can distinguish.

  For example:
  Search for literature about the nature of absenteeism, about absenteeism policy in general, about the causes of absenteeism for individual employees and within organizations and about the consequences of absenteeism for individuals and organizations.

- Then start searching for primary publications. For example, you could limit your initial search to recent (less than five years old) books and articles in high quality scientific journals. For an indication of the quality of journals, refer to acknowledged lists of journals where they are often classified as A (the top scientific journals) through E (lower quality, often application-oriented journals). The emphasis should be on international articles rather than books, since these provide a glimpse of more recent developments in a specific field and are supported by original empirical research. Books and textbooks often contain literature covering a somewhat broader field.

▌ 3.3 LITERATURE SEARCH

The search for relevant literature can be a complex task. It is infeasible to systematically read all the literature in the research field. Especially at the beginning of the literature study, it is unnecessary to read everything thoroughly. You only have to acquire global knowledge of the literature. Here are a number of suggestions to reduce the literature search to a feasible magnitude:

- Before you start, make a schedule for searching and studying the literature; otherwise you will have insufficient time left for your other research activities. In your planning, take into account possible problems with the availability of journals and books at libraries and difficulties with borrowing them.

- The title of a book or article in a journal often provides only a very global indication of the topic that is actually discussed. (This also demonstrates the importance of choosing a good title for your own report!) This means you should also search by topic and author. All kinds of synonyms are in use for the same topic. Therefore, to obtain as many *hits* as possible, map out the terminology concerning the topic beforehand by listing all the keywords and search terms that you can think of. The idea is to acquire a sufficient number of relevant hits. Sometimes there are too few, and sometimes there are far too many, only a small number of which may be relevant (this happens, for example, when you search for the keyword 'sick' when you are conducting a literature search concerning absentee-ism). Having far too many irrelevant hits is an indication that you should combine various keywords (for example, combine 'sick' with 'leave' or with 'job') so that only hits that are specifically applicable to the topic remain.

- Search for the abstracts of a number of relevant articles. If these are sufficiently interesting, it is worthwhile copying the entire article from a journal and studying it completely. Make notes about the authors, the dependent and independent variables, the hypotheses, the measurement instruments, the analysis techniques and the conclusions. This provides you with general insight into the magnitude and nature of the subtopics. By surveying these subtopics, you can limit the research area. This also clarifies the points on which the various research results agree and disagree.

- It is advisable to maintain a complete reference list from the beginning of the literature study which includes, for example, *the title of the journal and the volume and page numbers of the specific article in this journal* (see Chapter 9). Computer programs are available which you can use to maintain your own documentation system. Examples of such programs are *Endnote* and *Squarenote*.

- It sometimes happens that you accidentally encounter a relevant publication. By consulting the literature list in this publication, you can find other publications, and then you repeat this procedure. This is called the *snowball method*. One disadvantage of this method is that you go back in time (a publication from 1992 will contain only other publications from before 1992, for example). Another disadvantage is that the composition of a literature list can be subjective: authors frequently include only publications that agree with their argument and not those that deviate from it.

- It is advisable to see if there are other researchers active in your field and/or if there are relevant databases. This saves time, prevents errors and repeating work, and the results are more comparable. A number of extensive electronic databases are available for this purpose. You can also contact national research institutes to determine whether related research is taking place and to find out which other researchers are experts in this area.

3.3.1   The library

Libraries are the traditional location where you can find and collect information in person. You can look for relevant information in the journals in the library and scan the most recent volumes of these journals. The following are a number of suggestions for making in-person searches in libraries:

- At some university libraries, specialized libraries are attached to specific faculties, for example, the economics library may be located at the Economics Faculty. However, be aware that topics from organizational studies are often multidisciplinary in nature. Therefore, also consult the libraries of other faculties such as psychology and education, law or computer science.
- Consult as many different libraries at as many universities as possible; this is because different libraries often subscribe to different journals. You cannot only borrow books there in person, you can also use the Interlibrary Lending System (IBL); there is a fee for this service.

3.3.2   Bibliographies in printed form

One option for searching for literature on a specific topic is to browse through a few relevant bibliographies. The aim of bibliographies is to help the user systematically find literature in a specific field. Bibliographies contain lists of titles, but usually not the physical locations (at specific libraries) of the relevant publications. In principle, bibliographies therefore provide data on many more publications (or types of publications) than individual library catalogues. This is because bibliographies also include publications at other libraries and information about ongoing research. However, searching manually in annual or monthly bibliographic publications can be very time consuming. Luckily, besides the traditional printed form, bibliographies are increasingly available in cumulative electronic form (CD-ROM). You can use these CD-ROMs at many libraries.

- Examples of bibliographies are the *Social Science Citation Index*, which comprises an annual alphabetical list of authors whose work has been cited in many scientific journals, and *ABI/INFORM*, a bibliographic database of economic journals, which can be searched on keywords and authors. *ABI/INFORM* contains the abstracts of articles of more than 1000 English journals, primarily from North America, but also from Europe, Asia and Australia, published after 1986. It also contains the complete references from the articles and systematic codes for the articles.

- Other examples of bibliographies are *ATTENT* (contains not only titles, but also includes the entire text of some research reports in economics), *Exerpta Informatica*, *Psychlit* and *Econlit* (abstracts of publications in computer science, psychology and economic journals, respectively), *Eurocat* (all official publications and documents from the EU) and *SCAD*, a bibliography of documents about the EU and from the EU.

- Another possibility is to search for journal articles via the psychological, sociological, economic or management abstracts, which are published monthly. The indices of these abstracts contain a thesaurus (keyword list with synonyms) followed by a number. The following information about the article is listed next to the relevant number: title of article, author(s), name and volume number of the journal in which the article is published and an abstract of the article.

3.3.3 Searching for literature electronically

Besides using printed bibliographies, you can also conduct automated literature research (ALR) by using search engines on the Internet, for example. With the help of the computer, various networks are then searched for publications concerning a specific research topic.

- By using electronic databases you can search all member libraries, using a single search command. The system searches books and articles in journals and indicates in which library the material is present. If you have a subscription to *IBL*, you can then order the relevant books or photocopies of relevant articles. Manuals are available for using these databases.

One advantage for searching by computer is that you acquire an overview of the relevant literature quickly and inexpensively by combining keywords; you can then download or print out the information yourself. For example, you can use a search command to select only those publications that were published during the past five years in a specific field.

- The *Financial Times* is an electronic database that contains the full text of the articles, but the figures, tables, photographs and images of the printed version are not available. The *Statistical Masterfile* and *Accounting Digest* are other examples of electronic databases. The latter database, besides having articles from 450 journals, also contains information about books and articles from collections beginning in 1969. Finally, *Datastream* (this is a database containing primarily financial/economic and macroeconomic data, such as stock prices, exchange rates and company data from annual reports) is available.

Once you have found a promising title, you can then search for the shelf mark of this publication in the relevant catalogue of the library. Note that the catalogue does not contain titles of individual articles in journals, but only the titles of the journals themselves.

For example:
If you want to find the article 'What do managers do? A critical review of the evidence' from the *Journal of Management Studies*, then you should type 'Journal of Management Studies'.

If you have trouble finding scientific literature on a specific topic at a library, you can contact the relevant *information specialist*. These are library employees who specialize in a specific field. They specialize primarily in organizing and finding scientific knowledge in that field, but this does not mean that they have also mastered the contents of all material in the field. An information specialist therefore can provide you with valuable help in searching for the appropriate literature sources, but cannot help you formulate the appropriate research question.

3.3.4 The Internet

On the Internet you can view and download a wide range of freely accessible files. The addresses and home pages can be found with the help of various search engines (for example, Yahoo or the Dutch search engine Ilse).

The problem with searching for data using these general search engines is that this often results in many hits but little relevant information. For example, entering the key word 'absenteeism' results in 1657 hits via Ilse.

Another problem is that you are often denied access to scientific journals or databases on the Internet unless you are a subscriber. Such subscriptions are generally too expensive for an individual member. However, most libraries do have a subscription. The files can then be consulted using the Internet on a computer in the library.

▊ 3.4 PROCESSING THE LITERATURE

Based on a study of the relevant literature, you should briefly and accurately summarize the essence of the findings in your own words. Therefore do not structure the literature summary as a collection or list of summaries. Instead, you should provide an overview of various authors' standpoints and the results of empirical research. You can then discuss the findings critically and compare them in terms of their agreements and disagreements. Finally, you should indicate to what extent the literature summary is complete.

> For example:
> This summary includes references to the most important publications during the past five years.

Depending on the topic, it may be a good idea to discuss your own viewpoint. You should explain your viewpoint and relate it to the literature that has been discussed. It is essential that you clearly distinguish between the literature sources and your own opinion. You often do this in a fairly subtle fashion, however (for example, do not use 'I believe that . . .' or 'My opinion is . . .', but use 'On this basis, it can be concluded that . . .'; see also 'Writing Style' in Chapter 9).

■ 3.5   REFERENCES TO LITERATURE

In scientific organizational research it is customary to provide references to literature in the body of the text itself instead of using footnotes or endnotes. Depending on the context, you do this by reporting the last name(s) of the authors followed by the year of publication in parentheses, or the name, followed by a comma and the year of publication, all in parentheses.

> For example:
> 'According to the findings of Peterson (1994) (...)' or '(...) no confirmation was found (Peterson, 1994)'.

In principle you should use as many of the original sources as possible. If you still want to refer to an author who based his or her opinion on the conclusions of another author, you can do this in the following fashion:

> For example:
> 'Peterson (1971) believes that (...) (In: Jensen, 1994)' or 'based on Jensen (1994)' or 'partly derived from Jensen (1994)'.

In this case you would not include the publication of the original author (Peterson) in your bibliography, but that of the other author (Jensen).

If you use ideas from various sources, then you should report all these sources, separated by a semicolon. Publications are listed either chronologically or alphabetically based on the last name of the primary author.

> For example:
> 'Various researchers support this conclusion (Peterson, 1971; Meadow, 1980; Jensen, 1994)' or '(Jensen, 1994; Meadow, 1980; Peterson, 1971)'.

If you quote an author literally, then you must place the relevant text in another font and between quotation marks. If you want to leave something out of the text, you do this by using three dots between parentheses. If you want to add something to the citation, you do this by placing the addition between brackets, followed by a comma and the initials of the author who made the addition. The citation is followed by the last name of the author(s), the year of publication and the page number of the citation.

> For example:
> 'A good definition is, "Absenteeism is (. . .) the total absence of [all, vdV] employees in days per year" (Peterson, 1971, p. 25)'.

If a publication has two authors, then you should always list both names. If there are three or more authors, then you should list all last names the first time, for example, 'Peterson, Jensen and Meadow, 1987'. If there are additional references to this publication in the text, it is sufficient to use Peterson *et al.* (and others). In the bibliography, however, you should once again list all the authors (see Chapter 9).

If you use various publications from a single author from the same year, you can refer to this by adding the letters a, b, c, etc. to the year of publication. Use exactly the same system in the bibliography (see Chapter 9).

> For example:
> 'See Peterson (1974a; 1974b)'.

Finally, if you want to quote a citation or an original thought from a discussion with another individual, you can indicate this with the abbreviation 'p.c.' (personal communication). Be sure you ask permission from the relevant individual.

> For example:
> ' . . . (Jensen, p.c., 1996)'.

Also consider the author's rights and the copyright when using the figures and texts and when photocopying texts. If you use an idea or a text from another author, you must always provide a complete reference to the correct source. To use excerpts in textbooks, for example, you must report the use of short excerpts (fewer than 8000 words from a journal or 10 000 words from a book). To use a longer excerpt, you must ask permission from the publisher.

3.5.1 *References to the Internet*

The Internet is very dynamic. Pages that provide information today may be located somewhere else tomorrow, or may not even exist any longer. This is basically the problem of using the Internet as a literature reference. As indicated in Chapter 1, scientific research must be reproducible. You must describe the data collection process and the analyses in such a way that another researcher can repeat your research. This also applies to literature research. Since Internet pages are not always trustworthy at present, it is better to avoid referring to an Internet page. Use the published (printed) version of the page instead.

Chapter 4

RESEARCH DESIGN AND PLANNING

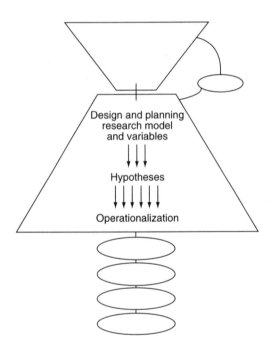

Design and planning
research model
and variables

Hypotheses

Operationalization

▮ 4.1 INTRODUCTION

In interaction with your literature study, the research question is further specified and accommodated to the other parties concerned with your research, such as clients (if any) and supervisors. It is important to plan what you are going to do beforehand. In the same way that you would not go on holiday without planning and preparation (for example, discuss the trip, make sure that somebody watches your home while you are gone, purchase currency, get travel insurance, etc.), you would not conduct scientific research without a plan. However, the difference is that when you plan scientific research, you must record exactly what choices you make during this planning. This is due to the methodological demand of public access to the research. During the planning phase, you establish the structure of the research. For example, how do you acquire data to test your hypotheses? Which research units are you going to use? How are you going to analyse the data? This general plan of how you are going to conduct your research is called the *research design*.

As stated above, your research design depends on the type of research question you choose. In addition, practical factors such as time and money certainly affect your choice of research design. In your research design you define the research units, the relevant variables of the research units, the data you are going to collect about the variables and how you are going to conduct this research. As a researcher, you must keep in mind that you can answer the research question or sub-questions based on the data you collect as determined by your research design. When drawing up the research design, you therefore ask yourself whether every aspect of the design contributes to answering the main research question or one of the sub-questions.

After determining a research question and performing a literature study, you formulate a research model (Section 4.2). From the research model, you derive the hypotheses that you are going to test in empirical research (Section 4.3). These hypotheses concern relationships between variables: which variables do you choose, where do these fit into the model, how do you define them and how do you operationalize them or measure them (Sections 4.4 and 4.5)? During this process, you must take measures that assure the reliability and validity of your research (Section 4.6). Then you must make a choice regarding the research population (or drawing the sample from the research population); which research units will be used (Section 4.7)? When making this choice, you must follow a number of behavioural rules (Section 4.8). The chapter ends with the research proposal (Section 4.9), which comprises all these elements. It also contains a time schedule and a financial budget. You must make a schedule and a budget beforehand because this will provide you with an indication of the feasibility of the investment that is required for your research.

◼ 4.2 RESEARCH MODEL AND VARIABLES

The first step in arriving at a complete research design is to draw a research model. A research model is an abstract figure in which you systematically indicate which relationships or correlations you assume between variables of the research units. Describe the most important variables in your research and the relationships you expect to find between them.

> # VARIABLES
> If the research units are people, variables would then be aspects such as gender or satisfaction with work. There are only two options with respect to the variable 'gender': male or female. With respect to the variable 'satisfaction with work', there can be much greater variation; some people may be very satisfied, others slightly satisfied and still others dissatisfied or very dissatisfied. An example of an assumed relationship between the variables 'gender' and 'work satisfaction' is that women are more satisfied with their work than men.

The research model therefore contains the terms of the research question: the domain of research objects or units (for example, individuals, companies, annual reports); the attributes of the objects that are variable (for example, height, absenteeism, satisfaction, profitability). The latter are the variables in the research model between which you establish relationships – preferably causal relationships (for example, employee dissatisfaction leads to more absenteeism). You indicate these relationships between variables by drawing arrows on your research model. A research model is a simplified presentation of part of reality.

Your research model is frequently derived from, or based on, a specific theory. A theory is a coherent whole of general assertions about a specific aspect of reality. These assertions are logically related and do not contradict one another.

For example:
You can establish a theory about absenteeism where the research units comprise individuals and the most important variables are absenteeism, tendency to be absent, work satisfaction and management style. In the theory, all these variables are placed into a causal relationship with each other.

You can use a theory in your research in two ways:

1. You can develop a theory to apply to the specific situation in your research topic.
2. You can adapt a general, existing theory to your specific research topic.

> For example:
> Apply the social comparison theory to the organizational science phenomenon of absenteeism. This theory states that individuals tend to adapt themselves to what is customary in their group. Applied to this situation, this means that absenteeism behaviour is not influenced by whether people feel sick or not, but by the visible absenteeism behaviour of their co-workers. Consequently, the absenteeism behaviour of an individual over the long term approaches that of the group average.

The development of a specific ad hoc theory is frequently viewed as less desirable than applying a general theory. This is because the ad hoc theory is less generalizable; this was one of the requirements of scientific research (see Chapter 1). In other words, it is less applicable to other phenomena. Therefore, first look in the literature to determine if there are existing theories that are applicable to your research.

A theory has to be formulated in such a way that specific, empirically testable expectations (hypotheses) can be derived from it. For example, from the theory of social comparison you could derive the hypothesis that absenteeism declines when your colleagues call in sick less often. Such expectations can be empirically tested.

An example of a research model in the area of absenteeism is shown in Figure 4.1.

In a research model, you make a distinction between four types of variables: independent, dependent, intervening and control variables. The variables assumed to have an effect on a specific result, which

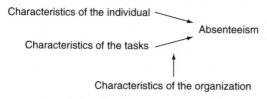

Figure 4.1 The characteristics of individuals, tasks, organizations and absenteeism are four categories of variables, and the arrows are the assumed relationships between them. An example of an expected relationship in this model is that the attributes of individuals affect absenteeism: poor mental health and low self-esteem lead to more absenteeism.

influence or even cause this result, are called independent variables (also known as determinants, predictors or explanatory variables). In Figure 4.1, the attributes of individuals and tasks are the independent variables.

Dependent variables are the results that you assume are dependent on how the independent variables are manipulated or varied. Dependent variables are also called consequences, criteria or variables to be explained. In Figure 4.1 the dependent variable is absenteeism.

Therefore, first look at the phenomenon you want to explain, in this case absenteeism. This is the dependent variable. Then look at the variables with which you are going to explain this phenomenon. These are the independent variables, in this case the attributes of individuals and tasks. Then consider whether there are variables that modify the relationships between the independent and dependent variables. These are defined as the intervening variables. The intervening variables can have a moderating or mediating role. If effects are dependent on situational attributes, this is called *contingency*.

EXAMPLE OF A MODERATING VARIABLE

In the research model, the attributes of individuals and tasks are assumed to affect absenteeism directly, where organizational attributes have a moderating affect. This is the case, for example, when the relationship between the attributes of individuals and tasks on the one hand and absenteeism on the other is different for people who score low on a specific organizational attribute (e.g. people in a bureaucratic organization) than for people who score high on this attribute (e.g. people in a flexible organization, for the time being not considering how you would operationalize this; see Section 4.4).

If the relationship between individual and task attributes and absenteeism takes place only via organizational attributes (i.e. when individual and task attributes have an indirect effect on absenteeism), then the organizational attributes have a mediating effect. For example, people with specific individual and task attributes tend to work exclusively in an organization with specific attributes. As a result there is more absenteeism or less absenteeism. The moderating and mediating effects of the variable C between variables A and B is shown schematically in Figure 4.2.

Finally, consider whether there are variables that you want to control (to correct for them or to keep them constant). You control such

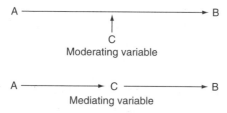

Figure 4.2 The moderating and mediating effects of variables.

variables if you don't want to attribute the results (the ascertained relationships between specific variables) to the effect of these variables. These are called *control variables* (also known as *co-variates*). Typical control variables are background and biographical variables such as age, sex, socioeconomic status and education, unless your research question is concerned with the effect of age or sex on absenteeism. In the latter case, they would be independent variables. The classification of variables therefore depends on the choices of the researcher. Of course, you must clearly explain these choices.

One way of controlling a variable is to keep the variable constant in your research design. This is called *experimental control*.

For example:
You can control for the effect of the variable of age by basing your absenteeism research on individuals who are all the same age.

Another possibility is to control this variable after the data collection, during data analysis (this is called *statistical control*; see Chapter 8).

For example:
If it is known that the culture of the organization is a variable that can lead to various results with respect to absenteeism, you can then choose to keep this variable constant. For instance, you can conduct the research within a single organization, or you can make a statistical correction during the analysis by including this variable as a co-variate. In the latter case, you actually conduct a separate data analysis for each organization. If these analyses provide different results, then you can argue that the culture of the organization indeed has an effect.

4.3 HYPOTHESES

As was mentioned earlier in Section 2.5, you can never test a theory or a schematic research model derived from this theory in its entirety.

Both the theory and the model contain too many variables and relationships between variables to test them all. By delineating your research question, you can focus on a limited group of variables, and the relationships between them, in your research model. Then you derive a number of hypotheses from your research model that you will test in your research. *Hypotheses* are your expectations, formulated as propositions or statements, concerning the relationships between variables, on the basis of theory. You can view hypotheses as a tentative answer to the research question. They are derived from the literature study and your own viewpoint. The latter is based, for example, on your experience with the topic you are researching. Hypotheses must always be established before your empirical research begins, but never afterwards as an explanation for relationships you have found in the data. Before you start collecting data, you must refine your hypotheses as much as possible so that they are well supported by theory and are feasible to test. Of course, after you have collected your data, you can no longer change your hypotheses.

EXAMPLE OF A HYPOTHESIS
Workers with low self-esteem call in sick more frequently than workers with high self-esteem.

Formulate your hypotheses in concrete, operational and measurable terms. This is because you can only test your theory through the hypotheses. They must be testable, so they must contain measurable terms. Stated another way, you must be able to disprove the hypothesis. Therefore always make sure your hypotheses satisfy the following primary requirement: the content of a hypothesis must always be falsifiable. This means it must be possible to reject the hypothesis by means of empirical research.

An example of a non-falsifiable proposition, that is one you cannot use in a hypothesis, is a normative or ethical proposition. These are propositions that use formulations such as 'must', 'should' or 'proper'. An example of an ethical proposition is 'it is proper for animals to be genetically manipulated'. An example of a normative proposition is, 'absenteeism must be avoided'. A normative proposition concerns a subjective value judgement that can differ from person to person. For example, one researcher agrees, but another may not. The propositions cannot be rejected by means of empirical research.

The tautology is another example of a non-falsifiable statement. These are statements that are obviously true in logical terms (for example, 'parents have children'). This is a very simple example. It becomes more complex if the tautology is not as obvious (for example, 'intelligent people score higher on an intelligence test'; this is a tautology because intelligence is in fact measured by such a test). On the other hand, a hypothesis must not be obviously empirically improbable. A hypothesis must therefore be interesting, i.e. it should be possible for it to be false. This aspect will be discussed further below.

The *form* of the hypothesis must satisfy three criteria. Make sure your hypotheses meet these criteria:

1. Certainty

Present the statement as an unavoidable *fact*. Therefore do not use any qualifying words such as 'maybe' or 'perhaps', since these make it impossible to reject the statement (consider the concept of falsification!).

2. Clarity

Provide operational definitions of concepts.

> For example:
> The hypothesis, 'As more sales employees feel affectively committed to an organization, fewer will be absent', can be operationalized by making the prediction, 'If more sales employees state that they feel at home in the organization, they will call in sick for fewer days per year'.

Concepts, such as affective commitment in the example, are frequently defined and explained first, so that the hypothesis can be formulated compactly using the concepts in the research model. A definition is a precisely formulated, summarizing description of a concept, which contains all the attributes that an object must have to be classified as an instance of the concept. For some concepts, a good definition is not much of a problem. Age and sex, for example, are very concrete. Other concepts, such as power and culture, are much more difficult to define because they are more abstract and vague. Be sure to give sufficient attention to the precise definition of concepts.

> For example:
> Various phenomena can be defined as absenteeism. For instance, it can be defined as the level of absenteeism measured by the frequency with which employees call in sick, or the total number of sick days per year. Furthermore, it can be measured at various levels, such as the individual or team level, and over various periods, such as a week, month or year.

You can use a definition directly from the literature, but you can also create your own definition from various literature sources. As a beginning researcher, you will most frequently use definitions directly from the literature. For example, there are good standard definitions of widely used concepts such as *work satisfaction, commitment, motivation, organization, self-managing work team* and *organizational process*. The definitions of these concepts are often summarized in indices in handbooks; they provide a good overview of the available definitions. Other social, economic and geographical concepts, such as classification into professional groups or study programmes, are also standardized.

> For example:
> The Central Bureau of Statistics in the Netherlands uses standard classifications for industrial branches, study programmes and professional groups.

Try as much as possible to link up with these standard concepts. This is important for the comparability of your research with other research results, unless you can properly support your criticism of these other results. Because organizational science is a multidisciplinary science, this may result in combinations of concepts and variables from widely divergent disciplines. An example of such a combination can be found in the *Balanced Scorecard*. This instrument uses not only financial performance concepts such as cash flow information, but also non-financial concepts such as client satisfaction, market share, innovation, product quality and product development. This makes it important for you to indicate precisely how you define these concepts.

3. **Precision**

You should not only precisely define the concepts, but also the *relationships between the concepts*. Remember that concepts refer to the variable attributes of research units from your research domain. Therefore, do not be vague. If you use relationships such as *more* or *less*, then define them precisely (i.e. more or less than *what?*). Or if you use relationships such as *many* or *few*, define these in numerical terms. Such terms are quite relative. For instance, 20 per cent would be many if the concept was staff turnover. Finally, if you state that there is a relationship between two concepts, indicate if possible the expected direction (positive or negative, for example satisfaction leads to less/more absenteeism) and the expected strength of this relationship.

Of course, you hope that your hypotheses will be supported by the results from your research. However, you should realize that even if a hypothesis is rejected, there is still scientific progress. The magnitude of this progress depends on the distance between your hypothesis and generally accepted theories or knowledge. For example, if there is a small distance and your hypothesis is supported, there is little scientific progress. If there is a large distance, but the rejected hypothesis was implausible, there is also little scientific progress.

In anticipation of the analysis of your data, which will be discussed later on in this book, it is important that you become acquainted with the difference between *one-sided* and *two-sided hypotheses*. In a two-sided hypothesis, you state only that a specific value is different than another value, but without indicating the exact direction of the difference (for example, purchasing department employees differ from sales employees concerning their level of absenteeism, but it is not clear beforehand which group scores higher or lower), or that a relationship exists, but without knowing or reporting the direction of this relationship. In a one-sided hypothesis, however, you do indicate a specific direction of the difference or relationship (for example, managers score higher on satisfaction than administrative staff). In Chapter 8 there will be a discussion about the difference between one-sided and two-sided hypotheses concerning statistical testing.

▮ 4.4 OPERATIONALIZING

If you have a hypothesis, which is clearly derived from the theory and from the research model linked to the theory, the following step is operationalizing the (relations between) concepts from the hypothesis. Operationalizing your concepts simply means that you make your concepts *measurable*. To this end, you must find a method, technique or procedure, or devise one yourself. This is the *measurement instrument*. Operationalizing a theoretical concept (or construct) means translating the concept into specific, measurable, observable and recordable aspects. Theoretical concepts (such as *absenteeism tendency*) are often impossible to observe directly. You must therefore translate this concept into aspects that link directly with all kinds of daily experiences. For example, if your experimental subject is an individual, you could ask him or her various concrete and understandable questions. Their answers would form an indication of the underlying concept that you want to measure (for example, 'How frequently in the past month did you plan on calling in sick?'). You can also observe the concrete behaviours of an individual, or study personal materials such as an employee's file or a diary. You can also use indices from other organizations (for example, the percentage of absenteeism in a branch of industry).

When operationalizing a concept, it is important that you indeed measure the concept that you want to measure (*What* are you going to measure? This is called *validity*) and that the measurement is conducted precisely and carefully (*How* are you going to measure? This is called *reliability*). In Section 4.6, these quality aspects of measurement will be discussed in greater detail.

It is advisable to use more than one indicator (*multiple indicators, multi-items*) to measure an abstract concept. If the research involves written questions/propositions (*items*), then the combination of multiple indicators or items is called a *scale* (*composite measure*). There are various types of scales. The Likert scale is the most widely used. In this scale you add all the items that measure a specific concept, and then you divide the sum by the number of items. This average is the score on the scale. The advantage of this scoring method is that it is less affected by random influences, which yields a more reliable measurement. It is assumed that every item contains random measurement errors that cancel each other out when the items are added together (see Section 7.2.2, 'Scaling and items').

THE LIKERT SCALE

An operational definition of the theoretical concept 'organizational commitment' can comprise various items such as 'feeling at home in the organization' and 'the fact that people are not looking for a job with another organization', to which a respondent can respond on a scale from 1 = 'disagree completely' to 5 = 'agree completely.' The scores on these items, added together (and divided by the total number of items) are intended to measure the concept of commitment.

When operationalizing concepts, you can use already existing instruments that are described in the literature, or you can use an instrument that you develop. Using existing instruments saves time, gives you more confidence in the reliability and validity of the measurement instrument and increases the comparability of the research results. You must, of course, carefully determine whether the existing instrument is compatible with your own research. You should also be aware that using existing instruments may lead to a certain degree of rigidity. Concepts can, for example, change their meaning over time due to societal or scientific developments.

If you use a self-developed instrument, you must conduct preliminary research (a pre-test) concerning its use in practice (do people understand the questions if you are working with a questionnaire?) or a more extensive pilot study concerning its reliability and validity (see Section 4.6). A pre-test or a pilot study is a small-scale study using a group of individuals or companies that are comparable to those in your main research, during which you test and study the measurement instrument (see Chapter 7). However, even if you use an existing instrument, you should determine whether this instrument is reliable and valid in your own research. After all, the group of individuals or companies in your own research can be totally different than the group of research units on which the measurement instrument was initially tested and studied (calibrated). *Calibration* is comparing the scores of a measurement instrument with another instrument (this is called the criterion) of which you are certain that you are indeed measuring what you want to measure (validity). You then expect to obtain the same results from the various instruments.

For example:
You can calibrate a self-developed questionnaire for work satisfaction with one from the many existing standard lists that are available for work satisfaction in the Netherlands.

▌ 4.5   MEASUREMENT LEVELS

Measurement means assigning numerical values to variables.

For example:
If someone states that they 'agree completely' with the proposition 'I am generally satisfied with my work', you can assign that answer a score of 5 if there is a five-point scale for that item.

However, these values do not always have the same meaning. Variables can be measured at various levels. Five levels are discussed below. In practice, organizational science research is concerned with the first three levels.

If you are making an inventory of a specific variable, then you measure at the nominal level. At the *nominal* level, scale values or numbers are used only to indicate that objects or units with different values are different with respect to the variable that is measured, and that those with the same values or numbers are the same (*equivalent*). In such cases, the specific numerical value assigned to an answer theoretically does not matter. The items male – female or dog – cat – fish are certainly different, but any numerical values assigned would be arbitrary and have no other significance in the case that the inventory is a human or an animal.

> An example of a nominal scale would be the possible reasons for absenteeism: broken leg, flu or a heart attack.

If you rank various research units with respect to a variable, this is referred to as an ordinal scale. With *ordinal* scaling, it is important not only whether the numbers are the same or different, but also whether one number is greater than the other (if there are two different numbers). The variables are *ranked* according to their size (for example, from less to more, from shorter to longer or from younger to older). However, the difference between two sequential values of variables does not always have to be of the same magnitude. For the variable 'education', it is possible to rank educational levels according to their degree of difficulty. You could therefore just as well assign the values 1, 5 and 10, as long as the *sequence* of the values does not change. The figure that you use for coding is meaningful only in terms of mutual ranking. It is customary that you assign a low value to the smallest, least or youngest object, beginning with 1.

For example:
You can ask people to rank or assign numbers of points to the different reasons for absenteeism according to the level of seriousness.

With an *interval* scale, the differences between numbers can also be ranked according to magnitude. In this case, however, the relative distance between the numbers also is important. Assume that we are conducting research into the readability (variable) of annual reports (objects) and have assigned the 'readability values' of 1, 3 and 5 to reports A, B and C. If readability is measured on an interval scale, this means that the difference in readability between B and C is equally as large as the difference in readability between A and B. In this case you cannot simply replace the readability values by 1, 7 and 9 (which would be possible if readability was measured at the ordinal level).

A widely used method for making an inventory of opinions is the five-point scale, which ranges, for example, from 1 = very dissatisfied to 5 = very satisfied (also referred to as the *Likert scale*). Although the distance between 1 and 2 in the experience of the respondent does not have to be equally as large as that between 4 and 5, Likert scales are nonetheless frequently used in practice as if the values were measured at the interval level or quasi-interval level. This is because it is often difficult to assign other values to the variables without changing the rank order of the research units on that variable.

A *ratio* scale has all the properties described above. In addition, however, there is a fixed natural point on the scale where the variable measured is equal to zero. But the value of the measurement unit can still be chosen freely. Age is an example of a measurement at ratio level; there is an absolute zero point of 0 years, and the interval between someone who is 10 years old and someone who is 11 is equally as great as the interval between an individual who is 44 and one who is 45. However, the value for the measurement unit can be days, weeks, months or years. Number of years are not variables at the ratio level since a natural zero point is lacking due to the differences in time calculation between various cultures. Years are therefore placed on an interval scale.

With an *absolute* scale, the numbers for the measurement unit are also fixed. Both ratio and absolute scales are used in organizational science research almost exclusively in the form of indices or percentages (for example, the percentage of individuals who are dissatisfied or the percentage who call in sick).

This classification into measurement levels of variables is important for the data analysis (see Chapter 8). Some analysis techniques require variables to be measured at a specific minimum level. There are differences in the number and type of allowable transformations between the various measurement levels.

For example:
You cannot add or divide the values of a nominal variable; you can only calculate the most frequently occurring value.

One could say that the higher the measurement level, the more types of analyses are possible.

A special case in this context is the so-called *dichotomous* variable. This is a variable that can have only two possible values: present or not present. Some variables are inherently dichotomous, such as the nominal variable sex: a male is a non-female and a female is a non-male. You can transform other types of variables into dichotomous variables.

For example:
The variable 'examination mark' can be transformed into the dichotomous variable 'passed'. If the examination mark is greater than or equal to 5.5, the individual passed the exam, otherwise he/she did not pass.

With dichotomous variables, it permissible to conduct analyses which actually require variables that are measured at a higher than nominal level. Of course, dichotomous variables provide less information.

For example:
If you dichotomize a five-point scale by converting scale values 1, 2 and 3 to 0 and scale values 4 and 5 to 1, the differences between the scale values 1, 2 and 3 and between the values 4 and 5 disappear. You therefore lose information.

▮ 4.6 RELIABILITY AND VALIDITY

Sometimes there can be major differences between the respondents in the interpretation of some items on the measurement instrument. A specific item, for example, may be taboo for one group of individuals but not for the other, or it may have a different meaning for different groups.

For example:
Calling in sick without a valid reason is entirely unacceptable behaviour for one sub-group of employees, but it is completely normal behaviour for the other sub-group.

You must determine to what extent these types of problems occur and the degree to which they distort your measurement. When searching for or constructing the measurement instrument, you must therefore pay attention to two important aspects: reliability and validity.

4.6.1 Reliability

The reliability of a measurement instrument concerns its overall precision and the accuracy with which (*How?*) a concept is measured. The measurement must be systematic; it must not be coincidental. The reliability of an instrument is virtually always defined in terms of repeatability. If you repeat a measurement on the same object, you should get the same result. The result must, for example, be independent of the time when the measurement is taken, such as after insufficient sleep or after a busy working day, and it must be independent of the individual who is using the instrument.

> For example:
> You use a ruler to measure an object. The first measurement in the morning is 83 cm, but when the same object is measured the following evening, the result is 91 cm. You would then conclude that the ruler is unreliable (assuming that the object has not grown in the meantime – after all, the object could have grown and acquired a different score, while the ruler actually measured reliably). The ruler would also be unreliable if a second researcher obtained different results than the first researcher using the same instrument.

One way that you can determine the reliability of an instrument is based on the *classical test theory*. This is not an actual theory, since it cannot be empirically tested (see Section 4.2). It assumes that a *measured score* is composed of two parts: a *true score* and a *measurement error*. The total variance of scores is also composed of two parts: the true score variance and the error variance. According to the theory, measurement errors have a totally random pattern. Moreover, there is no correlation between the true score and the measurement error. By taking repeated measurements, the true score can be determined because the measurement errors ultimately cancel each other out due to this random pattern: the sum of the measurement errors is zero. The measured scores begin to group themselves around a mean score, i.e. around the true score. Essentially, the determination of reliability means that you determine the relative dominance of the true part of the variance over the variance of the measurement errors. In other words, the reliability is a number that expresses the relationship between the true score variance and the measurement error variance: the lower the measurement error, the higher the reliability.

> For example:
> A gardener wants to know the exact length of a garden. He therefore measures the length 10 times and takes the average of the measurement results. The gardener is using classical test theory. After all, the gardener assumes that the measurement errors will cancel each other out, therefore that he will not always make the same error, for example by repeatedly measuring an excessive length. The same applies if you measure your own body temperature, find an unexpectedly high value, and check the measurement by taking your temperature again after 10 minutes.

There are a number of ways to determine reliability. An obvious method is the *test – retest method*, where you repeat the measurement with the same instrument at a later time. The correlation (see Section 8.6.4) between both tests then provides an indication of the stability and therefore the reliability. Note that this test – retest correlation only indicates the degree with which the relative positions of the research units on the instrument are maintained. A research unit that scores higher during the first measurement than another research unit should also score higher on the second measurement. The entire group of units can score higher or lower on average with respect to the tested attribute over time, but as long as the scores change to the same degree, the correlation is high.

> For example:
> The scores of three research units at the first measurement are 10, 15 and 30, and those of the second measurement are 20, 30 and 60. The correlation between the measurements is then very high, but the scores have clearly not remained the same. If there is no clear reason for this change in the scores, then the measurement instrument must be unreliable.

A problem occurs if some of the research units begin to score higher and others score lower. This reduces the correlation.

> For example:
> The scores of the first measurement are 10, 15 and 30 and those of the second are 20, 15 and 30. In this case, the correlation is low, but only one single measure has changed, namely that of the first research unit. For some reason, the instrument is therefore unreliable only for some of the research units.

Another disadvantage of retesting is that it is difficult to carry out in practice. After all, it is expensive and you have to bother the research units twice with the same questions. Therefore, the *parallel test method* is also used. Then there are two instruments that measure the same concept and are therefore expected to have the same true score (and are therefore parallel). With this method, you are actually measuring the same group of objects twice, where the second measurement immediately follows the first.

> For example:
> You can measure height by using a ruler and by using a questionnaire in which you ask respondents to indicate their weight and clothing size.

However, with the parallel method the first instrument may affect the second. Moreover, it is difficult in practice to find two instruments that not only measure the same concept, but also have the same mean scores, the same variance of scores around the mean and the same correlations with still other instruments. Yet another method is to split the instrument in two, if possible (as with a questionnaire), and determine the correlation between the two halves.

For example:
You can determine the reliability of a questionnaire for absenteeism tendency by splitting it into two instruments, the first composed of even-numbered questions and the second composed of odd-numbered questions. You then compare the scores of both new instruments. Because the instrument is divided randomly, you should therefore expect only random differences between the mean scores on both instruments.

In an *item analysis* (see Section 7.2.2), you go yet a step further: the instrument (the 'scale') is split into single questions or items. Each item is considered to be a distinct measurement instrument for the concept being measured. You then determine whether all items measure the same thing, by determining their mutual correlations. The most widely used measurement for the reliability of a scale composed of individual items is *Cronbach's* α (*alpha coefficient*). Alpha is approximately equal to the mean correlation of all items with each other. Alpha therefore rises as the mean correlation of the items increases. This coefficient must therefore be as high as possible in order for the total set of items to be reliable. In practice, .60 is considered a minimum, .70 is acceptable and .80 or higher is good. The level of alpha, however, also depends on the number of items: the greater the number of items, the higher the value of alpha. Consequently, you should try to obtain a sufficiently high alpha with the smallest possible number of items.

Finally, you could consider the possibility of using *analysis of variance* to determine reliability. This is based on the so-called *generalizabilty theory*. This makes less rigid assumptions than classical test theory. It assumes that there are various sources of variance – such as time of measurement, different researchers and research units – which can be explicitly described and measured instead of simply being defined as random measurement errors (implicit to classical test theory). This method determines the contribution in terms of variance of each of these sources to the total measured variance. The observed (measured) score is not split into a true score and a measurement error, but into different types of true scores: for example, a true score related to the time of measurement, a true score related to the attributes of the research units and a true score related to the influence of the researcher. Depending on the aim of the study one specific type of variance (e.g. the researcher) is considered as error.

4.6.2 Validity

Once you are certain that you have a reliable measurement instrument, you must determine the validity of that instrument. Validity is important because it provides insight into the degree with which a measurement instrument achieves its aim: does it actually measure what you want to measure? For example, does a driving test actually measure the driving skill of subjects or the degree with which they play up to the examiner? An instrument that measures unreliably can never measure in a valid fashion, but an instrument can be reliable without being valid. After all, reliability (how is the measurement conducted?) does not say anything about the content of that which is being measured (what is being measured?), but only says something about the way in which the measurement is conducted. Reliability is therefore a precondition for validity. Your measurement could be very reliable, but you could actually measure something totally different than you intended.

> For example:
> Research is being conducted into the popularity of a specific brand of ice cream by measuring sales. Are you actually measuring the buyers' appreciation of the ice cream or the effectiveness of the marketing?

Depending on the aim of your research, you can test for various types of validity. Authors use many different terms for these types of validity. Various types of validity are discussed below with respect to the *measurement of concepts* (*measurement validity*). Later on in this book (Section 5.3.3) various types of *experimental validity* will be discussed.

If you are concerned with the question of whether or not the content of your measurement instrument represents (all) the relevant aspects of the concept, then you are concerned with *content validity*. If you want to construct an instrument to measure a concept, you should therefore first have a clear idea about the content of that concept, i.e. what the concept is about. Content validity can be evaluated by researchers and experts.

For example:

According to experts, do all the items on a questionnaire actually refer to the theoretical concept of absenteeism tendency, and do the items completely cover the contents of this concept? In other words, experts decide on the basis of the content of the items whether the items are valid measures of the intended construct.

If the question concerns whether the concept correlates (or in fact does not correlate) with other concepts in a way that can be expected from the theory, then this is *construct* (or *concept*) validity. There is a distinction between *convergent* (coming together) and *divergent* construct validity. Both have to do with the relationship between two concepts or constructs. With convergent validity you determine with which comparable constructs the concept correlates. The expectation is that the correlation is positive and not too low. With *discriminant* validity, you determine how the construct correlates with other constructs that are comparable to a certain degree, but still different. The expectation is that the correlation will be positive, but not too large. Discriminant validity also includes the process of testing your predictions concerning variables with which the construct must absolutely not correlate.

EXAMPLES OF CONVERGENT AND DISCRIMINANT VALIDITY

Generally speaking, you expect that a low level of absenteeism will have a positive correlation with good physical and mental health. The correlation must not be 0 (it must converge), but it must also not be 1 (it must be discriminant).

If the items or observations in the measurement instrument form a good sample from the domain you are researching, then there is *sample validity*.

For example:

If you want to know whether someone can drive a car, then you subject this individual to a sample of relevant aspects of driving. This is exactly what happens during a driving test.

Note that in this case there is no theoretical concept that you want to measure (such as absenteeism tendency), but there is a population of items (such as a domain with all conceivable tasks in the case of driving or a textbook that represents all material to be studied for the examination), from which you simply draw a sample. The disadvantage of sample validity is that you go no further than observing whether one individual or a company possesses certain skills (for example, driving skills, sales skills or innovation skills). However, due to a lack of a suitable theory, you often do not have an answer to the question of *why* this individual or company has insufficient skills.

If you are concerned with the relationship between a *latent, unobservable, theoretical* concept and a *manifest* measurement instrument that aims to measure the construct (see Section 4.4, 'Operationalizing'' '), this is called *instrumental validity*.

If the relationship between two manifest instruments that are measuring the same concept is central to the research, the term *congeneric validity* is used. You then use various methods to measure the same construct. In this case there is *multi-method research*.

EXAMPLES OF SAMPLE, INSTRUMENTAL AND CONGENERIC VALIDITY

You want to determine the validity of the driving test. Generally speaking, you can do this using two lines of reasoning:

1. You can assume that the test is representative, and that especially the critical parts are a representative sample from automobile driving. In that case, you appeal to the sample validity of the driving test.
2. Based on previous research and theory, you could assume that the criterion 'good driving skills' has a high correlation with the individual attribute 'stability'.

Secondly, assume that the driving test is also a good measure of 'ability to withstand stress'. Finally, assume that ability to withstand stress is a good predictor of the criterion construct stability. The driving test is then a good predictor of the criterion good driving skills via the construct validity of ability to withstand stress as a predictor for stability.

Ability to withstand stress and stability are concepts that are not directly measurable, but which you assume form the basis of the relationship between the driving test and driving skills. In addition, the relationships between the predictor concept (ability to withstand stress) and the predictor (driving test) and between the criterion concept (stability) and the criterion (driving skills) must be valid. This form of validity is defined as instrumental validity.

Finally the agreement between the measurements of two instruments (two operationalizations) for the same construct (for example, a driving theory test and an actual driving test) is called congeneric validity. This can be summarized in Figure 4.3.

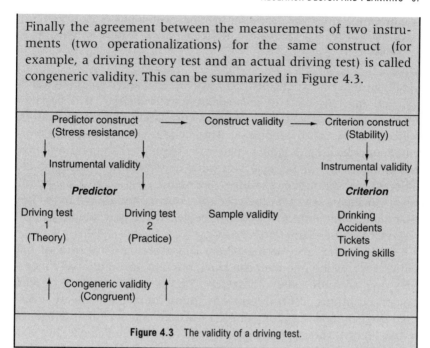

Figure 4.3 The validity of a driving test.

Figure 4.3 shows that another way to determine validity is to investigate whether the measurement instrument can predict another specific variable (this is called the criterion variable). This was the case in the above example concerning the driving test and driving skills.

Depending whether there is a time difference between the measurement of the predictor and the criterion, one refers to *predictive* or *concurrent* validity. In the case of predictive validity, there is a difference in the time when the instrument is used and when the criterion is measured. With concurrent validity there is no time difference; you use the instrument and measure the criterion at the same time. You then look at the correlation between the measurement instrument and a criterion that you think you can predict with the instrument.

For example:
In the context of research into personnel decisions, predictive validity is expressed in the correlation between the predictor (the score on the measurement instrument, such as an IQ test) and that, which is predicted (also called the criterion, such as the evaluation of the supervisor a year later). If the correlation between predictor and criterion is larger

(the evaluation of the supervisor improves with a higher IQ score), it becomes increasingly possible to predict the criterion score by using the predictor.

Finally in the context of construct, instrumental and congeneric validity, you must be alert to *contamination (confounding)*. This happens when you believe you have found a correlation between variables, which in fact exists by definition. This could occur because the theoretical concepts are the same or partly the same (for example, *dedication* and *involvement*), or because you have operationalized substantially different concepts (for example, *innovative capacity* and *competitive power*) in such a way that they are the same in operational terms (for example, you determine innovative power by the percentage of profit reserved for research).

Contamination also occurs when a measurement instrument not only measures the intended construct, but also unintentionally measures one or more other constructs. This is called *construct surplus*. Construct surplus occurs if too many unintentional, aspects are measured (for example, if a group of American students take an intelligence test in French, then you are measuring not only intelligence, but also knowledge of the French language). Construct under-representation can occur when the intended construct is insufficiently included (if it is measured by only a few items, for example). This is why you are advised to use multiple indicators or even multiple instruments to measure a construct. Therefore, ensure you take sufficient time and pay sufficient attention to making pure definitions and operationalizations of concepts to prevent contamination.

Face or impression validity concerns the question of whether the instrument is relevant to the concept and whether it is similar to the concept in the eyes of the respondents (the individuals whose responses are being measured with the instrument). As more people agree that the instrument appears at face value to be valid, the higher the face validity of the test. Note that content validity is comparable to this. However, while content validity concerns the viewpoints of experts, face validity concerns the opinions of respondents and possible clients.

For example:
Of the available selection instruments, the assessment centre (AC) has greater face validity than, for example, the psychological test. It is easier for applicants to see the relevance or value of the AC in connection with being selected for the job than is the case with the psychological test.

They believe that they can better demonstrate what they can do with the AC test than with a psychological test. As a result, the AC is more widely accepted by applicants than is the psychological test.

▌ 4.7 POPULATION AND SAMPLING

Besides formulating the hypotheses, defining and operationalizing the variables and determining the reliability and validity of the measurement instruments for the variables, you must also focus on the object or the unit of research: the *research population*. The first step is to select and define your research population. Population refers to every complete collection of research units or objects that collectively form your research domain (for example, people (respondents or subjects), households, departments, annual reports or companies). Further limitations are often placed on the population in terms of geography, age (minimum and maximum ages?), and other characteristics (for example, only males, only individuals with a minimum educational level, only mid-sized companies?). If the population is not too large, you can involve the entire population in the research. However, if you have a large population, then researching the entire population is an expensive and time-consuming task. In that case you can confine yourself to part of the population. However, this part must be representative for the relevant population as a whole. You do this by drawing a sample. A sample is a representative subgroup of the population.

The advantage of using a sample is that you don't have to study the entire population, even though you are going to make conclusions about this population. The bridge between sample and population is built by using statistical tests. It is therefore important to use a random sample. Drawing an adequate and responsible random sample can be a time-consuming task, which is frequently limited by practical considerations.

For example:
As part of a tutorial, organizational economics students wanted to conduct a study involving graduate economists. Based on the results, they could determine the opportunities and problems that they would meet after completing their own studies. One of the first and most important questions is which economists should they approach? Approaching economists from all possible specializations was objectionable because the results could be less relevant for organizational economists. Taking such a standpoint limits the population. A second limitation to the potential population is the amount of professional experience the

respondents are supposed to have. Economists who graduated between two and five years ago seemed best able to provide the necessary information. Economists who graduated before this were perhaps too far away from their study, while more recent graduates could perhaps be too close to their study. An important problem in this context, which placed clear limitations on the population, was the addresses that were available. For example, if the address file of the faculty newsletter was used, this could lead to a non-random group of respondents.

Once you have determined the required attributes of the sample, you must find a sampling frame. If this frame does not exist, you must establish one yourself. A sampling frame is a type of record in which research units and/or their attributes are registered (for example, the research units registered in the citizen registry of the municipality or an address list from the personnel department of the organization). This list of research units must be as similar as possible to the complete research population.

For example:
If you use the membership list of the Association of Graduates for a study of graduate economists, you can expect that you are using a random sample and that the results of the research will therefore only be applicable to the group of graduate economists who are members of this association.

Problems can occur if such lists or files are out of date or incomplete, if they contain undesired elements or if certain units in the list have more probability of being included in the sample. This could happen if they appear twice on the list for some reason (for example, a membership list on which married women appear both under their maiden names and married names).

Sometimes it is difficult or impossible to arrive at a good sampling frame. For example, a list of unemployed individuals is frequently contaminated if it is not properly updated. It may not only list people who have found jobs in the meantime, but it may also fail to list people who have recently become unemployed. Telephone books are another example of incomplete sampling frames because they do not contain people who have an unlisted number. Moreover, people with low incomes or those from certain ethnic groups are under-represented in comparison to the composition of the entire population, because such individuals often do not have a telephone. To avoid these problems, you could randomly dial telephone numbers (*random digit dialling*), but there are also practical objections to this method. For example, you might dial numbers that do not exist or numbers that do not answer. Even if they do answer, the answering individual may be a child and therefore not meet the requirements for the sample. And people without telephones are still excluded from the sampling frame. It is important to think carefully about such issues, since you ultimately obtain your sample from such sources.

For example:
If you want to conduct a study into how employees spend their free time, and you decide to conduct interviews during the day at a museum, then individuals who do not regularly visit a museum will have a much lower chance of being included in the research. In addition, units can be included in the sample (such as foreign tourists), which do not belong to the intended population of employees.

If the sample elements are smaller units than required by the research question, then you can consider whether it is possible to combine a suitable quantity of units into a single unit; this is called the choice of *level of aggregation*. For example, you could collectively define the behaviour of all individuals in an organization as an attribute of the organization.

For example:
You decide to measure the culture of an organization by measuring and adding the scores of individual organization members on a culture questionnaire. Or you could combine various groups of employees who are members of a team. The various teams together then represent the organization.

It is generally recommended that you collect and analyse data wherever possible at the same level as your research question. Does the research involve individuals, teams or parts of the organization?

A recent development is *multi-level research*. This is where group membership is taken into account, and groups within groups are considered (for example, individuals within a department and departments within companies).

4.7.1 Representativeness of the sample

The method used to draw a sample is important for the interpretation and generalization of the research results. An important concept in this regard is that of *representativeness*. The important question here is, to what extent is this sample comparable with (or representative for?) the total population? Representativeness cannot be used in general terms. A sample can only be representative for one or more specific variables or attributes of the population.

A sample is representative for a variable if the values of the variable for the units or objects in the sample have the same relative *frequency distribution* as in the total population of objects from which the sample is drawn.

> For example:
> In a sample of students, the age distribution must be the same as the age distribution in the total population (defined as all students enrolled at the university).

A sample is *biased* if it is no longer representative, that is it does not provide a good picture of an attribute of the population. You can never say that a sample is completely representative, since the frequency distribution for some variables in the population is unknown. Moreover, the number of variables is theoretically infinite.

> For example:
> A sample of young, beginning companies is only representative by approximation because every day more new companies are launched and may quickly go out of business.

However, as a researcher you should make this approximation as accurately as possible.

4.7.2 Sample size

It is not an easy task to determine the minimum sample size. In any case, the sample size is not – or only marginally – determined by the size of the population to which you want to apply the results, unless the population is relatively small (fewer than 100 units or objects, for example). Therefore, you do not necessarily need a certain relative percentage of the entire population as a sample to acquire a representative picture of the total population, nor is a specific absolute number of research units required. However, a number of analysis techniques, which will be discussed in Chapter 8, do require a minimum number of research units in combination with the number of variables.

For example:
Factor analysis (see Section 8.6.5) requires a minimum number of 10 research units per variable. This type of analysis also requires a minimum absolute number of research units (at least 100, for example).

For most statistical tests, the sample size must not be too small, since it is otherwise difficult to discover significant correlations. It is therefore important in this phase of your research to think about the analyses that you plan to conduct.

Sample size also varies according to the data collection method (see Chapter 6). For example, a smaller sample size for interviews is often used than for a questionnaire that is mailed. This is due to the high investment of time and money that is required for such research. The data collection method is in turn related to the quantity of knowledge that is already available about the topic. If there is little knowledge available during the inductive research phase, small samples are more acceptable than when you are testing knowledge on a large scale. For example, it is better to first determine which instruments you can use to measure which constructs by initially using a small group of research units. You can then use these instruments on a larger sample.

Sample size is determined in part by the following factors:

- The level of imprecision of the results. If you want to have more precise and reliable results, you must have a larger sample. As a result, errors and coincidence will have a smaller effect on the mean score of a group, among other things.

  For example:
  An individual has been on sick leave for 30 days this year. If this individual is part of a sample with nine others who have each been on sick leave for three days, then the mean is 5.7 days of sick leave per year. If this individual is part of a sample with 99 other individuals who have all been on sick leave for three days during the year, then the mean is 3.3 days per year.

- The non-response percentage (these are respondents who have been approached for the research, but have not taken part) can distort the results if there is a correlation between the non-response and the measured variables. To check whether such a correlation exists, you can, if possible, ask several core questions to non-respondents to find out more about the reasons for their non-response (for example, is the non-response caused by illness, moving, a refusal to participate, or other aspects that concern the topic?) in order to determine the effects of the non-response on the results of the research. You can also make a comparison between the attributes of the sample and the population. In this way, you can compare rapidly responding individuals with those who respond later. If these groups differ on a specific variable, you can assume that the sample is not representative for that variable.

> For example:
> Late-responding respondents may be more frequently sick on average. If frequency of illness is an important research variable, you should not allow the results of your research to be distorted because you only included the data from the respondents who responded rapidly (who were sick less frequently).

- The frequency distribution (see Section 4.7.1) of variables in a population. To study the relationship between all kinds of variables, you must have sufficient numbers of research units with differing combinations of variables. A rule of thumb is that you should have at least 20 research units for each possible combination of variables.

> For example:
> If you want to study men and women in various age categories in various organizations, use a data matrix (see Chapter 8) with many cells. For each cell, there should be at least 20 research units. This is because statistical analyses, such as the mean or the standard deviation, which are calculated with at least 20 research units, (see Chapter 8) are reasonably reliable.

4.7.3 Types of sampling

There are two ways to draw a sample:

1. If it is required that every element in the population has an equal chance to be included in the research, a *random (non-systematic)* sample is preferable. Random means that the sample is chosen by a random draw. It refers to the way in which the sample is drawn (the *sampling method*); the representativeness discussed earlier is related to what kind of sample is ultimately chosen (the *sample result*). Virtually all statistical tests assume that a random sampling method has been used. Although there are major advantages to random samples (for example, little previous knowledge of the population is required, and the acquired data are easy to analyse), it is not always used. This is because it is not always the most efficient way to draw a sample. Since you often have some previous

knowledge of the population, you can choose a more efficient method of drawing a sample, such as stratified sampling (see 2 below).

You can also draw a *systematic* sample. First determine the total number of research units in the sampling frame (for example, all 350 enrolled first-year students) and the number of units to be selected (for example, 70 students). The fraction is the ratio between both numbers. It is important to choose a random starting number in the sampling frame. Then select at a certain interval (for example, every fifth individual from the list or draw a sample of students based on their student number).

The danger of systematic sampling is that you don't know beforehand how strong the selection will affect the result. For example, if the list is arranged according to a characteristic that is partly related to the research topic, and this is not immediately obvious, the selection method can affect the result. You can check whether this is the case by determining whether you systematically get a different result by using a different starting number. In that case, you could perhaps re-order the list. Sometimes an analysis of the data can provide an answer, for example by comparing individuals in the sample with those who are not in the sample according to various characteristics. If you do not find any difference with respect to a characteristic, then you can conclude that the sample is representative for that characteristic.

2. If you aim for the highest possible precision in the results, and you want to obtain the best possible distribution of the total sample across all the layers of the population, then a *stratified* sample is an obvious choice. An important advantage of a stratified sample is that you know beforehand that you have sufficient numbers of research units to conduct statistical analyses. With this method, you divide the population beforehand according to attributes (such as age or number of personnel), which you expect are related to research variables (such as absenteeism). To draw a stratified sample, it is necessary to know which attributes are important, that these occur in the population and that they are easy to assess or measure. Then draw a random sample from these various layers (sometimes called *sub-populations* or *strata*) of the population. The units in various layers do not have equal chances to be drawn for the sample. By using this method for drawing a sample, you can make sure that the sample is representative for those specific variables.

For example:
A random sample of companies contains primarily small companies, since these occur most frequently. But if you also want to involve large companies in the research because you suspect that the size of the company affects absenteeism, then you can first make layers (strata) according to the size of the company and then draw a random sample from this layer. However, you must then be able to properly measure the size of the company.

If a stratified sample leads to a small, but very important group being under-represented in the research, you can deliberately aim to have this group over-represented. This is called a *non-proportional* stratified sample.

For example:
As part of a study of employees and supervisors in a company where supervisors make up only 3 per cent of the total staff, you can choose to study all supervisors (100 per cent of all supervisors in comparison to, for example, 25 per cent of all employees) in order to arrive at a sufficiently large number of supervisors to conduct specific analyses.

In order to draw conclusions about the entire, combined population, weighting techniques can be used to compensate for the fact that a specific group is over-represented with respect to other groups. You can also draw a sample all at once (*simple*) or in steps (*multiple*). An example of a multiple sample is when companies are randomly selected and then another random sample of the employees from these companies is taken.

With a *quota sample*, an absolute number of research units with specific attributes is established beforehand, which must be included in the research. For example, as part of a study into the causes of absenteeism, it can be desirable that at least a sufficient number of 100 long-term sick individuals and 100 long-term healthy individuals are included in the sample.

Finally, there is the *snowball* sample. In this method a limited number of people are asked about other people they know with specific attributes (or combinations of attributes) that are important for the research. These individuals are then asked whether they know other people.

For example:
During research into specific inherited attributes that can cause illness, a patient is asked about other family members with the same inherited attributes.

This type of sample can be used, for instance, when no suitable sampling frame is available. The disadvantage of this method of drawing samples is that it can lead to a select sample.

▌ 4.8 BEHAVIOURAL RULES

Before and during the research, a number of behavioural rules must be followed. These rules concern ethical/political and practical issues. The most common ethical issues have to do with the respondents. Political issues are frequently concerned with the clients. An example of such a problem is the situation where the research produces results that are not beneficial to the client.

With respect to the respondents, make sure that they are not needlessly bothered and that they do not suffer any negative consequences from participating in the research. Examples of ethical questions you should ask yourself are:

- *Is the research necessary?*
  Organizational science research not only requires time and money, it frequently involves people as well. Before the research begins, you must be certain that:
  – the research into this topic is necessary;
  – the necessary data cannot be found somewhere else;
  – there is no other, less disturbing way to answer the research question (for example, surveying the number of absenteeism reports during the year by studying the employee information system instead of questioning employees);
  – you are not asking any unnecessary questions.

- *Do you know any individuals in the research sample?*
  Try to avoid having to involve people you know in the research. If this is unavoidable, decide beforehand how the research might affect your relationship with them or vice versa.

- *Is the privacy of the respondents assured?*
  Many people and companies will participate in research if the results cannot be traced back to specific individuals and companies. Respondents should only participate in research voluntarily. You must determine if they object to being reported by name or if they are recognizable in some other way.

For example:
Do not use the following formulations in your report, 'The shoe manufacturer in the southern part of the UK, the grocer who pays attention to the small details, the largest private employer in the US', because it is quite obvious which companies are being referred to.

- *Will the respondents be given sufficient, honest information about the research?*
The respondents must be informed that they are the objects of research in one way or another. Sometimes it may be necessary in the interest of the research to withhold some information, since this can increase the risk of influencing the respondents.

  For example:
  Research is being conducted into the changes in the degree of pre-paredness to participate in research. It is quite possible that respond-ents will respond differently if they know the aim of the research and that the results will consequently provide a distorted picture of reality.

- *What will happen with the results of the research?*
What are the consequences of the results of the research for the respondents and for society? Are the results in their interest, or do they in fact damage their interests? Is a grievance procedure available?

- *Should confidentiality agreements be signed?*
Some companies require such an agreement. However, these can be so vague that they include almost everything, even research results they do not like! Therefore check carefully to see which topics are included under the confidentiality agreement and what the consequences will be for the research report.

Besides the ethical side of research, there is also a practical side. A great deal of time, expertise and money is involved in the development of a good research instrument. The question is, what will happen with the research instrument and the results? Are they your property or that of your client (if you have one)? For example, if a questionnaire is generalizable to other companies, it could indeed be a commercially interesting object. You could then sell the questionnaire, or part of it, to recover the initial investment. It is important to make such arrangements beforehand.

Besides the commercial aspect, there is also a scientific aspect linked to the ownership of the questionnaire and the results. The method that was developed and the results that were found can be scientifically interest-ing. You can use the topic, the method and the results as part of a scientific article. The question is then, what can be included in such an article? Of course, you can make certain that the organizations are not recognizable. Make agreements about this before the research begins.

▋ 4.9 RESEARCH PROPOSAL

The preparatory work and the choices that made up to now must be written in a research proposal. This proposal includes the following parts:

- The aim and research question, the expected output and the applicability of the research. What are you going to do, why are you going to do it, what is already known about the topic, what can this research contribute to existing knowledge, what results will it produce and what can you do with the results?
- The clients and supervisors, links with other research and frameworks of cooperation.
- The theoretical framework, the research model, the operationalization of variables and the method for drawing a sample from the population. What does the research model look like, what are your hypotheses, how do you measure the variables and how exactly do you arrive at the research units?
- The quantity and nature of data to be collected. What kind of data are you going to collect, when and how and from whom are you going to collect? Check to make sure the effort required is in balance with the relevance of the research question and the means that are available.
- A global plan of analysis. What data are you going to compare, how are you going to compare, which methods are you going to use and in which sequence? It is a good idea to think beforehand about the analyses that are going to be possible in general, and what conclusions and interpretations would be possible with which level of precision.
- A realistic and complete (financial) budget. Include, if applicable, expenses for staff for data collection, processing and analysis, apparatus, the reporting process, travel and lodging, meeting and office expenses, office space and storage expenses, advisory expenses and the financial consequences of possible setbacks. Determine whether you can acquire funding for the research. If you can, stipulate where and how you can acquire such funding.
- A timescale. This provides a summary of all the steps in a research project. For each part of the research, estimate how much time it will require, when it will take place and by whom it will be carried out. Here are several suggestions for planning:

– Plan the data collection in such a way that there is sufficient time beforehand to read the relevant literature and draw hypotheses that you are going to test in your research, but also make sure that there is sufficient time afterwards to process the results and draw conclusions.
– Do not leave any holes in the schedule. For example, you could write a report on the literature study in the meantime. Take account of holidays. Order materials in a timely fashion and design the research instrument in plenty of time so that you can make it, test it and adjust it.

- Have the research proposal critically evaluated by your supervisors and clients. Clarify the mutual expectations: does your client want to have a say in the research or in the reporting? Does the client want to do something with the results?

In closing:

- Plans are not so definitive that you can never deviate from them. They are only useful if you keep them up to date and change them if necessary. Therefore check your progress regularly and write progress reports.

Once the research proposal is ready, you have to decide how you are going to conduct the research. Are you going to set up an experiment or are you going to do extensive survey research? The following chapter will discuss such research strategies.

EXAMPLE OF A RESEARCH SCHEDULE

Activity
- Formulate research question
- Conduct literature research and discussions with experts
- Consult with clients and modify the research question if necessary
- Establish research design: find or develop measurement instrument, test it and modify it
- Recruit research units, draw sample
- Collect data
- Process data
- Analyse data
- Write draft report
- Consult with parties involved and modify draft report; write definitive report
- Presentation

Chapter 5

RESEARCH STRATEGIES

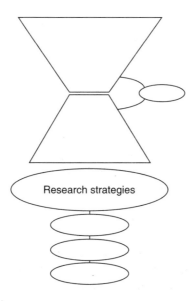

■ 5.1 INTRODUCTION

In Chapter 2, it was stated that the type of research question had consequences for the design and implementation of the research. This relationship will be discussed more extensively here. There are a number of research strategies. In Section 5.2, two classification principles are discussed, which characterize types of research strategies. In Section 5.3, the three main strategies will be discussed: survey research; the case study; and the experiment. These strategies differ according to the degree in which they show causal links between concepts. This is why the topic of causality is discussed at the end of the chapter in Section 5.4.

▮ 5.2 CLASSIFICATION PRINCIPLES

One classification principle, which can be used to characterize the various types of research strategies, is the distinction between structured and unstructured research.

5.2.1 Unstructured research

If you have a descriptive or explorative research question (see Section 2.3) or your research is still in an orientation phase and you therefore have little information available beforehand, unstructured research is a good method. Unstructured research means that you begin looking for indications for possible links between concepts, perhaps by making observations and asking questions.

> For example:
> A high level of absenteeism has been noticed at a department. You do not know what this absenteeism is caused by, so you decide to search for various, possible explanatory factors that are related to absenteeism.

In addition, unstructured research is often used to illustrate structured research. Sometimes a citation or an anecdote can provide good support for a presentation of quantitative material (figures) or be used as an example. The disadvantage of unstructured research is that it takes a relatively large amount of time and money, but it does provide a great deal of information. There is a risk, however, that you will be swamped by a large quantity of data that is not immediately relevant. You can prevent this to some extent by working from a very precisely defined research question.

> For example:
> If you want to investigate the causes of high absenteeism, then you could draw up the following list of attention points:
> – types of illnesses;
> – working conditions;
> – changes in the structure of the organization;
> – style of leadership.

With unstructured research, you therefore do not collect data without any preparation. You generally draw up a list of points of attention beforehand. However, this list can change somewhat during your research – you may add a point of attention or remove one. You must document these changes in your research report.

You can then analyse the substantive results of the unstructured research by categorizing and qualifying the various parts of your research. However, because you will later provide an interpretation (possibly a subjective one) as a researcher, this can reduce the objectivity of the research.

5.2.2 Structured research

If you know beforehand exactly what data you require (to test specific hypotheses, for example), you will conduct structured research. You will then focus on finding support for your expectations. In comparison with unstructured research, structured research requires relatively little time and money. After all, you know beforehand what concepts you are searching for, and you can collect data in a focused manner. The risk in structured research is that you may not notice other relevant correlations and therefore collect no information about them. Consequently, structured research can bring up questions concerning the possible relevance of other variables, thereby leading to further research.

Table 5.1 provides a summary of characteristics of structured and unstructured research.

Table 5.1 Summary of the characteristics of structured and unstructured research

Structured research	Unstructured research
Research to test hypotheses	Explorative research
Data are often quantitative	Data are often qualitative
Relatively low costs	Relatively high costs
Closed questions: requires more time beforehand during the construction of questions	Open questions: requires more time afterwards when processing data
Relatively many options and high dependence on the researcher	Relatively high dependence on respondents
Risk: may forget relevant variables	Risk: information overload

5.2.3 Qualitative and quantitative research

The distinction between structured and unstructured research also has to do with the distinction between quantitative and qualitative research. This distinction is made on the basis of the data collected. Quantitative research is where the results are numerical in nature. Qualitative research is where the results are *not directly* numerical in nature, but are composed, for example, of words, narrations or descriptions of behaviour, which must later be categorized and quantified (converted into numerical values).

> For example:
> If you do not provide possible answers beforehand, a question such as, 'How do you assess the level of absenteeism in this company?' is a qualitative question: the respondents can state what they think in their own words. To quantify this question, you can provide a number of possible answers to the respondents, such as:
>
> | 1 | 2 | 3 | 4 | 5 |
> |---|---|---|---|---|
> | very low | low | normal | high | very high |
>
> In this case, it is possible to assign a numerical value directly to the answers.
> An example of a quantitative question is, 'How many people call in sick each month at the purchasing department?'

The degree of structure in your research and the data you collect are often related. If your research is unstructured in nature, then the data are generally qualitative in nature. If your research is structured, then the data are often quantitative. However, quantitative data are sometimes collected as part of unstructured research. If you ask someone's age as part of an unstructured interview, this is an example of a quantitative piece of information.

Besides qualitative and quantitative data, there are also qualitative and quantitative *data analysis methods*. Generally speaking, qualitative research requires more time *afterwards*, during the data analysis phase, since you then have to quantify the various answers. Quantitative research requires more time during the design phase of the instrument because you have to design your answer scales *beforehand*. In qualitative research, however, you still have to make calculations, and you still have to understand statistics. The only difference is that you quantify your data afterwards instead of beforehand.

For example:
Establishing a frequency distribution of the use of specific words in an interview, or ascertaining the amount of attention a company pays in its annual report to the theme of 'the environment' by counting the number of words used to discuss this topic.

In summary: with quantitative data, the respondent directly chooses the number that best expresses what he/she thinks and/or feels. With qualitative data, the researcher determines afterwards which figure best expresses the data from the respondent.

▮ 5.3 MAIN TYPES OF RESEARCH STRATEGIES

The three main types of research strategies can be categorized using the following two dimensions:

- *The degree to which the researcher intervenes*. In some kinds of research, the researcher may intervene – sometimes literally – with the research units (experiments, for example). In other types of research, there is no intervention, and the research units may even be unaware that research is being conducted in which they play a role (theoretical literature research and computer simulations, for example).
- *The degree to which the researcher wants to make generally valid conclusions*. In some kinds of research, the researcher wants to generalize the results (survey research, for example). In other types of research, the researcher may want to study a very specific case (a case study, for example). This dimension was previously discussed in the section concerning the three requirements for general, simple and exact research (see Figure 1.1 in Chapter 1).

Figure 5.1 shows the effect of placing these two dimensions on a graph.

Figure 5.1 shows that the laboratory experiment is a strategy that intervenes with the research unit and focuses on arriving at generally applicable conclusions. In contrast, theoretical literature research entails absolutely no intervention, but still focuses on making general assertions. A case study involves less intervention than a field experiment because in a case study you simply observe natural processes. Both the case study and the field experiment are less generally applicable because there is no population from which they are drawn as a

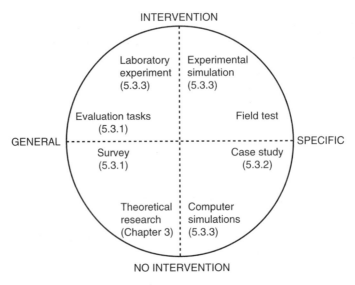

Figure 5.1 Classification of research strategies based on two dimensions (adapted from Runkel and McGrath, 1972). Reprinted with permission.

sample. During evaluation tasks, carefully selected individuals on a panel are asked to give their opinions about specific topics.

The three main research strategies are discussed more extensively in the following sections: survey research; the case study; and the experiment. Especially in organizational science research, mixed forms of these main strategies are used. Survey research, for example, can be part of action research (*survey – feedback*). In this mixed form, you use the report of the survey research as an intervention in the organization, instead of it being the end point of the research. Survey research can also be part of a case study (the *case survey*).

Various methods of data collection can be used within a main strategy. For example, during an experiment you can make observations, use a questionnaire and measure physical responses (see Chapter 6).

5.3.1 Survey research

If you are dealing with a large number of topics and a large number of research units (in a survey, these are called *respondents*), survey research is an obvious method to choose (for example, research before elections concerning the preference for political parties). Survey research is often used in organizational science research. The research units are usually sampled from the total population. If you draw a good sample, the results of a survey can be generalized to the total population. The strength of this research design is that you can then draw general conclusions.

The relatively large number of research units and topics that are studied in a survey means that you generally work with quantitative data which yields research results that are easy to process. Survey research is therefore relatively efficient in terms of time and money. It is very suitable not only for descriptive research questions, but also to test hypotheses.

Survey research concerns the opinions, attitudes, motives, values and norms of research units, or their actions. This generally means that you have to question people, by using an oral interview, for example, or – much more commonly – the written questionnaire (see Chapters 6 and 7).

For studying some concepts, such as interaction processes between people or groups of people, the survey is less well suited; this is because the respondents themselves are in the midst of the process and are therefore less capable of looking at themselves and their relationship with other individuals of groups. (For example, how do the Employees Work Council and the management behave with respect to each other? Or, how does a management team develop?) It is preferable to investigate these concepts by means of observation as part of a field experiment or case study. Observation is the best way to study the *behaviour* of research units. In survey research, however, specific behaviours can also be investigated, such as behaviour that took place at an earlier time ('How did you previously behave as a supervisor?'), behaviour that is quite seldom ('What kind of behaviour do you display as a supervisor when you discover that an employee is improperly using sick leave?'), or behaviour that occurs in private (during closed management meetings). These behaviours are much more difficult to study using observation.

There is also a number of disadvantages to survey research. First of all, survey research is susceptible to viewpoint and memory effects; after all, you are asking people to remember something or to formulate an opinion. A related problem is that survey research depends on the willingness and the ability of respondents to answer. In addition, as a researcher you can cause a distorting effect during an oral interview or a written questionnaire. This can occur, for example, if you lead the respondents, consciously or unconsciously, to answer in a socially desirable manner.

You can conduct survey research at one point in time or at multiple points in time. The latter is called *longitudinal research*. This type of research is suitable for mapping out changes in variables over time and cause–effect relationships between variables. A special variant of longitudinal survey research is *panel research*, where you ask the same questions to the same group of individuals at various points in time (in Figure 5.1, this research strategy was defined as evaluation tasks). For example, a researcher follows the same group of people who are questioned every five years about the important developments in their work and their health. If you want to ascertain *trends* over time, you can ask the same questions to different people at different points in time (for example, young people between 20 and 30 years of age during the 1970s, 80s and 90s). The advantage of this type of research is that it makes it easier to investigate changes in variables and cause–effect relationships between variables, since there is a difference in the time periods when the variables are measured. This is one of the three demands you must satisfy to conclude that there is a causal relationship between variables (see Section 5.4).

Finally, if you want to map out developments, you can conduct *continuous research*. With this type of research, you do not conduct research at different (discrete) times. Instead, you continuously conduct research during a certain time period. For example, as part of a study into the effects of work behaviour on physical stress reactions, you can attach various types of measurement apparatus to people. This apparatus is worn for several days, so that as a researcher you can link their work behaviour to their physical responses at any time of the day. You should take account of the fact that the analysis of such data is more complicated than of data that is collected at a single point in time.

5.3.2 Case study

If the aim of your research is to conduct an intensive study of a phenomenon within the total, natural surroundings, then a *case study* is the appropriate method. The case study is often used to describe, rank and explore data with the aim of generating hypotheses or illustrating an existing theory. In the latter situation, the case study is typically used to illustrate or clarify a theoretical argument. In situations where the case study is used as a basis for theory development, this is referred to as *grounded theory*. This method attempts to develop a theory from the 'ground up', i.e. without making any assumptions beforehand. In this way you will allow as few ideas as possible to affect the theory development. However, this is difficult to accomplish because you always require certain assumptions in order to arrive at useful interpretations.

The most important characteristic of a case study is that you systematically describe a single case; this case could be a company, a department or even a single individual. In contrast to the survey, you therefore have a small number of research units. In some cases, you have only a single research unit, $N = 1$ (N is the number of research units).

Note: Although you are studying a single case, you can still collect data from multiple sources, such as various sources within a single company. If the study concerns only one company, and this company is treated as a unit in the analysis, the results and the report, this is still defined as a case study even if multiple data sources are used.

In a case study, there are often more variables than research units.

For example:
For his research, which had the aim of developing a theory concerning management styles, Mintzberg tracked a small number of managers for a certain length of time in order to study what managers actually do. The number of characteristics that he observed in the behaviour of the managers and their surroundings was very large, however, much larger than the number of managers.

In a case study you therefore often collect data about the same phenomenon in more than one way. This certainly places high demands on you as a case researcher, since you must be capable of applying various data collection methods. For example, you often conduct interviews with various individuals in the organization and you make observations. As part of a case study you can also collect information in a quantitative fashion. It is possible, for instance, to conduct a survey within a single company (a 'case survey'). An important aspect in this situation is therefore the degree to which the results and the conclusions of the various data collection methods point in the same direction.

An advantage of a case study is that it can provide deeper insight into the ways in which people and departments respond to each other, have mutual expectations about each other and accommodate their behaviour to each other. A disadvantage of the case study is that the results are not *statistically generalizable*. They are only valid for the specific situation of the individuals, company or the department that is studied. After all, you have not drawn the case from a population (in a select manner). For this reason, a case study is not generalized to a population of cases (to other departments or organizations, for example), but to a theoretical domain. This is called *analytical generalization*. If you conduct case study research, you should preferably have a theory in mind. If you conduct many individual case studies without the unifying principle of a theory, your research will be hit or miss.

> For example:
> A study of strategic decision making in teams of top managers is being conducted. Before the researchers began to study a specific team of managers, they identified a number of important concepts, such as 'conflict' and 'power' that were based on the relevant literature. These concepts were then measured by means of interviews or questionnaires. It turned out that a number of the concepts that were selected for theoretical reasons were indeed related to characteristics of the decision-making process.

However, selecting and using specific theoretical concepts beforehand must not prevent you from keeping your eyes and ears open while conducting the case study.

In case studies, it is important for to have a correct and complete description of the case. If the case is an organization, you must first describe the *organizational chart*. This is a schematic diagram of the various parts of the organization. However, it primarily shows the hierarchical structure of the organization, not the relative importance of the various departments. To define the mutual relationships of the various parts of the organization, the following aspects can be described:

- The work floor: what does the work floor look like where the employees carry out work that is directly related to the company's products or services? How does the transformation process of *input → throughput → output* take place?
- The top management of the organization: how does it ensure that the aims, mission and long-term strategy of the organization are attained? How are internal events (within the organization) tuned with external events (in the organization's surroundings)?
- Middle management as a link between the work floor and top management: how does it give shape to its role?
- The technical structure: how are work processes given shape, how are activities planned and implemented? How are the employees on the work floor trained to conduct these activities? Which control and evaluation mechanisms are built into the system to assure the continuation of the processes?
- Support staff: which departments provide support services to the rest of the organization? Which support services are outsourced?

Other factors that can be described include:

- The history of the organization, its beginning and development to the present (for example, the age of the company).
- The type of organization (for example, who owns the company and what kind of product does it make or what kind of service does it provide?).
- The size of the organization (for example, sales and profit figures).
- The composition of company staff with indicators such as the total number of employees.
- Growth or shrinkage in recent years.
- The most important demographic developments that are expected.
- The degree of centralization and formalization within the company.

To acquire an impression of changes that take place in time, it is also useful to study the organizational charts from previous years. In this way you can discover trends, such as a reduction in the number of hierarchical levels within the organization and an accompanying increase in the staff/supervisor ratio. Finally, it is useful to make comparisons with companies who operate under comparable conditions or in similar sectors (this is called *benchmarking*). These issues will be discussed more extensively in the following chapter in the section about using existing material in the form of indicators.

> For example:
> If the research topic is to assess the level of absenteeism and the reason for absenteeism at two departments, it is important to determine not only the level of absenteeism at these departments, but also the absenteeism figures that apply to the entire company or the entire sector.

As stated previously, the case study can also comprise multiple individual cases. If you are conducting this type of research, you need to map out specific phenomena by comparing various cases in terms of similarities and differences. Depending on your aim when making this comparison, select as many similar or different cases as possible. The minimization of the differences between cases regarding a single variable is referred to as minimizing the variance on this variable. This may concern either the independent or the dependent variable (see Section 4.2). You can also maximize the differences between cases regarding a single variable; this is called maximizing the variance on this variable. Consequently, there are four possibilities for comparing cases with each other, as shown in Table 5.2.

Table 5.2 Research strategies for selecting cases

	Minimizing the variance	Maximizing the variance
For independent variables	(1) Cases are as similar as possible concerning independent variables: do similar cases produce the same result?	(3) Cases differ as much as possible regarding independent variables: do differing cases also produce a different result (or in fact the same result)?
For dependent variables	(2) Cases are as similar as possible concerning dependent variables: which factors are important for the results with similar cases?	(4) Cases differ as much as possible from each other concerning dependent variables: which factors are important for the results with different types of cases?

From Swanborn, P.A. 1994. Het ontwerpen van case-studies: Enkele keuzen (Designing case studies: some choices), *Mens & Maatschappij, 69,* 322–35.

1. If your underlying research question is, 'Do similar cases also produce the same results?' then you must select cases that are as similar as possible regarding the independent variables, such as the size of the company or the type of technology at the departments. This ensures that the variance for the possible causal variable is minimal.

   For example:
   'Are companies that are equal in size and that operate in the same sector also similar in terms of their absenteeism profile?'

2. If the aim of the research is to find possible causes of similar success with different cases, you must design the research in such a way that the cases do not differ very much in their results. In this situation, you should minimize the variance for the possible result variables. Here as well, you should select cases that are as similar as possible, but with respect to the dependent variables. You then attempt to determine what possible causal factors the cases have in common. These could be the cause of success. However, you must be careful to not only select successful cases (sometimes called *best practice* cases). Such a research design is weak because it is unknown if the same conditions are also present with less successful cases: after all, there is no control group. Cases are selected based on

the successful results at one point in time. Such results are usually not exactly the same at another point in time. You therefore run the risk of indicating specific variables as causes when they actually contribute nothing or little to success. They are defined as success variables simply because they occur in all the cases that were studied. It is only when you can link the presence or absence of success to the presence or absence of a specific variable that you can be more certain about drawing this conclusion.

> For example:
> At the beginning of the 1980s, Peters and Waterman conducted research into the success factors of large organizations in America. In 1990, Pascale studied the current situation of the 43 companies that Peters and Waterman defined as 'excellent'. Approximately half of these companies had either grown weak or were in serious trouble. Pascale concluded that theory is essential to such research and that researchers should not only look at the best companies in the long term, but also at the worst companies.

3. Another possibility concerns choosing cases that differ as much as possible as the independent variables. The research question is then, 'Do differing cases produce a different result or in fact the same result?'

> For example:
> The causes of the success of the US economy can also be studied by comparing it with the historical causes of an equally successful economy of a totally different type of country, such as Japan.

4. If your research question is, 'Which factors are important for the results of different types of cases?' then the variance is maximized for dependent variables. When using this strategy to distinguish successful cases from less successful ones, you must be careful that you do not establish two groups that differ simultaneously regarding a number of causes. This would make it nearly impossible to separate the effects of these causes.

When conducting either a single case study or a multiple one, it is essential that you summarize and/or structure the results. The study cannot simply be a collection of individual cases. You can structure the data in various ways to acquire insight into the entire case study or to make a comparison with other case studies possible. Yin (1984) distinguishes a number of possible structures. The most important of these are the linear–analytical, the comparative, the chronological and the suspense structure.

1. You would choose the *linear–analytical* variant if you intend to make a comparison between theory and practice. This is the most common form of case study, especially in scientific reports (see Chapter 9). It operates as follows: formulate a research question from the existing literature. Then study a single case or multiple cases. After that, analyse the resulting data. Finally, compare the theory with your findings. Then draw conclusions and make recommendations for further research.

2. If your aim is to compare more than one case or to ascertain a development within a case, the *comparative method* is the appropriate variant. You then describe the cases to be compared with the aim of ascertaining differences between the cases or changes over time within a single case. The advantage of comparative research is that you can always make conclusions. This is because the conclusions can always be related to something. Generally speaking, there are three types of results in comparative research.

   > For example:
   > The absenteeism at company A is higher than company B/or higher than a year ago.
   > The absenteeism at company A is equal to company B/or equal to one year ago.
   > The absenteeism at company A is lower than that at company B/or lower than a year ago.

3. If your aim, for example, is to describe a reorganization process at one or more companies or to describe a development over time, then the *chronological variant* is appropriate. The sequence of events determines the line of your argument.

4. If the aim of your research is to explain certain results, then the *suspense variant* is the recommended approach. In the same way that mystery novels begin with the murder, the suspense structure begins with the results of the case study (or studies). During the remainder of the report, you discuss the reasons or causes for your findings. Consequently, the suspense structure is in fact the reverse of the linear–analytical structure.

A specific example of a case study concerns *evaluation research*. This is used to evaluate whether an intervention has been efficiently implemented and has been effective in a specific case. One of the first problems with this approach is determining what costs and benefits must be included. A second problem is how these costs and benefits must be quantified.

For example:

The research concerns an evaluation of a technical training programme to reduce production staff absenteeism and increase performance by reducing the risk of industrial accidents. Which costs should be taken into account? Only the costs that are incurred with the training itself? Or also the costs resulting from the fact that some of the personnel are not present on the work floor due to the training? What method will be used to measure performance? Finally, if an improvement in performance is observed, is that actually the result of the training?

A third important problem concerns when the cost–benefit analysis will be conducted. *Ex-ante research* is used if the analysis is conducted before the intervention (such as the above training programme) is in force. *Ex-post research* is conducted after the intervention has taken place.

Evaluation research comprises the following steps:

1. Define the aim.

   For example:
   Is the training budget used to improve the technical expertise of the staff (or part of the staff) or to develop their social skills?

2. Identify the main principles concerning how the intervention works; possibly map out alternatives.

   For example:
   Is it better to use the training budget for a small number of special- ized, costly courses or is it better for the company if everyone follows a less expensive, more general course?

3. Draw up a list with assumed costs and benefits. Quantification of costs and benefits entails hanging a 'price tag' on the various costs and benefits.
4. Determine how these costs and benefits can be estimated and which assumptions will be made in this process.
5. Interpret the results and make recommendations.

5.3.3 Experiment

If you want to determine whether one variable affects another variable and also determine the magnitude of this effect, experimental research is the most appropriate choice (for example, what is the effect of the temperature of the workplace on absenteeism?).

In an experiment, you create systematic variation in the independent variable (*manipulation*). For example, you change the temperature settings of the air conditioning. During this process, you control as many aspects of the environment as possible. You deliberately create various situations for groups of research units in order to study the effect of a manipulation (also called an *intervention* or an *experimental treatment*). You require at least two groups of research units, where you manipulate one group (the experimental group), but not the other (the control group). Both groups should preferably be subjected to a measurement beforehand and afterwards to determine if a change in the variable actually occurred due to the manipulation. Moreover, all other conditions must be the same for both groups. The process of establishing this situation is called *matching*. To determine whether the change is actually and exclusively due to a specific variable, the groups must therefore differ only with respect to that variable. Whenever possible, you should assign research units randomly to the two groups. Randomization is the assignment of research units to groups by allowing chance to determine which research unit becomes part of which (experimental or control) group.

The main difference between the case study and the experiment is that case study research is conducted as much as possible in the natural surrounding, while experimental research takes place as much as possible in an isolated situation. Another difference is that the number of variables in an experiment is limited, while in a case study there are many variables, sometimes even more variables than research units.

There are various forms of experiments. The most well-known form is the *laboratory experiment*. Laboratory experiments have the advantage that you can conduct research under strictly controlled conditions. The laboratory experiment is rarely used in organizational science, but it is possible.

> For example:
> By using carefully compiled, artificial, model annual reports that are quite realistic, you can determine what elements in the annual report are decisive for the evaluations of investment analysts.

In organizational science research, it is often difficult to achieve randomization. As a researcher, you are generally unable to control which research unit undergoes what intervention (for example, the researcher cannot determine beforehand which company goes bankrupt and which does not). Therefore, quasi-experimental research (in contrast to true experimental research) is more common. This is where the differences between already existing, *non-equivalent* groups are studied (for example, you can compare two production departments concerning the level of absenteeism, where one department undergoes an intervention and the other does not). A non-random, systematic difference between the groups can already exist before you apply the intervention. The question is then what the actual effect of the intervention is. This has a negative effect on the validity of the research. Moreover, there may be a situation where a specific intervention is experienced as very desirable, or very undesirable, by one or both groups. Consequently, one group of research units may respond in an extremely positive or negative way to the research.

> For example:
> A specific measure initially appears to have an unexpectedly positive effect on shortening the duration of absenteeism. Nevertheless, it is crucial to maintain the research long enough to determine whether or not the measure actually works. The chance is high that the research will be halted prematurely because the control group also wants to benefit from the measure.

To prevent this, you can draw up an agreement beforehand with the research units in which they agree that they will continue to participate regardless of which group they are assigned to. *Blind research* means that the research unit is not informed about what group (experimental or control) he/she (or it) belongs to. *Double-blind research* means that the researcher also does not know to which group the research units belong. This measure has the aim of preventing undue influence by the researcher, for example in the form of a different approach to, or treatment of, the two groups.

> For example:
> Research is being conducted into the effect of a medicine where at least two groups are used: one group receives the medicine and the other group receives a placebo. Neither the physician/researcher nor the patients know whether they are receiving the medicine or a placebo.

Another example of an experiment is the *simulation*. This is the situation in which you attempt to simulate the relevant aspects of the actual situation on a small scale in an experiment so that you can bring the conditions properly under control.

> Examples of simulations include computer simulations, man-made simulations (such as the interactive simulators on which pilots are trained and evaluated) and experimental simulation (such as the assess-

ment centre). Another example of an experimental situation is when students act as test subjects with assigned roles that simulate the situation. For example, they may act as fruit sellers at an auction or as a bank manager making a decision about a loan.

An advantage of the experiment and the simulation is its repeatability. Moreover, processes can be studied in time. However, you should pay attention to the *reality value* (or 'ecological validity') of the simulation: the artificiality of the simulation can reduce the generalizability of the results in a practical situation. Therefore, you must make sure that the conditions (the characteristics of the research units, the locations and the times) in the research situation are as similar as possible to those in the situation to which you want to generalize. Other factors must not play a role, or at least not a dominant role.

For example:
Besides allowing pilots to land on virtual landing strips that are as similar as possible to actual strips from around the world, the interactive simulators in which pilots are trained also simulate all kinds of weather and all possible day/night situations.

This concerns the context of the research design, therefore not the research design itself. It concerns the generalizability of your research results to other groups of individuals, organizations, conditions, locations and times. This illustrates the importance of a good research design and the importance of providing a detailed and exact description of the organization, group of employees, time, location and surroundings in your research report. You should also describe the statistical tests and significance levels (see Chapter 8). In this way, others can form an impression about the breadth of application of your research results.

For example:
If you conduct research into absenteeism in a specific subgroup of purchasing employees at a mid-sized company in the middle of the country, then you must ask yourself whether the results are generally applicable. For example, do they also apply to sales employees or only to specific jobs and job levels? Do they apply to all companies or only to mid-sized companies? Do they apply to all companies in the country or only to companies in that specific region? You must also explain why the results are applicable or not in all the above situations.

Before you can conclude from experimental research that a specific effect has been caused by an intervention, you must also make sure the research is sufficiently valid, and you must support your reasoning afterwards. This has been stated several times previously. The following section addresses various types of experimental validity.

▮ 5.4 CAUSALITY

The research described up to now usually involved discovering links or correlations between variables. These correlations do not by definition have to be causal (cause–effect) relationships between variables. If you want to conclude that a causal link exists between two variables, then you must simultaneously satisfy the three demands of causality:

1. *Covariance*: there must be statistical correlation between the two variables (for example, a change in one variable is accompanied by a change in another variable).
2. *Time sequence*: the causal variable must precede the effect variable in time (for example, first the patient is given medicine and then he becomes better).
3. *Non-spurious correlation*: the correlation between two variables may not be caused by a third (distorting or crossing) variable. If this is the case, it is referred to as *spurious correlation*.

> For example:
> If a correlation between two variables is discovered, such as stress and health, then this is usually interpreted in a causal fashion, i.e. stress causes poor health. However, one of the conditions for causality is that the effect of a third (distorting) variable must be eliminated. Perhaps age is such a variable. This would be the case if a correlation exists between age and stress, between age and health and if the correlation between stress and health disappears when the effect of age is removed from these variables. This means there was a spurious correlation between stress and health.

It is sometimes difficult to meet all three of the above demands. It is especially difficult to meet the third demand. After all, when do you know that you have eliminated all other possible explanations? An explanation for a organizational science phenomenon is virtually never unequivocal. There are always an infinite number of partly unknown factors. You must measure variables that you think may affect the results, so that possible spurious correlations can be eliminated. This is also a reason why theories and hypotheses are falsified instead of verified (see Section 2.5). After all, showing that a specific expectation has been supported with one set of data does not verify a theory. Theories and hypotheses become increasingly valid to the extent that they withstand *rival* hypotheses, which propose other variables as causes, or to the extent that increasing numbers of other hypotheses are rejected.

However, if you ascertain that there is no correlation between two variables, even though you expect that there should be one, you should check to see if there is a *suppressor* variable. This is an erroneously omitted variable that hides or suppresses the correlation between two other variables. A plausible explanation for the unexpected absence of a causal correlation between the two variables is an important aspect of your research analysis in the eyes of experts, for example.

You must therefore have specific expectations beforehand about the correlations between variables. It is not necessary to correlate all variables with each other. If you do attempt to correlate all the variables, this is usually a sign that your research question and hypotheses are insufficiently refined. It is better to test specific correlations between variables as much as possible on the basis of a theory. If you attempt to correlate a large number of variables, you will always find some significant correlation due to *chance capitalization*. These correlations are based on chance. By studying a large number of relationships, there is always the chance that you will find something.

Generally speaking, causality can be demonstrated most clearly by using an experimental research design and least clearly by using a non-experimental design, such as the case study. With experiments, 'third' factors can be eliminated very effectively, while with case studies, many different factors become mixed together. A pure experimental research design is, as previously stated, much less common in organizational science research than non-experimental research designs. If properly conducted, experimental research is better than other research designs in excluding alternative factors as an explanation of behaviour.

To this end, you must take as many control measures as possible to exclude these factors: you must exclude them beforehand in the design, or afterwards by controlling for the effect of other, distorting factors during the analysis (see Section 4.2, 'Control variables'). It is impossible to prevent all the threats that are listed below. In practice you must often make an explicit choice. A few examples of threats to the experimental validity of research are:

1. **History**

   Besides a specific intervention, certain events in the *surroundings* of the research unit may take place between the initial (pre-test) and the second (post-test) measurement. As a result, the effects can no longer be exclusively attributed to the intervention.

For example:
If a higher salary is given to employees (intervention or independent variable), and a decline in absenteeism (dependent variable) is then observed, this must not be caused by other variables, such as the fact that there is always a decline in absenteeism after the summer holiday and the measurements were conducted after the summer holiday.

2. Spontaneous growth or change

Specific processes may take place within the research unit itself between the first and second measurements that are not the result of the intervention.

For example:
Resistance to an organizational change can also disappear spontaneously due to the research units becoming accustomed to the change, without there being an actual effect from the intervention of an organizational consultant.

3. Test effects

The experience of the initial measurement has certain effects on the second measurement.

For example:
After someone has taken an IQ test once, they become more skilled at taking the test, so they score higher on the second test. But this does not have to mean that there has been an actual improvement in IQ.

4. Instrumentation

There may be differences or changes between measurements due, for example, to a different calibration of the instrument or attention being focused on the phenomenon itself by the instrument.

For example:
If a great deal of attention is focused on absenteeism, absenteeism figures sometimes rise simply because there is more careful registration, or they may fall because attention is focused on this phenomenon and people are therefore less likely to call in sick.

Another example is the Hawthorne study. In this experimental study into the influence of working conditions on productivity, it turned out that not only good working conditions led to higher productivity, but obviously poor working conditions also had this effect. This result was explained later as a consequence of the unusual extra attention for employees during the experiment: this extra attention had a much stronger effect than the potential productivity decline resulting from the poor working conditions used in the experiment.

5. **Statistical regression towards the mean**

This is a phenomenon that occurs when research units are selected for a study based on unreliable measurements. If a measurement is repeated, there will be fewer extreme scores in a group than with the first measurement. Generally speaking, observations have the tendency to concentrate around a mean. There is therefore a statistical regression to the mean that is not caused by the intervention.

6. **Selection**

This is caused by bias in the research, which is the result of differing selection procedures for the research units for the experimental group and the control group. The research units do not all have the same chance of being placed in either of the two groups.

> For example:
> Measures against absenteeism can be tested primarily with individuals who are present at work, therefore those who are not absent very often. This means that the research group could be somewhat healthier and more motivated than the control group.

7. **Experimental mortality**

The research units who stop participating in the research usually form a select (sub)group of the total group of research units. They are, for example, less healthy, less motivated or in fact more mobile than the research units who continue to participate. The results of the research are valid only for the remaining, select group – as a result they are distorted positively or negatively.

> For example:
> If you give a test to a group of employees and then offer them training, after which the same test is given again, the employees with a low test score might have dropped out (and do not participate in the second test) because, for example, they found the training to be too difficult. In this case, the results of the research would be distorted. A higher score on the second test in comparison with the first is not only caused by the training, but also because the low scoring individuals are no longer counted when calculating the average.

Part II

CONDUCTING THE RESEARCH PROJECT

Chapter 6

DATA COLLECTION METHODS

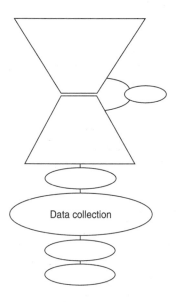

▌ 6.1 INTRODUCTION

Various data collection methods can be used as part of the research strategies described in the previous chapter. We will discuss these methods in greater detail in this chapter. We will focus on the following questions: what data are going to be collected, where and when are they going to be collected and by whom will they be collected? The collected data must then be systematically analysed to arrive at an answer to the research question (see Chapter 8).

For every research question and the research strategies derived from it, one or more data collection methods are most suitable.

> For example:
> An appropriate way to answer an explorative research question is generally using a case study consisting of interviews with open questions; while survey research using a written questionnaire with closed questions is more suitable for an analytical research question.

The choice of a data collection method also depends on certain research limits (such as limits on time, funding and the availability of people) that pertain to researchers and research units. Some data collection methods require more time and money and/or result in more interference with the research units than others.

> For example:
> If the research units live in many parts of a country and only a single researcher is available who must collect all the data during one week, then telephone interviews or a written questionnaire are preferable to in-person oral interviews.

The accuracy of the file containing addresses/contact list then determines whether you choose telephone interviews or a written questionnaire (for example, are the names and addresses sufficiently accurate for the questionnaire to be mailed?). It is therefore important that you take into account the practical limitations of the research when formulating your research question. It is essential that you make a deliberate evaluation of the available research methods and explain your choice of method in the report (see Chapter 9).

In this chapter, four widely used methods for acquiring data will be discussed: using existing material (6.2); observation (6.3); the oral interview (6.4); and the written questionnaire (6.5). The final section of the chapter (6.6) will discuss combinations of various methods. In Chapter 7, a number of practical tips will be given for implementing the latter two data collection methods.

■ 6.2 ARCHIVING DATA

The collection and analysis of existing material is often the first step in your research. The literature research phase discussed in Chapter 3 is in fact one form of collecting and studying existing material.

6.2.1 Statistical and written records

You can initially collect and study existing company-specific data such as *ratios* or *performance indicators*. Such internal data can give you insight (at the economic or technical levels, for example) into human behaviour in the work situation. Examples of company data include figures for absenteeism, accidents and turnover; data regarding employee selection and education level; the training requirements of the staff and their willingness to accept training; the placement and transfer of employees; organization charts and production figures at the departmental and company levels. You can also study annual reports and minutes of company meetings. With this data you can create a snapshot of an organization at a specific time. This is called *vertical analysis*. If you use similar types of data to illustrate developments over a number of years, this is called *horizontal analysis*.

Moreover, you can also study external material – data at the national level – such as that found in publications from *Central Bureau for Statistics* in the Netherlands, the *National Planning Bureau*, the *Economic Information Service* and the *Chamber of Commerce*. You can then compare these external data to internal data to determine where the relevant company stands with respect to the national average. This is called *comparative analysis*. Especially with the latter type of analysis, it can be difficult to establish a fixed norm (i.e. a standard definition of the indicators). This depends on how the units are compiled in these various types of reports.

> For example:
> Units expressed in workweeks in one report and units expressed in percentages of turnover from another report cannot simply be added together. You must first convert both units to a standard measurement.

It is important to make a distinction between indicators that are applicable for both profit and non-profit organizations. Common financial indicators used in profit organizations are earning power, solvency and liquidity. Earning power is the ratio of profit earned per unit of capital. Solvency is the degree to which a company is capable of meeting its long-term obligations (the ratio between assets or equity capital and debt). Liquidity is the degree to which a company is capable of meeting its short-term obligations (the balance of income and expenditures). For non-profit organizations, figures relating to earning power are often unavailable, and criteria for measuring effectiveness and efficiency are often more difficult to apply directly. These organizations do not have much of a tradition of using such indicators.

There are two advantages to using existing material: the costs are relatively low and you do not have to approach any other people. However, you must take account of the fact that the collected data often provide an incomplete picture. For example, minutes taken at a meeting may not provide a good description of the atmosphere in which the meeting takes place. Moreover, indicators are only 'symptoms' of an organization's performance. They do not explain *why* the organization operates in this way. As a result, additional methods are generally used to supplement the existing material.

6.2.2 Archived documents

As outlined above, a great deal of data about organizations can be found in existing records. For example, aggregate data about Dutch companies are published by the Central Bureau for Statistics (CBS). You can find these data in the statistics collections of libraries or electronically via data networks. Also refer to the electronic database *Data stream*. This can be accessed at libraries that subscribe to this service.

It is also advisable to determine whether you can answer your research question with data previously collected by other researchers. This is called *desk research*. Data are not only available on the Internet (where you can download them to your own PC), but many researchers also deposit data records in archives such as the ESRC (Environmental Social Science Research Council) Archive. You can use this material for *secondary analysis*. During this process, it is important to determine how the data have been acquired and archived. For example, if the data are raw or processed, how the data have been collected, from which group of people the data have been collected, if the data are suitable for your type of research, how old the data are, what the quality of the data is, if demands are placed on the users of the data by its owners/administrators and if there is a charge for using the data.

6.2.3 Meta-analysis

It is also possible to link the results from various existing studies. This is referred to as *meta-analysis*. This method is used to aggregate or compile the statistical results of many different studies concerning a specific topic to arrive at a single 'meta-result'. Unlike secondary analysis (discussed above), it therefore does not concern the re-analysis of basic data from previous research, but the analysis of the *results* of various studies about a specific topic. Meta-analysis can help draw more accurate conclusions about inconsistent research results in a specific field. In this method, statistical procedures replace traditional literature research. This is because traditional literature research is affected by the bias of the researcher. Researchers often disregard large amounts of relevant information from the original research reports, such as the size of the sample and the magnitude and significance levels of the effects that are found, and may not take these factors sufficiently into account when making conclusions. In meta-analysis, however, this information is taken into account.

For example:
It is interesting to determine the general relationship between work satisfaction and absenteeism. Many studies have been conducted in this area, but the results do not all agree. For instance, because the sample size of the studies differs a great deal and different questionnaires are used that vary in their reliability for measuring work satisfaction, the correlation (see Section 8.6.4) can range from .05 to .60. The question is what the underlying 'true' correlation is between work satisfaction and absenteeism, independent from irrelevant issues such as the size of the sample or the unreliability of the measurement instruments. By conducting a meta-analysis of all these previous research results, it is possible to answer this question.

▌ 6.3 OBSERVATION

Observation is a suitable method if you want to investigate the complex interactions between people and the actual behaviour of people in organizations in situations where the respondents do not know exactly what they do or how they do something. This is because people's beliefs do not always relate to their actions (for example, certain individuals might say that they provide people-oriented leadership, but in fact they only provide task-oriented instructions). Observation focuses on the concrete behaviour of an individual, group or organization. As a result, it has a high face validity. In addition, you can use observation research as part of a preliminary study, for example before conducting interviews or distributing a written questionnaire.

Participatory research is a special form of observation – this is sometimes referred to as *ethnographic research*. This means that you (as an observer) take an active role in the situation, and do not observe purely as an outsider. Participatory observation allows you to acquire an impression of such aspects as the emotional experience of work, the work atmosphere and the company culture.

> For example:
> The German researcher Günther Wallraff reported his participatory re-search where he took the role of a Turkish labourer to study discrimination against Turkish workers and the effects this can have on an individual.

If you do not make yourself known as a researcher, this is called a *hidden strategy*. This obviously has ethical implications that you should consider carefully before applying such a strategy. Ethically speaking, you must not harm the welfare or interests of a respondent, all respondents must theoretically be informed that they are test subjects and all must partici-pate voluntarily in the research. The downside of such informed con-sent is that the respondents may behave differently if they know that they are being observed as part of a study. For example, they may display more socially desirable behaviours than they do normally.

Unlike questionnaire-based research, observation is not limited to a single measurement. The information is often collected over a longer period. You can make written notes or work with a video or audio recorder. Recording your observations is strongly recommended since it allows you to continue your observations afterwards by viewing the video or listening to the cassette tape. Be aware of the risk of the presence of a video or audio recorder disturbing the situation. Most people behave differently in the presence of a video camera or tape recorder; it takes some time before they become sufficiently accus-tomed to its presence that they start behaving naturally.

When collecting data using observation, an *observation chart* or *obser-vation form* is generally used. This is a list of categories of behaviour (in contrast to intuitive observations that are not pre-structured). The observation chart lists all relevant possible descriptions of specific behaviour, such as its frequency, duration and intensity. This depends on whether you are conducting *time sampling* or *event sampling*. Time sampling means that you are only observing at specific points in time. You would use this method, for example, if you wanted to acquire an impression of the frequency of behaviours. You would use event sampling if you are interested in specific types of events, conducting observations only when these events occur.

You must be certain that the categories on the observation chart are complete and exclusive (see Section 7.2). The observer fills out this chart during or after the observation, or records the intensity and duration of the behaviour when it occurs.

For example:
A chart can comprise various columns, with one column for each observed individual. Various behaviours are listed on the rows. The observer has a stopwatch and records the duration and intensity of the behaviours for the various individuals.

Make sure that the name (or code) of the subject, the observer, the date, location and time are clearly recorded on the chart. Any unusual conditions should also be noted. You should also test this chart beforehand to make sure it is understandable and usable before the main research takes place (see Section 7.5).

When conducting observation research, you must explicitly distinguish two phases. The first phase concerns the observation itself. The second phase concerns the analysis and interpretation of the observation. When determining the observation scores (the *rating*), you should be as objective as possible and exclude your own subjective interpretation wherever possible. In the following phase, however, you must analyse and interpret the large quantity of information that has been acquired. During this process you should in fact use your own insight, judgement and interpretation. Due to the required objectivity during the first phase, it is usually necessary to train observers in observation. You must also provide very clear instructions to the observers: all observers must score the same behaviour in an identical fashion. Finally, after the observations are completed you must determine the reliability of the various observers (including yourself). The reliability criterion is whether the observers classify the same behaviour in the same behavioural category.

One disadvantage of observation research is that it is frequently difficult to control the research variables: you must simply wait until the behaviour occurs. Moreover, there are often no subtle distinctions in observation research: an individual either shows the behaviour or does not. In addition, it requires much more time, preparation and training than interview-based research, and is therefore more expensive. As previously stated, it also requires a relatively large amount of interpretation from the observers (for example, 'Which category of behaviour is this?'). As a result, objectivity can be compromised and individual differences between observers can lead to differences in observations (unreliability). For instance, using an electronic apparatus to measure how many people enter a specific shop often provides a more reliable result than when observers are used to count the number of people crossing the threshold.

For example:

You want to conduct a study into dominance. You assume that one indicator of dominance is the degree to which an individual interrupts other individuals. This may concern the number of times that someone interrupts others and the type of interruption involved (e.g. does the interrupter change the topic entirely, or does he interrupt to add something to the story of another individual?).

A group of people begins a discussion without knowing exactly what the topic of the research is – they know only that they are the object of the research. The discussion is recorded on a video tape. An observation chart is made for all test subjects in the group. The observers are trained in using the chart. During a preliminary study, the deviations in observations were discussed with the aim of arriving at an unequivocal scoring method (to improve the reliability of the measurement). The researchers initially indicate their general impression of the degree of dominance of the test subjects immediately after seeing the video, or they score them on a five-point scale and then rank the subjects according to their degree of dominance. After this, they score the entire video tape using the observation chart. The number and type of interruptions are counted for each individual, and it is then determined whether the person initially evaluated as being the most dominant also made the most interruptions (based on Willemsen, T.M. 1984. Groups in discussion. A methodological and substantial study of interaction in small groups (PhD thesis, University of Leiden. Meppel: Krips Repro).

▌ 6.4 INTERVIEWS

If your research concerns the knowledge, facts and opinions/attitudes of individuals, the oral interview (and the written questionnaire, see following section) is the most suitable data collection method (for example, research concerning the exact opinion of an individual about management must be asked directly; by means of observation, you can acquire only a global impression of this aspect). In addition, an interview can help you gain access to other existing sources of information, such as annual reports of companies (see Section 6.2). You can also use interviews as part of a preliminary study . This method is therefore primarily used with explorative research questions, and much less with analytical ones. When conducting interviews as part of a preliminary study, it is important that you interview a wide range of individuals, for example by including people from all functional groups and hierarchical levels. Take into account the fact that these initial interviews will be less thorough than later ones. Regarding the number of interviews to be taken, a good rule of thumb is the following: continue conducting interviews until you no longer hear any new information.

For example:
In preparation for a major questionnaire study into the reasons for absenteeism, you can conduct a number of interviews with various individuals from the organization. After a certain time (often quite a short time), you will notice that the list of possible reasons for absenteeism is complete. You can then use this list for constructing a written questionnaire.

The oral interview differs from observation and written questionnaire research primarily due to the direct interaction with the respondents. *Active listening* is at the heart of interviewing. You must pay attention to both the content of the interview and the intention behind the words of the respondent. You do this, for example, by looking for non-verbal cues. In concrete terms, this means making sure that the respondents understand that you respect them and that you are interested in what they have to say.

An important advantage of the oral interview is that it generally produces a higher response rate than a written questionnaire. In addition, during an oral interview you can address more topics than in a questionnaire. There is also a smaller risk of questions being skipped because you can monitor this yourself and restore any omissions if necessary. In addition, it is possible to acquire more detailed background information because follow-up questions can be asked. Finally, interviews yield a relatively large amount of information in a relatively short time.

There are also disadvantages to oral interviews. For example, oral interviews require more manpower, time and money than written questionnaires. It is more difficult to process, analyse and generalize the results of the interview afterwards because the respondents may vary greatly in the way they formulate their answers. This can be prevented by offering previously formulated answer options with every question (this option will be discussed in more detail below). When conducting an oral interview, also take into account the factor of time, since you make individual appointments with the respondents and often have to travel as a result.

Another problem with interviews can be the reliability of the data. Possible causes of unreliability are that the respondents may be affected by a limited and/or selective memory, and that they may have a greater tendency to provide socially desirable answers than on a written questionnaire. This is because respondents lose their anonymity due to direct contact with the interviewer.

As a result of these problems, *partial* non-response occurs relatively more frequently in oral interviews than in other kinds of research. Although respondents may participate more easily in an interview than in a written questionnaire survey, they might not answer certain questions. It is a well-known fact that in large cities, the *general* non-response rate for interviews is higher than in smaller communities, that individuals with a higher education refuse to answer more frequently than individuals with a lower education and that older individuals and women refuse more frequently than younger people and men. With written questionnaire surveys, on the other hand, older people and individuals with lower education refuse to answer more frequently than young people and individuals with a higher education.

Partial non-response occurs especially with unpleasant, threatening questions. You can try to prevent this by paying careful attention to the introduction and formulation of questions and the possible answer categories. However, to do this properly you require a great deal of knowledge about the population that you are studying. You have to know what topics are sensitive among the groups concerned.

There are two types of interviews: structured and unstructured. If the research is analytical in nature and if it is important that all questions and choices are presented, then you would conduct a structured interview. If the research is more explorative in nature, where the aim is to generate a hypothesis, an unstructured interview is a more suitable choice.

In the structured (or standardized) interview, you use closed questions with fixed answer options that are presented in a specific, fixed sequence. You are not allowed to explain the questions or answers. Such an approach is taken by political polling organizations. This organization conducts interview surveys using a number of pollsters. Pollsters ask the questions and also read the possible answers to the respondent. The answers are often processed immediately, usually with computer support.

An example of an unstructured interview is the *free-form* or *in-depth interview*. This usually concerns an oral interview. This type of interview provides a great deal of information and is often used as part of explorative research or during a preliminary study with the aim of acquiring more insight into the issue. In this technique, only the topic and the initial question are fixed beforehand. You ask people about their opinions, not about facts (for example, 'What do you think of (the topic)?' instead of 'What do you know about …?'). You intervene during the free-form interview only if the respondent deviates from the topic (non-relevance) or if you feel that the words of the respondent do not reflect his/her actual opinion. Be careful with this type of intervention!

During the free-form interview, you must listen actively. You should pay attention to both the content and the intention of the respondent's words. Encourage the respondent to answer, but do this in a natural way without being directive or suggestive. You are interested only in the actual answers of the respondent.

The *half-structured interview* is an intermediate form. You have a questionnaire with previously formulated questions, but you also have the flexibility to go more deeply into important matters. You can use this type of interview if you are not entirely certain of the completeness of your questionnaire or if you want to assure the respondents' cooperation by giving them the impression that you are making your own contribution to the interview.

Finally, three special types of the oral interview will be discussed below: the group interview; the telephone interview and working with *proxy respondents*.

6.4.1 Group interview

Oral interviews can be conducted both individually and in groups. This latter technique is used for example with consumer panels. This is where a group of 'model' consumers are asked to provide their impression of a new product or shop design (evaluation tasks, see Figure 5.1 in Section 5.3). Another example is conducting an interview by means of a group discussion with the aim of studying the opinions about redesigning a shop or surveying the opinions about a new method for allocating tasks in a department. With this aim in mind, a discussion takes place where you are present as an observer and/or discussion leader. The input for the discussion is previously formulated questions and themes in a previously determined sequence. The result of such a discussion, the narratives and opinions of the participants, must then be processed and categorized before the data can be analysed.

6.4.2 Telephone interview

Besides conducting in-person interviews, you can also conduct telephone interviews. This data collection method is increasingly popular. It is often used, for example, by market research institutes. A sample of telephone numbers is drawn at random from a telephone book, or a specially created list is used (for example, employees older than 60, alumni from the student almanac or managers with a foreign name).

One advantage of telephone research is that you do not incur any travel costs. Another advantage is that it requires less time. In addition, you can ask questions using a 'funnel' system and you can use complex cross-references. In this way, you lead the respondent through the questionnaire. After monitoring the answers, you can skip non-relevant parts of the questionnaire. This prevents irritation and consequently reduces the non-response rate of the respondents. You can also use *Computer Assisted Telephonic Interviewing* (CATI) or a computer, which is equipped with an electronic version of the questionnaire. The answers to the questions are entered directly into the computer while you are talking with the respondents on the telephone. One disadvantage of telephone interviews is that you cannot provide any visual aids, such as answer cards. Another problem is that the respondents cannot look anything up. Moreover, you cannot observe the respondents while they are answering the questions. Finally, due to widespread use of telephone interviews by market research institutes, potential respondents may have already been approached quite frequently and are therefore less willing to participate in an interview. One way to gain their cooperation is to send a good introductory letter beforehand (see Section 7.6.1).

6.4.3 *Proxy respondents and non-obtrusive measurements*

Another way to acquire information is by using *proxy respondents*. These are individuals whom the respondent knows well (for example, co-workers, colleagues, supervisors, friends and family members). Take into account the fact that such proxy respondents can only report on the behaviour of the respondent and may be able to say little or nothing about the opinions of a respondent.

The term *unobtrusive measurements* should also be mentioned here. These measurements do not depend on the cooperation of the respondent: the respondent does not know that he or she is being observed (for example, the quantity of paper on a desk as a measure of the orderliness of an individual).

▌ 6.5 QUESTIONNAIRE

If large groups of companies or individuals have to be studied in a short time, then the use of written questionnaires is the most suitable research method. The most important advantage of a written questionnaire is its relatively low cost in comparison to the oral interview. This is primarily because fewer people are involved in conducting the research. Another reason for using a written questionnaire is that it is simple to collect and process the data since you do not have to categorize the answers afterwards. In addition, the respondents have the advantage of a much greater feeling of anonymity; consequently, they are more inclined to answer certain personal questions. There is also less risk of result influence by the researcher than with an oral interview.

One disadvantage of a written questionnaire is that you have to invest a great deal of time in constructing the questionnaire. You cannot provide a personal explanation. Everything the respondent needs to answer the questions must be put clearly and unequivocally on paper. The most important disadvantage of the written question-naire with respect to the oral interview is the lower general response rate. This is often due to the lack of a personal bond. Generally speak-ing, a response rate of 50 to 60 per cent for a written questionnaire is considered good. The most important characteristics of the oral inter-view and the written questionnaire are summarized in Table 6.1.

6.5.1   Questionnaire by means of the Internet or email

Written questionnaires are increasingly being distributed on the Inter-net or by email. When using the Internet, the questionnaire is placed on a web page. The respondents can enter the answers using an answer field, or the answer categories can be ticked as required. Special programs are available for making such pages, which are increasingly inventive and easy to use. Make sure that the background and the illustrations are not too distracting; after all, the aim is to allow the questions to be answered as correctly and as completely as possible.

One disadvantage of using the Internet as a distribution medium is that you cannot always monitor who is filling out the questionnaires. Results of research via this medium can be contaminated by 'acciden-tal visitors', who provide random answers. You can prevent this to some extent by asking control questions and excluding deviating answer forms from the analysis. However, to do this you have to be able to interpret the answers. Another way to exclude unintended respondents is to protect the page using a password. You can send this password to the intended respondents beforehand.

Another possibility for excluding non-intended respondents from the research is to send the questionnaire via email to a specific group. In this case you can send the questionnaire as an *attachment*. After the respondent has filled in the questionnaire electronically, he or she can return the completed questionnaire as an attachment.

A second disadvantage of using the Internet for these questionnaires is that the respondent groups in any case have a single characteristic in

Table 6.1 Summary of important differences between an oral interview and a written questionnaire

Oral interview	Written questionnaire
Usually applicable to qualitative/explorative research	Usually applicable to quantitative/analytical research
Relatively low non-response rate, but much less anonymity	Relatively high non-response rate, but more anonymity
Focus on information richness/depth	Focus on comparability and/or reliability/breadth
Information can be included about what is relevant for the respondent or what is spontaneously stated	Only data that have been explicitly asked for are available
Requires relatively high amounts of labour and money	Requires relatively little labour and money
Requires relatively more time afterwards for processing and analysis	Requires relatively more time beforehand during construction
Relatively high degree of influence by the researcher	Relatively little influence by the researcher
Researcher requires relatively little previous knowledge about the possible reactions of the respondents	Researcher requires a relatively large amount of previous knowledge about the topic and the respondents
Ad hoc formulation and explanation, can be adapted to the individual respondents	Fixed formulation carefully tested by the researcher; is the same for all respondents
Generally used for a very small number of respondents or a very heterogeneous group of respondents	Generally used for a large number of respondents with a reference framework that is more or less the same
Assumes that the respondents have a large verbal capacity	Can be used if respondents have a small verbal capacity

common: they all own computers or are people who have access to computers. By using this medium you therefore reach a selected group of respondents.

▌ 6.6 MULTI-METHOD

In organizational science, it is common to use a combination of the methods described above as part of a study. This approach is called *'method triangulation'*. The researcher combines qualitative research (usually defined as observation research and interviews) and quantitative research (usually existing data and written questionnaire surveys). In this way data sources can complement each other and the researcher has the possibility of checking the information (do the various sources provide the same results or in fact different results?).

For example, as part of your orientation to the problem, you first study existing material and make observations within the organization. Then you conduct a number of interviews with experts. These are people who are involved in the problem and can tell you something about it from their experience. Based on the above, you can refine the research question and link the question and its characteristics to the experience of the respondents (and to the client (if any)). You can establish hypotheses and design a questionnaire to test these hypotheses. You may also be able to expand this process after you have obtained the results from the questionnaire by conducting a series of interviews to gain more insight into the material. Or you can determine whether the client, the respondents or the experts recognize the picture that emerges from the results. When you use a combination of methods, it is important to take into account whether they affect each other in an undesirable fashion (for example, if you first conduct an interview with respondents and then give them a questionnaire to complete at home, the answers they gave and the impressions they gained during the interview could affect the answers that will later be given on the questionnaire).

Finally, understand that you eventually have to collect and combine all the data for each research unit. You somehow have to establish an administrative link between the various results from the same research object.

For example:
Questionnaires with closed questions are used as part of the study. To explore the answers on the questionnaire in greater depth, an unstructured interview is conducted during which the most important themes from the questionnaire are used as the topic of discussion. The researcher promises that the respondent's answers will be held in confidence. This means that an administration must be established in which every respondent is given a unique number for the questionnaire. A record must be kept of which respondent has returned which questionnaire. Then an appointment must be made for an interview. The results of the interview (the cassette tape and transcript) must then be assigned the same number as that on the questionnaire.

Chapter 7

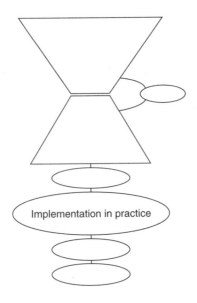

QUESTIONNAIRES AND INTERVIEWS

Implementation in practice

▮ 7.1 INTRODUCTION

In the previous chapter, a number of methods for collecting data were discussed. They will again be addressed in this chapter, but in more concrete terms: how do I make a questionnaire and how do I conduct an interview? Instructions for constructing a written questionnaire and conducting an oral interview will be given. These methods are emphasized because every researcher will have to use them and because questionnaires or interviews are part of almost every research strategy. Questionnaires are commonly used not only as part of a survey, but also during an experiment, and people are often interviewed during a case study.

By formulating your research question and your hypotheses, you focus your research on a specific number of topics. These are often the variables in your study (for example, absenteeism, work satisfaction or unhealthy working conditions and the relationships between them). The core of every study is a list of topics for which you want to conduct measurements. With this aim, these topics can then be converted into a list of questions and presented to a respondent. This can take place by means of a written survey or an oral interview. It is important to have the list of topics ready before beginning the practical implementation of the research. After all, this will form the common theme of the questions to be asked, and you can generally ask the questions only once. In contrast to the phases of hypothesis formulation and research design, you cannot do the practical part of the research over again: it has to be right the first time!

When the questions for the questionnaire or the interview are ready, you can organize a pre-test to test and modify the questions as required. A number of suggestions are given below for such a pre-test (see Section 7.5). After that we will discuss making contact with the research units with whom you want to conduct the research (Section 7.6). The final section of this chapter (Section 7.7) will address the difference between anonymity and confidentiality and will provide a number of suggestions to assure confidentiality.

7.2   QUESTIONNAIRES – GENERAL REMARKS

Constructing a questionnaire is an important and time-consuming phase of the research. Avoid vague or incorrectly formulated questions in questionnaires and interviews. Such questions may lead respondents to make an unintended interpretation, or various respondents may interpret the questions differently, making it impossible to compare the resulting data. For example, respondents generally look for an interpretation that allows them to answer the question easily. If you do not stipulate specific conditions in the question, they may also relate the question to their own circumstances. Of course, this may be your intention.

You can assure validity, reliability and efficiency by asking clear questions that adequately measure what you *want* to measure by providing well-written instructions and using standardized answer categories. Before formulating the questions, you must have a clear idea of exactly what information you want to collect. The best way to determine this is by writing up the research questions and the hypotheses explicitly and in simple terms.

> For example:
> Employees with low self-esteem tend to call in sick more frequently than those with high self-esteem. In this example, the concepts 'employees', 'low self-esteem', 'high self-esteem' and 'calling in sick more frequently' must be operationalized: how do you define an employee, what is high self-esteem and low self-esteem and how do you define calling in sick more frequently?

Generally speaking, a measurement becomes more reliable as you ask more questions about a specific topic. You can then determine to what degree the answers to these questions correlate with each other (see Section 4.6).

7.2.1 Open-ended versus closed-ended questions

The choice for open or closed questions is related to the aim of your research. In explorative research, you generally use open questions because this allows you to collect as much information as possible. Essentially, you are asking the respondent 'Could you say something about absenteeism in your company?'. In analytical research, you often use closed questions. In this case, you know beforehand the type of answers you can expect, and you therefore include them as the choice options in a multiple-choice question. You can also use closed questions when making a survey of respondents (for example, according to sex, education and living situation) in the biographical part of the questionnaire or the interview.

The difference between both types of questions has to do with the degree of freedom that you want to give the respondent when answering a specific question. With closed questions, you offer a limited number of answer categories with which the respondent must answer the question. The respondent has the fewest choices with yes/no questions. *Multiple-choice* questions, where the respondent is asked to select a single answer from a limited number of options, offer more possibilities. The *multi-response* question offers the most possibilities in a closed question: multiple answers to the same question are possible (for example, 'Which aspects (X, Y, or Z) of your work are important to you?'). However, you must tell the respondent how many answers are allowed and whether the answers should be prioritized (for example, 'Rank your answers from "most important" to "least important"'). You must also decide whether to weigh some answers more than others during your analysis. Generally speaking, it is advisable to ask as few multi-response questions as possible. It is often better to break up such a question into separate multiple-choice questions (for example, 'How important is X for your work?' 'How important is Y for your work?' 'How important is Z for your work?'). The advantage of the latter approach is that the respondent does not have to choose between various issues (he or she may believe that everything is equally import-ant) and also does not have to rely on what he or she can think of at the time. Because all respondents are presented with identical questions and answer possibilities, their answers are more comparable.

Research with closed questions offers a simple and fast method to collect and process data. It is a pleasant method for the respondent because it requires little time to answer the questions and because the answer simply has to be ticked. For the researcher, it also simplifies the analysis phase: you can immediately use the answers in the analysis because the coding takes place beforehand by assigning a number to each answer category.

As a rule of thumb, you can assume that you will primarily ask closed questions and will use open questions only when this is clearly beneficial (such as questions that ask for an explanation of an answer). In all cases, it is very important that all respondents are given exactly the same questions. Apparently minor differences in a question can lead to major differences in answers.

Constructing closed questions does require a great deal of previous knowledge about the topic. After all, you have to decide beforehand what answer categories you will provide. For example, if you want to define salary levels by using categories, then you must establish mean-ingful boundaries between categories within which every respondent can provide an answer, but which still allow the respondents to be sufficiently distinguished from each other (for example, you have to decide what answer possibilities should be joined together). It must be possible for every respondent to answer the question. The answer categories must therefore be *exhaustive*. This means that all possible answers must be present; otherwise the respondent cannot provide an answer (for example, 'What is your civil status, married, unmarried, living together?' – in this example, the variant 'single' is absent). The answers must be clearly described and presented unequivocally to the respondents. The answer categories must also be *exclusive*. This means that there is no overlap between the various answer categories; other-wise the respondent cannot choose a single answer (for example, 'How many pairs of shoes have you purchased in the past year: 0–5 pairs; 5–10 pairs; 10–15 pairs?' – in this example it is not clear in which category 5 and 10 pairs would be placed). This of course does not apply to the previously cited multi-response questions. It can sometimes be difficult to completely satisfy the requirements of both exhaustiveness and exclusivity. After all, you cannot always think up all possible answers in advance that a respondent could give. Moreover, you never know exactly how respondents are going to interpret answer categories. It is therefore quite possible that the answer categories will still overlap in the experience of the respondent.

Another disadvantage of using closed questions can be that the respondents are unable to make any subtle distinctions in their answers. As a result, you can lose information and the respondent can become frustrated and may no longer want to participate in the research. The more exhaustive the answer possibilities, the less information loss and frustration there will be. However, this also makes the questionnaire longer. You must therefore make a good trade-off. This is why you sometimes use an intermediate form between open and closed questions: the half-structured question. This is where you specify the answer alternatives, for example, but then provide an open space to allow the respondent to explain the answer. To prevent an answer possibility from being disregarded when you are using closed questions, you can offer a fill-in option as a last category (for example, 'Other . . .'). The answers for this last option can then be treated like those for an open question. This provides extra work, however, since you must categorize these answers afterwards.

Open questions give the respondent complete freedom to formulate an answer; they do not offer any standard answer options. During the interview or while completing the questionnaire, the respondents can tell their story in their own words with all kinds of subtle distinctions. This may prevent the respondent from feeling frustrated, and the researcher acquires a great deal of information. However, this information is sometimes not entirely usable. The advantage of this method is that you require little previous knowledge about the topic when formulating the questions. Open questions are therefore frequently used in explorative research. One disadvantage of an interview with open questions is that it requires a great deal of verbal skill from both the interviewer and the respondent. Such an interview also lasts longer and is more difficult, thereby requiring more motivation from the respondent. You must record these answers as completely as possible. Afterwards you can assign figures to these answers (*coding, categorizing* or *quantifying*). Writing complete answers is objectionable for some researchers. As an interviewer you have to simultaneously listen, write, evaluate answers and possibly ask follow-up questions. Therefore, some researchers only write a brief summary or use a cassette recorder to record the answer.

Another problem when using open questions is that you must apply a category system afterwards in order to process the answers. To conduct an analysis it is necessary to quantify the data (see Chapter 8). This can be difficult.

> For example:
> To the open question 'When did you last call in sick?' you may get the following answers: 'Last week', 'When my boss chewed me out', 'Actually I've never called in sick', or 'It was a while ago, I don't remember exactly'.

When creating answer categories, be aware that you are also making a subjective interpretation of the data. You can deal with this problem by involving multiple researchers in the interpretation process. In this way you can determine to what extent the various researchers (evaluators) agree with each other. This is referred to as *intersubjectivity* or *interrater reliability*. There are coefficients of concordance that indicate the extent to which evaluators agree in their observations. This provides an indication of the reliability of the observations. Examples of such standards are *Cohen's kappa* and *Kendall's w*.

7.2.2   Scales and items

Some questions form a *scale* when combined (see Section 4.4). With this *multiple operationalization* you attempt to measure a specific concept or theoretical construct (such as absenteeism tendency). As stated in Section 4.6 ('Construct validity'), this is generally assumed to be more reliable than a single item measurement. A *Likert scale* is used especially for attitude measurements: it comprises various items or statements. The respondent can indicate to what extent he or she agrees with these statements. The term scale can be used only when the answers from a respondent to the various items can be combined into a single score. This usually involves the addition of all scores to arrive at a single total score, divided by the number of items. Generally speaking, the higher the score, the stronger the measured construct. This transformation means that the items cannot be measured at a nominal level. After all, you cannot add names together and divide them by the number of names!

It is not easy to formulate a number of items that can be expected to represent an underlying concept. Therefore it is advisable to first look in the literature for a suitable scale that has been tested for reliability and validity. These are often included in the appendices of articles in journals.

When formulating statements (*scale construction*), the following rules apply:

- Preferably use no more than 20–25 words for each statement.
- Avoid statements that concern factual knowledge: the scale is intended to measure an opinion or attitude.
- Do not ask any questions about future behaviour; the answers are often unreliable (for example, 'Assume that you have to fire someone, how would you do this?'). With this type of question, respondents tend to provide socially desirable answers. Recent behaviour in comparable situations is a better predictor of future behaviour than plans or intentions regarding future behaviour (for example, 'Have you recently fired someone? If yes, could you explain how you went about this?').
- Use simple, clear and direct language in the statements.
- Avoid statements that could be explained in various ways. Therefore do not use any long sentences with double meanings, double negatives/illogical constructions and complex words or sentences.

  For example:
  It is illogical to respond to the statement 'Scientific research usually has no social relevance', with 'sometimes/always'. Nevertheless, people do respond to such statements in this way, even if they understand that it is illogical. This response may arise from indifference or perhaps from an intense desire to cooperate. People often assign meaning and logical consistency to a question or statement even if these qualities are absent in reality. Of course, this negatively affects the validity and reliability of the research.

- Do not use vague words.

  For example:
  The question, 'What is your income?' can be interpreted in a number of ways: as individual or family income, wages, income from a grant, monthly or yearly income.

- Do not use words such as 'always', 'never' or 'everyone'. Statements that include these words are suggestive: almost no one can agree with such absolute statements.

- Do not refer to multiple topics in a single question or statement (*parallel linking*). In parallel linking, two independent statements are combined (to save time, for example). Be cautious with questions such as, 'Is absenteeism at this time higher or lower than five years ago? And do you believe this a problem?'. Within such linked questions, the answer to one question depends on the answer to the other (for example, the answer to the question, 'How high is absenteeism?' depends on the answer to the question, 'Is there absenteeism?').
- Do not ask irrelevant questions or make irrelevant statements; these cause irritation (for example, irrelevant questions about whether the respondent has felt attracted to a co-worker in a questionnaire concerning effective management behaviour).
- Do not ask contradictory statements (for example, 'I have high organizational commitment, but would be open to job offers elsewhere in any case')

Common response categories or answer options to these types of assertions are:

1 = disagree completely	or	1 = very unimportant
2 = disagree		2 = unimportant
3 = neither agree nor disagree		3 = neutral
4 = agree		4 = important
5 = agree completely		5 = very important

In a scale, always work from left to right:

1	2	3	4	5

where the left end of the scale is smaller, more negative or lower than the right. Such an answer scale is called a five-point scale. You can provide all answer possibilities or only the two extremes and the middle possibility.

When constructing answer categories, the researcher generally uses an odd number of possibilities: this must of course be at least three. The most commonly used scale has five possibilities. If necessary, you can combine the two categories at the ends of the scale (for example, combine 1 with 2 and 4 with 5) at a later date.

If you want to offer the respondents more possibilities for making subtle distinctions in their answers (with complex questions, for example) then you can increase the number of answer possibilities to seven. Be aware that the choice you make concerning the number of answer categories and the method of answering them can affect the results of the measurement. Using 'extreme' terms for the ends of the scale could lead to respondents avoiding these categories. This causes regression to the middle of the scale. If there is a scale with more than seven answer categories (such as a 10-point scale), respondents will generally avoid the most extreme categories (the categories 1, 2 and 9, 10 with a 10-point scale). In effect, a 10-point scale then becomes a six-point scale ranging from 3 to 8.

The middle answer category (answer number 3 on a five-point scale) is neutral. For example, individuals who neither agree nor disagree with a specific assertion can choose this category. The problem is that people who have no opinion about the topic because they do not understand the question or because they do not have any experience with the topic, and therefore guess or gamble about the answer, will often choose this category. This can result in many people choosing the middle answer category. After all, it is often easier to not have an opinion about something than to think about it or to admit that you know nothing about it. In order to prevent this, you can use the forced choice, where there is an even number of choices. You can also include two separate categories 'neutral' and 'don't know/no opinion' as answer possibilities.

7.2.3 Drawbacks in scale construction: answer tendencies

It is important to prevent *answer tendencies* (*response sets, response styles*) of respondents. Respondents may have a preference for specific answers that have nothing to do with the concept you want to measure.

Different respondents may have different types of answer tendencies. For example, some respondents like to agree with an assertion that is formulated in a somewhat positive fashion, regardless of the content! They mark 'yes' or 'agree' more frequently. In contrast, other respondents prefer to answer 'no' or 'disagree', regardless of the content of the question. The latter tendency is less common. You can prevent such answer tendencies by formulating half of the questions in such a way that the negative answer (for example, 'disagree completely') is in fact a positive indication of what you want to measure. Other respondents tend to choose one of the extreme alternatives: 'very positive' or 'very negative'. As stated previously, there is also a common tendency to choose the middle category: 'no opinion' or 'neutral'. Finally, some respondents want to be consistent in their answers, while others tend to alternate their answers.

You must also be cautious about the possible occurrence of the 'halo effect'. The halo occurs when the question concerns the opinion of a respondent about an individual, a characteristic or an object. This question then results in the respondent having a generally positive or negative reaction (such as irritation or anger). This general feeling then affects how the rest of the questions in the questionnaire are answered.

In addition, some people prefer to guess or gamble on the answer. Deliberate sabotage also occurs. Finally, it is important to understand that respondents are often more reluctant to provide negative information than positive information. You can counteract these effects by making an answer scale that is made up of multiple items or statement formulated both positively and negatively, where the items preferably vary in emotional charge with respect to the research topic (for example, 'I believe the two-phase structure is a travesty' and 'The two-phase structure is the wrong step' – both statements are negative with respect to the research topic (the two-phase structure), but clearly differ in their emotional charge). However, make sure you recode the negatively or positively formulated items later when processing the data (you 'invert' the values, i.e. $1 = 5, 2 = 4, 3 = 3, 4 = 2, 5 = 1$); without recoding, you cannot add these items together to calculate an average score on a scale. After you recode the items, you can determine the final score on the scale in the usual fashion (add the values and divide by the total number of items). By varying between positive and negative formulations and then recoding the values, you can eliminate the statistical effects referred to above.

You can prevent socially desirable answers by asking neutrally formulated questions wherever possible. For example, make sure you do not ask any threatening, suggestive, global, presumptive, multiple or hypothetical questions. Respondents tend to answer such questions in a socially desirable fashion instead of providing another type of answer. An example of a suggestive question is, 'Of course you believe...?'. You must not influence the actual answer of the respondent positively or negatively. Even if it is quite obvious what the answer will be, the respondents must still answer the question themselves. An example of a global question is, 'How do you evaluate the current situation in the world?'. An example of a presumptive question is, 'How often are you absent every month?'. With such questions you are assuming a specific situation or event that may not be relevant. An example of a multiple question is, 'Do you read two or three newspapers per day or do you read no newspapers at all?'. An example of a hypothetical question is, 'If you were allowed to provide leadership, then what would you do?'. The risk of hypothetical questions is that the respondent may act in a totally different way if the actual situation were to occur.

You can use the *funnel* model to place the questions in the correct order. You would use this method if you want to introduce a complex topic or focus the respondent's attention on a specific topic, such as a memory. In the funnel model, you begin by asking general, open questions. Then you focus more specifically on the concrete situation regarding the respondent using closed questions (for example, 'What are the working relationships like within the company in general?', 'How are the relationships between the supervisors and the staff?', 'Can you indicate how well you get along with your boss on a five-point scale that ranges from 1 = very poorly to 5 = very well?').

There are also special scales to determine the tendency to provide socially desirable answers (the so-called *lying scales*). Such scales contain non-existing answers that help you determine the tendency of a respondent to provide socially desirable answers. You can use this information afterwards, for example to determine to what extent social desirability has distorted the results and/or to correct this distortion statistically. Such a correction often occurs by making a regression analysis (see Chapter 8) of the questionnaire score with respect to the score on the lying scale. You can then determine the extent to which the questionnaire score can be predicted by the lying score. This makes it clear which part of the score on the questionnaire is the result of socially desirable answers. By using the results of the regression analysis, you can then correct the questionnaire score for the effect of social desirability.

Of course, it is better to prevent such problems beforehand than to try to correct them afterwards: when constructing the items, you should take into account the possible answer tendencies. One problem is that you do not always know exactly what a socially desirable answer is for a specific group of respondents. For example, you can make a suggestive question more neutral by including all answer possibilities or perhaps only a few. Another approach is to offer answer alternatives that are all equally socially desirable or undesirable. You can also indicate that large numbers are not unusual by the way in which the answer alternatives are delineated (for example, 'Every year I call in sick without a medical reason: two times, five times, 25 times'). Or you can introduce the question to show that an answer that is not particularly socially desirable can simply occur. Finally, in the question you can assume that the respondent believes something displays certain behaviour by asking this directly (for example, 'How old were you when you first called in sick?'). However, note that this is a presumptive question (see above). You can also distribute socially desirable items through the questionnaire; the tendency to provide socially desirable answers generally decreases as a respondent continues to work on the questionnaire. A structural aid is to make answers to 'socially sensitive' questions more anonymous by distributing them on a separate sheet of paper in a closed envelope. However, in this case make sure that you write down the corresponding respondent number beforehand.

7.2.4 Translating questionnaires

The appendices of scientific articles sometimes contain the actual questionnaires with which the reported research was conducted. It is worthwhile to search for these questionnaires and, if necessary, to translate them for your own use. In this way you can save the time that would otherwise be spent in developing the questionnaire. Moreover, such questionnaires have usually been tested for validity and reliability. Finally, using an existing questionnaire makes it possible to compare various research results.

However, translating questionnaires causes certain problems. A well-known method for making sure the questions retain the closest possible meaning in another language is *back translation*. In this method, for example, an English questionnaire is translated into another language. Another individual then translates the questionnaire back into English. After this, you compare the original and the back-translated version and see whether both versions are the same. After correction, this procedure is repeated until you have a definitive translation. The technique of back translation only solves language problems, however. You must also be aware that cultural differences can make it difficult or even impossible to compare questionnaires. Topics that are important in the United States, for example, may be totally unimportant in the UK or may have a different meaning (for example, the concept of 'discrimination').

▮ 7.3 STRUCTURE OF THE QUESTIONNAIRE

Every questionnaire contains a fixed number of elements in a specific sequence:

- Begin the questionnaire with a question that is interesting and easy for the respondents to answer, but is still neutral. If the first question is boring, difficult or threatening, then the motivation of the respondents to complete the questionnaire will decrease. Work slowly towards questions that are more sensitive. The background or biographical data, such as sex and age, are usually included at the end of the questionnaire, but sometimes at the beginning.

- Make clusters of questions in which the respondent can ascertain a logical sequence. Introduce these clusters to the respondents (for example, 'Here are a few questions about...').
- Number all questions and sub-questions. Keep each question together on the page (make sure it does not run onto the following page).
- If certain questions are applicable only to specific respondents make sure there is a logical and clear *routing* in the questionnaire (for example, 'If you answer question x with 2, then you can now go to question y').
- Consider the relationship between the various questions; this is because questions can influence each other (for example, consider the 'halo effect' described above). Therefore work from easy to difficult questions and from popular to less popular topics.
- Finish with a friendly, open question to the respondent (for example, 'If you have remarks or questions concerning this questionnaire, you can write them here. Thank you for your cooperation') Make sure you read any comments that are written here and learn from them.

7.3.1 Language use in the questionnaire

Besides the sequence of the questions, you should also pay attention to language use:

- In terms of language use, it is important to write the questionnaire with the target group in mind, such as production staff, young people, newcomers to the company or managers. The use of specific *jargon* can have a stimulating effect on a specific research population. The respondents then have the feeling that the questionnaire is indeed intended for them. However, consider beforehand whether the target group is familiar with such jargon.
- Do not give commands or assignments to the respondents. Instead, formulate questions in a polite fashion (for example, do not write 'Explain your answer here!' but 'Could you please explain your answer here?'). Ask the questions in such a way that the respondents

have the least possible difficulty in answering them. You should do any calculations (such as percentages) yourself, either beforehand or afterwards.

7.3.2 Layout of the questionnaire

A third aspect you should pay attention to is the design of the questionnaire. The following suggestions may come in handy when making the questionnaire:

- Make sure that the questionnaires have a perfect appearance: this prevents people from disregarding them due to a sloppy first impression. You should pay attention to the following aspects: a handy format, for example in the form of a booklet; good quality paper (preferably white paper); an attractive first page with an intriguing title (which of course is relevant to the content of the questionnaire), a graphic image and the names of the researcher or researchers; no questions on the first page or the back page of the questionnaire and a careful layout.
- The more time it takes for your respondents to complete the questionnaire, the lower the response rate. Moreover, a longer questionnaire is more expensive: it requires more paper, more typing time, more time for writing the items, more coding work and more input and analysis work. In addition, the longer the questionnaire, the less reliable the answers are in general. Therefore, the questionnaire should not be too long (or appear to be too long). Make sure that every item has a relevant function in the research.
- It is important to include good instructions with the questionnaire. The instructions state the aim of the research (and of the questionnaire) and explain how the questionnaire should be filled out.

> For example:
> 'This part of the questionnaire contains 10 statements. Indicate to what extent you agree with these statements by circling the answer that is closest to your opinion. Please don't skip any questions'.

Separate instructions should be included with each type of question or statement, including an example and a possible response. Make sure that these examples have a totally different content than the actual items to prevent possible influence on the respondents.

Other aspects that you could address in the instructions are: 'It is important to not think too long about the answers; your first reaction is the most important'. Or, 'There are no correct or incorrect answers; we are only interested in your opinion'.

- Finally, do not ask the respondents to provide their own envelope or postage stamps to return the questionnaire. Therefore, make sure a postage-paid return envelope is included which can be used to return the questionnaire at no cost to the respondent.

As stated previously, it requires a great deal of time to construct a questionnaire. However, it is crucial for the research to have a properly constructed list; after all, once the questionnaire is mailed to the respondents, it is impossible to make any changes or additions. Even the statistical analysis methods and the type of results that can be obtained are already fixed at the time the questionnaire is distributed. It is therefore very important to make sure you have not forgotten anything. You can do this by conducting a pre-test (see Section 7.5).

■ 7.4 INTERVIEWS – GENERAL REMARKS

As an interviewer, you must simultaneously take many different roles. You can learn to do this through practice. In the first place, as an interviewer you must make sure that the respondents provide as much relevant information as possible. To achieve this aim, put the respondents at ease, encourage them, reward them in an immaterial fashion, be a good listener and give the impression that you understand them (the *relational aspect*). In addition, you must make sure that you get an answer to your research question. To this end, you must structure, categorize, process and analyse the narrations of the respondents (the *substantive aspect*). In other words, as an interviewer you take an active role: you make the appointment with the respondent, ask questions, evaluate the answers, ask follow-up questions if necessary and close the interview. But you also take a passive role: the interviewer must show interest in the respondents and in their answers, listen well and must not judge the answers positively or negatively.

Instructions for all these tasks will be provided in the following section. This concerns preparation, the structure of the interview, verbal and non-verbal communication, and the interview's location. An interview is not a normal conversation between two individuals. There is not an equal relationship between the interviewer and respondent. For example, as an interviewer you are not allowed to express your own opinion; this is difficult because it is a natural tendency to say what you know about the topic, even more so if the respondent explicitly asks you to do so. Nevertheless, avoid doing this. Do not enter into a discussion with the respondent.

7.4.1 Preparing the interview

Here are a number of suggestions for preparing an interview:

- If multiple interviewers are required for data collection, think about how they will be recruited, selected and trained. During recruitment, consider the similarities between the interviewer and the respondents regarding a number of relevant characteristics. For some research topics, it is best to use interviewers who are similar in one way or another to the respondent (for example, older managers should be interviewed by older managers, individuals from other countries should be interviewed by people from their own country). This is because people are more likely to trust their 'equals' with respect to sex, age, socioeconomic status, language use and body language.
- When selecting interviewers, it is a good idea to have the candidates conduct a test interview, ask them to make notes and deal with problem situations.
- Train interviewers so that there are as few differences as possible between them (once again, consider the reliability of the measurement instrument). They must be given the same instructions, ask the same questions and provide the same explanation to the respondents. Such training often takes one or two days, depending on the complexity of the questions.
- Finally, it is important to continually supervise, monitor and correct the interviewers during the data collection process. For example, use cassette tapes to record the interviews; you can listen to the tapes to check whether the interview actually took place and to provide feedback about the interview technique. Of course, you must ask the respondent's permission to record the interview.
- Make sure that you have a good supply of all necessities such as spare questionnaires, spare pens, paper, batteries and cassette tapes.
- Consider supplying a form of identification that your interviewers can show to the respondents.
- Consider whether it would benefit the research to provide the respondents with information about the topic and/or the questions beforehand.

7.4.2 Structure of the interview

There is a standard procedure for conducting an interview:

- Put the respondent at ease – Having an informal chat before the actual interview can relax the respondent; the topic of this chat should be separate from the context of the interview topic. For example, stick to topics such as weather, the interview room or the respondent's trip to the interview.
- Introductions – This creates a link with the respondent and reduces the chance of non-response (saying 'no' to someone with a name and a face is more difficult than disregarding a letter or saying no to a voice on the telephone). For example, 'Good morning/afternoon/ evening Ms/Mr ... My name is ... I am from the bureau/office/ university ...'.
- Discuss the reason for the interview – This explains why the respondent is being interviewed. For example, 'We are conducting a study into ... I would like to ask you several questions about this'. In other words, you are telling the respondent, 'You are an expert in this area'.
- Discuss the relative positions of the interviewer–respondent–client – This affirms the independence, interest and trustworthiness of the interviewer. For example, 'You can tell me anything without there being any consequences. You can trust me'.
- Discuss the plan for the interview – Inform the respondent about the content, structure and duration of the interview. This provides the respondents with a feeling of control over the situation; they know what to expect.
- Ask questions – Prepare these questions as much as possible in advance. The interviewers should present the questions to the respondents in exactly the same manner and sequence. This assures the comparability of the answers. Of course, you must do this in a natural fashion (do not simply read the questions in a monotone). As stated previously, seemingly small differences in the formulation of a question can lead to major differences in the answers from the same respondent.
- Evaluate the answers in terms of completeness, relevance and validity – The criteria for evaluating the answers are that the answers actually relate to the question and that the answers include all the information you intended to acquire.

Follow-up questions – Based on the above evaluation, ask follow-up questions if necessary. This allows you to check whether the respondent has finished answering the question, and you can indicate to the respondents that you have listened to them and were interested in what they had to say. You have to make a trade-off between asking more follow-up questions to obtain more information but possibly influencing the respondent in an undesirable way. In any case, do not show any agreement, disapproval or admiration about the answer. Do not provide your own opinion about the topic or any information about yourself during the interview. If the respondent appreciates this, you may provide this information after the completion of the interview.

Summarizing – By repeating/summarizing the answer, checking and taking notes (the *Listen, Summarize* and *Ask follow-up questions model*), you indicate to the respondent that you have listened to them and understood the answer. In addition, it offers the possibility of comparing and equating language use, thereby helping the respondents to supplement or improve their answers and enabling the interviewer to structure the discussion. Reflect the words of the respondent as much as possible without repeating them literally. Do not provide your own interpretation, opinion or judgement. (For example, 'OK, let's see if I understand what you have said. Essentially you said … But I might have forgotten something. Do you have anything to add?' 'Do you think there are still topics that we haven't discussed?' 'Do you have any questions or remarks?')

Closing and word of thanks – The interview should not end abruptly, but must be closed smoothly and actively by the interviewer. (For example, 'This was the last question of the interview. Thank you very much for taking the time to participate. Your answers will be processed in a report; you will receive copy of this report, probably in about one month'.)

7.4.3 Verbal communication

During an interview it is important to pay attention to verbal communication. This is not so much about *what* you say, but *how* you say it. By using the following elements, you will express interest in the respondent, and you can make sure that the interview proceeds smoothly:

Interpolations – By saying 'Yes' and 'I see' at the right time (that is, not prematurely), you encourage the respondent to begin or continue a narration. Be careful about using fillers such as 'you know'. These have no communicative value; it is best to leave them out.

- Repeat a portion of the last answer of the respondent with a questioning intonation – This acts as a follow-up question. ('Can you say something more about...?' 'Can you talk about this in more depth/ explain it?' 'Keep talking about that. Can you cite another example?') Never ask 'Why?' or 'How do you mean?' if you want the respondents to explain their answer. This is often experienced as threatening.
- Announcement of new parts of the questionnaire – You can use this to close the previous section and focus attention on something new ('That was the last question about topic X. Now we will go on to topic Y').
- Pauses and moments of silence – This provides the respondent with an opportunity to think, or it can 'force' the respondent to say something. However, an excessively long silence can cause the respondent to become agitated.
- Do not interrupt – Avoid interrupting the respondent halfway through a sentence. If the respondent persists in providing irrelevant information, you can carefully attempt to interrupt ('We have already talked about the provocation, now let's talk about the cause').
- Language use of the respondent – Listen carefully to the respondent's formulation; why does the respondent say something in a specific way? If necessary, ask follow-up questions.
- Returning to previous topic – Always take notes during an interview so you can return to relevant topics ('I heard you refer to ... Shall we talk about this for a minute?').
- As stated above, it is advisable to use a tape recorder during an interview. You then have more time to listen and you do not lose any information. Once again, you have to acquire the permission of the respondents to record the interview. Make sure you use good quality apparatus; also consider having extra cassette tapes and batteries.

7.4.4 Voice

- Volume – Talking too loud is threatening to the respondents. They will then be ill at ease and can become less cooperative.

- Intonation – A statement that ends in a questioning tone can bring forth a confirmation or a denial. In this way you can determine whether the question or answer is correct. However, there is often no correct or incorrect answer; the important thing is the opinion of a respondent.

7.4.5 Non-verbal communication

- By means of body language you can indicate that you are interested in the respondent, put them at ease, encourage them to continue to speak and that you are not making any judgements or are not prejudiced. You can do this by leaning slightly forward, keeping your arms, hands and legs open (so they do not touch), maintaining adequate eye contact, nodding at the correct time at the end of a sentence, smiling and having a friendly facial expression.
- The body language of the respondent can also tell you a great deal. If their arms or legs are crossed, if they sit far away from you, look away, do not maintain eye contact and sit stiffly, this can indicate a defensive attitude. If they shift back and forth, are restless, smoke many cigarettes or smoke them without finishing them and have restless eye movements, this can indicate that the respondent feels ill at ease. Observe these signals and bring this possible defensive-ness or discomfort up for discussion, but do so carefully ('I see that you ... Are you troubled by ... ?'). This is called *emotional reflection*. Something might have been said that the respondent did not under-stand or experienced as threatening or painful.
- It is important to look at the respondent when asking a question to observe whether he or she hears and understands the question. If the respondent does not understand the question, then you should not be tempted to give examples. In this way you can unintention-ally influence the respondent. Instead, repeat the question. If necessary, use synonyms.

7.4.6 Space and time

- The distance between the respondent and interviewer plays a role during the course of the interview. Maintain a distance of between 0.50 m and 1.25 m. A distance of less than 50 cm is often experienced as being too intimate ('He/she wants something from me') and a distance greater than 1.25 m is often experienced as being too aloof.

When determining the distance, take into account the cultural differences. In some cultures, it is considered more normal to sit closely together. There are also differences regarding the accepted seating distance between men and women. If you sit too close to a respondent, this may lead to incorrect conclusions or may be intimidating.

- Make sure you have comfortable chairs and a table. Never sit directly opposite each other (at a 180° angle) or right next to each other, but allow enough space to move the chairs (at a 90° angle). This makes it possible for the respondent to temporarily avoid eye contact during personal questions.
- Make sure something to drink is available and writing materials are supplied.
- Pay attention to the lighting in the room. The sun should not shine directly into your face or the respondent's face.
- Reserve sufficient time for the interview. For example, do not conduct 10 interviews in a single day.
- Make sure there is sufficient privacy so you are disturbed as little as possible by third parties, mail or telephone calls.

Making a literal transcription of an interview generally requires four times the length of the actual interview. You can also make a summary of the interview. It can sometimes be useful to present the report to the respondent in order not to make any errors. You can then analyse interviews by, for example, determining the frequency of specific words. You can also determine co-frequencies (for example, how often is the word 'sick' used in the same sentence as the word 'pressure'?). When coding the interview, you can also assign numerical values to words in the text. However, these words must be theoretically relevant. This means that you must determine beforehand which words and concepts you will pay special attention to in the interview based on your theoretical framework. If you do not do this, you then run the risk of being led or distracted by the coincidental content of the interview. When processing the interview, you can use a glossary that you created yourself. Make sure that individuals who code the interview agree in their interpretations and/or that their interpretations are stable over time (once again, this is important to the reliability).

There are also computer programs for analysing qualitative data, enabling you to analyse interviews in an automated way. To this end, you must first select, define and operationalize categories of words (for example, verbs, nouns and adjectives, as well as the positive, neutral or negative content of such words). During this process pay attention to *synonyms* (different words with the same meaning) and *homonyms* (words that are spelled the same but have different meanings). In this way, a keyword list is established. You must then check this list against a sample of the text, thereby allowing you to determine the reliability beforehand. If the reliability is adequate, you can then apply the list to the entire text, where you again have to determine the validity and reliability afterwards (see Section 4.6). The advantage of this explicit system is its comparability over time, allowing results to be accumulated.

▌ 7.5 PILOT STUDY/PRE-TESTING

A great deal of research is currently being conducted by research institutes, etc.. Consequently, there is a declining percentage of respondents who are prepared to participate in research. This is referred to as *respondent attrition*. To obtain the maximum amount of cooperation and the minimum amount of resistance from potential respondents, it is a good idea to invest a great deal of time and effort in the implementation of the research. A pre-test can bring irregularities in the research to light. This allows you to make improvements before the actual research takes place. The pre-test can involve not only the various researchers/interviewers, but also the respondents. For example, you can use a pre-test when developing closed questions. You could initially formulate open questions concerning a specific topic. Based on the answers to the open questions that emerged during the discussions with respondents, you would then formulate closed questions and answers for the main study.

Once you have draft versions of these questions, you can then invite a few people from the target group to 'think aloud' about completing the written questionnaire or answering the questions during an interview. These individuals must not belong to the actual sample, but must be as similar to the sample as possible. There is little use in studying your acquaintances or family members because they are probably accustomed to your language use. The observations and criticisms that emerge during these sessions with the individuals from the target group can be used to improve the questionnaire. For example, are the questions formulated sharply enough? Are any answer categories missing? Do all individuals interpret the questions in the same way? After this first session, you would again approach a number of respondents, after which you would evaluate whether or not the questions indeed provide the intended information. Finally, it is advisable to fill out the questionnaire or take the interview yourself. This gives a great deal of insight into the experience of the respondents.

There is a difference between testing a questionnaire and conducting a more extensive *pilot study*. In a pilot study, for example, not only the question and answer formulations are tested, but you also determine the reliability of the scales using a somewhat larger group of respondents. In this pilot phase you can even begin keeping a file in which all the data are stored every time the questionnaire or test is used. Eventually, this can be used as the basis for a *norm set*, which you can use to indicate how an individual or department compares to other individuals or departments. It can also be used to make a statement about the score of a respondent at a specific time compared to a previous time. However, you should be careful with such comparisons. There can be all kinds of differences between individuals and conditions over time, which can affect scores or result in changing scores.

▌ 7.6 MAKING CONTACT

Making contact with companies and individuals is obviously very important to your research. It is useful to begin making contact at an early stage with individuals who have sufficient influence and authority about conducting the research within a company. Specific points of attention in this regard include:

- First of all, write down exactly what data are needed from which companies and which respondents (for example, names only, or addresses as well?) and in what form you want to have this data (for example, printed lists or computer files?). If you suspect that the respondents will be difficult to reach or may refuse to cooperate, make sure there are sufficient 'reserve individuals' to replace them.
- If possible, use your network – such as parents, family members, neighbours and friends – to make the initial contacts with individuals from the companies.
- You can obtain the addresses and telephone numbers of companies from various catalogues of companies of from the Chamber of Commerce. You should initially make contact by telephone, try to make an appointment and then write a letter in which you refer to the telephone conversation. This increases the probability that you will write to the right person. Therefore completely spell out all names and titles when addressing such letters.

- Take your time. This is not only important for establishing goodwill, but also for steering a research proposal through various decision-making bodies. Sometimes people want to see and approve the questionnaire. The meetings of, for example, co-management councils, or employee's councils are often rather infrequent. This is especially the case during the summer and in the month of December; during these periods it is very difficult to acquire permission to conduct research.

- Carefully formulate the aim and the nature of the research and give yourself plenty of latitude. A request that is formulated in purely scientific terms is often rejected. A research question with detailed sub-questions that are precisely formulated beforehand is not always very inviting. Especially when conducting evaluation research, formulate your research questions in close cooperation with the company.

- Contacts with individual respondents should be made very carefully. It is best to do this personally if you have the time and manpower for this. The response rate is better if you can develop a more personal bond with the respondent. Make sure you have a good introduction for the first few seconds of the initial contact. Research has shown that people who speak relatively quickly, who have a relatively loud voice and radiate self-confidence and expertise have relatively more success in convincing people to participate in a study.

- Deal seriously with the company's concerns regarding the amount of time that is required for the study and its confidentiality. When writing the research report, it is very important to assure the confidentiality of the data. A widely used solution is to provide two types of reports: an internal report that contains all data and an external report from which confidential information has been removed. In addition, many large companies often have a house style for reports, and they are very appreciative if you use this house style when writing the report. Theoretically speaking, scientific reports are accessible to the public without restriction. In cases where a report contains confidential information from a company, there must be supplementary agreements between the client, student, supervisor/instructor and university regarding access to the report.

- Another suggestion is to not challenge the arguments of people who do not want to participate in the research. Empathize with such individuals and try to keep the conversation going. However, make sure that you have a number of counter arguments prepared to encourage them to participate in the research. Give complete and correct answers to any questions from the potential respondent. Do not make complex explanations, for example, about the process of drawing a sample. Do not make any promises you can't keep (for example, do not say that the interview lasts half-an-hour while in reality it will last one hour). The maximum length of an oral interview is between one and one-and-a-half hours.

- When making contacts by telephone, pay attention to proper voice use. If there is no answer, try to call at various times throughout the day. Decide beforehand how you are going to make notes during the conversation, for example, by filling in a pre-printed form, taping the conversation on a cassette tape or entering the information directly into a computer.
- Ask if the previously mailed letter has arrived, has been read and understood. If necessary, remind the individual of any appointments that have been made and confirm these in writing.

7.6.1 The introduction letter

You can use an *introduction letter* with interviews as well as questionnaires. This letter should fully inform the respondents and encourage them to participate in the research. You can send the introduction letter first and then contact the respondent by telephone to explain the letter and to make an appointment. Or, after making an appointment on the telephone, you can send the respondent an introduction letter in which you confirm relevant aspects and possibly list the aspects that will be discussed during the interview. An introduction letter should be short (not more than one or two pages) and should answer the following questions:

- What is the subject and aim of the research?
- What is the background of this research and in what framework will it be conducted?
- How have the respondents been selected? How have you acquired the names of potential respondents?
- How is confidentiality guaranteed? Protecting the privacy of people is very important; privacy is stipulated by law. However, complete anonymity can almost never be guaranteed.
- How long will the research take? People have busy schedules, therefore indicate how long the interview will last or how long it will take to complete the questionnaire. For example, in some cases

you can mail the questions before the interview takes place so that the respondent knows what he or she can expect.

- How will the respondent benefit from the research?
- Reward the respondents by sending them a ballpoint pen, a gift certificate and/or a report with the research results. You should enclose this gift with the introduction letter, but of course not with the research report.
- What is the deadline for returning questionnaires and where can the respondent send the completed questionnaire? Consider enclosing a self-addressed postage-paid return envelope.
- Who can the respondents contact if they have questions about the research?
- Finally, thank the respondents for their cooperation.
- Also consider the following aspects: a personalized address with correctly spelled names, initials and titles, handwritten or hand-typed to the respondents; real postage stamps instead of 'post-paid' stamps; official stationery and an envelope, including a personal salutation; correct gender and a personalized opening sentence (such personalized aspects cannot be used on the questionnaire itself due to the possible conflict with anonymity); an attractive closing sentence; and a personal signature in blue ink from a respected individual, such as the project leader. These aspects can all increase the response rate. This is the *Total Design Method of Dillman* (see Dillman, D.A.1978. *Mail and Telephone Surveys*. New York: Wiley). *Total* means that the various parts of this method must be used in combination; if used individually, they do not have much effect on the response rate.

7.6.2 Non-response and reminders

There may be people who do not return the questionnaire or who refuse to participate in an interview. According to Dillman (1978), it is customary with questionnaires to send three *reminders* after the deadline for returning the questionnaire has passed; these are sent after one, three and seven weeks. In these reminders, you make a friendly request to fill in and return the questionnaire. You can also include a new questionnaire with the second and third reminder letters. These reminders should be addressed personally. You must therefore keep careful records of who has returned the questionnaire and who has not. If you were to send a reminder to the entire sample, this would cause irritation among the respondents who had already returned the questionnaire. If this is not possible (because a study is being conducted anonymously for instance), then include an apology in the letter and explain that you have not kept track of the names of those who have returned the questionnaire. Also thank those who have already returned the questionnaire and ask those who have not yet returned the questionnaire to do so. Try to have the respondents at least return the questionnaire with an explanation of why they did not want to participate.

In large studies involving a number of interviewers, you can use response forms to record when contact was made with the individual respondents, how this contact was made (by telephone or in person) and the result of the contact (interview completed, respondent sick, deceased, moved, or refused to participate; with the latter, include the reasons for refusal if possible).

▌ 7.7 ANONYMITY AND CONFIDENTIALITY

An important aspect for preventing non-response is *anonymity*. The respondent must feel safe enough to provide honest answers. However, oral interviews can never be anonymous by definition. Written questionnaires can theoretically be anonymous, with the exception of longitudinal research. After all, to make repeated measurements you must be able to approach the same respondents again.

It is advisable to take as many precautions as possible to improve the *confidentiality*. With interviews, the names and addresses of the respondents do not have to be recorded. You can also work with respondent numbers instead of names and addresses; the researcher is then the only individual who can make the link between respondent numbers and names. Moreover, you should never interview acquaintances. You can also tell the respondents that the data will be dealt with confidentially. Individuals who deal with confidential data can, for example, sign a confidentiality agreement. You can also state that the report will focus on the group level, not individuals. This is because it is sometimes possible to recognize individuals from 'anonymous' data in a report due to unique combinations in the data (for example, a 'male marketing manager, 35 years old who has worked for the company for five years' could only be Peter Stone). Finally, you can state that the questionnaires will be destroyed after the research is completed. But it is unwise to promise this; in that case you can no longer check anything on the original questionnaires. Moreover, the majority of scientific journals require that the data on which publications are based are stored for several years after the study itself.

Chapter 8

DATA ANALYSIS

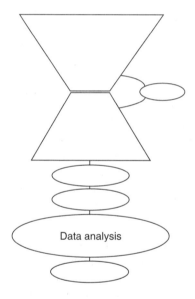

8.1 INTRODUCTION

The previous chapters addressed various data collection methods. In order to answer the research question on the basis of this collected data, you must *quantify* the data. This means that numbers are assigned to various answers and these numbers are entered in a data file. As previously stated, this quantification can take place either before data collection (usually the case with quantitative research) or afterwards (usually the case with qualitative research).

This chapter will address the steps that follow data collection: first *coding, data entry* and *pre-processing*, then applying statistical *data analysis techniques* and finally reading the *output* and summarizing the results. However, this chapter will only touch briefly on the technical formulas used in these techniques and the actual commands (*setups*) used in a computer program such as SPSS.

■ 8.2 THE CODEBOOK

Before beginning data analysis, the data has to be coded, entered and processed so that statistical analysis techniques can be applied. Therefore you must first list all variables in a *codebook* and assign a numerical value to all answer possibilities. For example, if a questionnaire is used to collect data, then you can use a copy of the questionnaire for the codebook. When coding the questionnaire, check the following points:

- Is every question or statement provided with a distinct code: the *variable name*? Treat every question as a separate variable. Later on, you can make new, composite variables (scales) from groups of questions that measure the same concept, for example by calculating the mean scores of the research units for the individual questions that form the scale. If more than one answer to the same question is possible, you must make each answer into a separate variable that can assume two values: ticked or not ticked.

  For example:
  Sometimes more than one answer can be given to a question, such as when a respondent is asked to state the two most important reasons. Although this is a single question in the questionnaire, it actually concerns two variables: the most important reason and the second most important reason. You must then reserve a column in the data matrix (see 8.4) for each variable. Because you 'create' new variables in this way, the number of the questions on the questionnaire does not always correspond with the number of variables. The statistical analysis applies only to the variables, not to the questions themselves.

- Have all answer possibilities been assigned a number? This may be a problem for unstructured interviews or observations. After all, in such cases the list with possible answers is almost never exhaustive.

■ 8.3 COMPUTER USE

It is advisable to enter the data into a computer; once the data has been entered in a file, all further analyses can be conducted in a simple way. It is only when using strictly qualitative data or if there are such small numbers of research units that a calculator would probably be faster. However, you still need to have the formulas for the relevant analysis techniques and the tables for the various tests. You can use the tables to read off the desired significance level based on the number of research units (N) or to determine if a specific test value is significant (see Section 8.7).

Various data entry programs are available for entering data on a computer. Examples are *SPSS* and *Excel*. Currently, data that is entered using one of these programs can be exported to most other programs. You therefore do not have to re-enter the data to use a different program. You can also enter the data in *ASCII* (American Standard Code for Information Interchange) format.

The advantage of working with such programs is that they can be used for quality control. You can enter the entire questionnaire into the program. During this process, you can stipulate the *range* of all possible answers and include controls for illogical combinations of answers (for example, a male respondent who says that he is pregnant). This helps to prevent errors when entering data. For example, if an answer to a specific question has to be given on a five-point scale, then you can order the program to sound a warning tone if you accidentally enter a figure other than one through five ('the range test'). You can also enter the questionnaires twice and compare them with each other. Finally, you can print out descriptive data (frequencies) for all variables in order to discover illogical answers. Note that you cannot replace these afterwards with other, 'logical' answers!

After the processing and analyses that follow data input, always make sure you keep the original file on a separate disk. Make backups of the files. Always name files and sub-files and make sure they have a date and a short description. Take into account the fact that the original questionnaires must be stored for at least 10 years following data input.

Most spreadsheet programs have rudimentary calculation functions. SPSS for Windows contains all the necessary formulas from which you can make a menu-driven choice. With most other analysis programs that are not menu driven, the computer must be provided with exact commands. These are called *syntaxes*. The advantage of creating and saving syntaxes is that a record of your work is kept. You can also repeat analyses with a simple click on a button if you have made an error or accidentally entered extra data. The computer starts calculating and then provides the results of the analyses as output that you can save and print out.

> An example of a menu-driven task in SPSS for Windows is the following: you want to test whether the purchasing and sales departments differ in their levels of absenteeism. In the analysis program, click on the menu command that states you want to conduct a t-test (for differences in means between two independent groups). The menu choice is 'compare means/t-test for independent samples', where the numerical dependent variable is 'level of absenteeism' and the nominal independent variable is 'department' (1 = purchasing, 2 = sales).

▌ 8.4 DATA MATRIX

To analyse data, the answers must be placed in a data matrix or spreadsheet. During data entry, the information from the research units (such as individual employees, teams, annual reports or organizational characteristics) is linked to the codebook. This results in a data matrix where the variables (the scores on the series of questions) are used for the columns and the individual research units comprise the rows. This arrangement is chosen because the number of research units is generally larger than the number of variables. In the cells of the resulting matrix, you enter the scores for each research unit on each variable. You can now read all answers from all research units for every question. You can use this data matrix to conduct various analyses. For example, you can explore relations between different variables by examining and comparing columns (such as the relation between work pressure and absenteeism). For research involving differences and similarities between research units or groups of research units, the rows are compared with each other (such as differences between sales and purchasing staff concerning absenteeism). An intermediate form is conducting an analysis of variables for only part of the research units. Figure 8.1 shows how questions from a questionnaire can be placed in a data matrix.

The standard procedure is to reserve the first column for a number. This is a unique number for each research unit written beforehand or afterwards on the questionnaires of the research units. The advantage

The questionnaire	The codebook
1 What is your sex?	Sex (variable name)
☐ male	1 (value)
☐ female	2 (value)
2 How old are you?	Age
..... years	....
3 What is your year of study?	Year of study
..... year	.....
4 What is your household situation?	Household
☐ Room with shared facilities	1
☐ With parents/guardian	2
☐ Own house/apartment with my own facilities	3
☐ Other, (please explain).........	.....
5 If you engage in a sport, how often do you train?	Sport
☐ Once a week	1
☐ Twice a week	2
☐ Three times per week	3
☐ More than three times per week	4
6 How would you classify your study programme?	Study programme
☐ Humanities	1
☐ Exact sciences	2
☐ Social sciences	3

The accompanying data matrix

Number	Sex	Age	Year of study	Household	Sport	Study programme
001	1	22	3	1	2	3
002	2	23	4	2	3	1
003	9	24	3	1	4	9
004	2	22	4	2	2	2
005	1	21	5	2	9	3
006	2	25	3	1	1	3

The above matrix shows that research unit number 001 is a 22-year-old man in his third year of study in a social science study programme who is living on his own and trains twice a week. For research unit number 003, it is unknown if the respondent is male or female, therefore a code for a missing value is used.

Figure 8.1 Example questionnaire and data matrix.

of this numbering method is, among other things, that it makes it easier to find the relevant questionnaire afterwards. Therefore, place the original questionnaires in numerical sequence. If there are fewer than 100 research units, two digits are sufficient. The answers to the questions are placed after every number. The result is a long row with figures. Each row contains the answers on the questionnaire from one research unit.

If you do not use a special data input program or spreadsheet to enter data onto the computer, you must indicate which number positions belong together (in columns) and what these columns mean by assigning a variable name to each column and giving it a more complete description. This is shown in Section 8.2. Syntaxes must satisfy a number of rules. For example, some data entry programs limit variable names to a maximum of eight positions. The syntax also stipulates that commands must end with a specific type of punctuation (e.g. full stop, forward slash or back slash). There are many more syntax rules, which are listed in the manuals for the relevant data entry programs. Generally speaking, making a data entry *setup* requires great precision.

Before you begin the actual data analysis, you often have to *re-code* certain variables and then make scales of these questions. One form of re-coding is called *mirroring*. This is used on either all negatively or all positively formulated statements or questions. This means that you tell the computer that the lowest score (for example, a 1 for 'disagree completely' on a five-point scale) must actually be interpreted as its 'mirror image', therefore becoming the highest score (in this case, a 5 for 'agree completely') and that the highest score must be interpreted as the lowest score (for example, a 5 becomes a 1). The same principle is used for the scale values 2 and 4; these scores must also mirror if there is a mix of positively and negatively formulated questions or statements on a scale. You can do this by entering the following in the computer:

> To measure organizational commitment, two statements have been included to which a respondent can answer on a scale from 1 (disagree) to 5 (agree):
> a   I feel at home in the organization.
> b   I am looking for a job at another organization.
>
> The second statement must be mirrored because then the same ranking method would be used for both items: a higher score means the individual feels more committed to his or her organization.
>
> Recode (variable name) (1 = 5) (2 = 4) (3 = 3) (4 = 2) (5 = 1)

This recoded file must often be resaved and reopened in order to use it in the analyses. It is always faster and more accurate to do such recoding afterwards (after data entry). The individuals responsible for data entry should therefore enter only the original (raw) data in the file.

Another example of recoding is when classes of values that belong together are grouped at a later date. For example, after data collection and entry, you might want to make several distinct age categories (such as 20–30, 31–40, 41–50) from the *continuous variable* of age (where you ask the respondent's exact age in years – 'How old are you?') instead of providing the respondent with these age categories and asking him or her to choose from them. The latter option results in loss of information.

The difference between continuous and *discrete variables* can be described as follows. A discrete variable means that this variable can only have a limited number of values and that there are no values in between these discrete values (for example, the total number of staff cannot be 34.67, but can be 34 and 35). The best way to graphically portray a discrete variable is therefore a histogram. With continuous or semi-continuous variables, such as age or turnover, there can be all kinds of interim values. With such variables it is generally not very useful to calculate frequencies, because then there will be far too many classes (there are sometimes as many classes as values; the frequency of every class is then 1). In this case, you can do the following. You can make a limited number of classes by recoding (reducing the number of possible values for a variable) and then calculating frequencies, or you can limit yourself to calculating descriptive statistics such as means and standard deviations.

After this you can add the scores for the various items that are intended to measure the same concept to arrive at a total score for that concept. This results in a single scale. During this process, you assume that these questions actually measure the concept as intended (that is, they are *valid*) and that they are sufficiently correlated with each other. You can check this latter assumption by means of *reliability analysis*. The most commonly used method is *item analysis*, where the correlations between the answers on various questions are calculated. The degree to which all questions are correlated with each other is expressed in the homogeneity index *Cronbach's alpha* (discussed in Section 4.6.1).

This alpha coefficient (a type of mean correlation between all items) can theoretically have a value between -1 (where the questions have completely opposite correlation) and $+1$ (where there is perfect correlation; the questions overlap each other completely). In practice, these extremes virtually never occur. Moreover, a negative alpha can sometimes be made positive by recoding some items (mirroring). The alpha coefficient must be as high as possible. In practice this usually means a value of 0.60 or higher. However, the magnitude of alpha also depends on the number of items: the greater the number of items, the higher the alpha coefficient. Therefore, you should aim to have a sufficiently high alpha coefficient with the smallest possible number of items. Therefore consider the *item rest correlations*: which items have a negligible or even negative effect on homogeneity? You could possibly remove these items in the scales before the final analyses. The reliability analysis indicates what the alpha coefficient would be if that item were to be removed or not included in the total score.

It is then important to have descriptive data (*descriptives*) for all variables (individual items and scales), to determine on which level the variables have been measured and to ascertain whether they have a normal or skewed distribution (see below). These aspects can be the preconditions for specific analysis techniques. Specific preconditions will be discussed with individual analysis techniques.

▋ 8.5 MISSING VALUES

It sometimes happens that respondents skip certain questions when completing a written questionnaire, that certain questions are accidentally skipped during an oral interview or that specific responses are neglected during observation (*partial non-response*). In these cases data must be entered into the appropriate cell of the data matrix. This is called a missing value.

But now you have to make it clear to the computer that there is a missing value. You do this by entering a code at the location of the missing value. Theoretically speaking, every code that is not a valid value of a variable is a missing value, but missing values are usually coded by using the number 8 or 9. Of course, you can use these numbers only if they are not actual values for the variable (if there are more than eight or nine answer possibilities, you can use the numbers 88 or 99). Some data entry programs also accept a space or a dot as a missing value.

Make sure that you do not interpret the answer 'does not apply' as a missing value. This answer has a different meaning than 'skipped' or 'forgotten'. You must make missing values recognizable to the data entry program, otherwise this 'value' (such as 8 or 9) is simply interpreted as an actual score and could be used to calculate the mean scores of research units on variables, for example. It is inadvisable to use 0 as a code for a missing value.

The next question is what to do with the missing values when analysing the data. You should first understand how the missing values occurred. For example, were the missing values caused by the respondents themselves (such as a refusal to answer, a 'don't know' or a 'does not apply') or does the cause lie elsewhere (with the researcher, for example, who made an error during data entry)? In the latter case you can replace the incorrect value with the correct value by referring to the original questionnaire. You then determine whether there is a structural pattern of missing values (with respect to research units and variables), or if the error is the result of chance. One way to answer this question is to compare respondents with individuals not involved in the research. You can also examine the comments made by respondents during interviews or those that they have written down on a questionnaire, for example.

You can choose from a number of options, each of which has a specific consequence. During the analyses, one option is to disregard all research units for whom at least one variable in the data is missing. In computer language, this option is called *listwise deletion*. This option entails a risk that the total number of research units will rapidly decrease. If there are only a few research units, this is therefore not a very good strategy. A second option when conducting an analysis with specific variables is to use only those research units who actually have a score on those relevant variables. This option is called *pairwise deletion*. This can mean that every analysis is based on a different number of research units. A third option is to replace the missing values by the mean score on the variable for the total sample or population (for example, if the mean score of the sample for the question about satisfaction with work is 4, enter this value for respondents who forgot to answer this question). The fourth option is to fill in the most logical answer by considering the respondent's answers to comparable questions.

For example:
If a positive answer is given to three of the four questions concerning organizational commitment, and the respondent has forgotten to answer the fourth question, it is logical to assume that the answer to the fourth question would also be positive.

All of the above options have specific consequences for the reliability of the results. For example, replacing the missing answer by the mean value makes variance estimates less valid. After all, many values are artificially included that are exactly equivalent to the mean, causing the frequency distribution to become concentrated around the mean. As a result, the variance becomes artificially smaller, as can be observed in Figure 8.2.

In addition, the frequency distribution is distorted, which can reduce correlations. The fourth option has the disadvantage that correlations in the data are amplified because systematic patterns in the data are

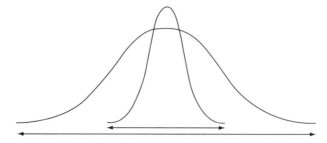

Figure 8.2 Decreasing variance.

taken into account. Depending on the type of data, this can lead to more rapid confirmation of the hypotheses. With both options, modifications are done on the basis of patterns in the sample data that could be entirely coincidental; as a result, the results become less generalizable. Regardless of the option you choose, it is important to be careful and to properly describe and explain your choice in the report (in the 'Research Method' section). Once again, in this case it is better to avoid the problem than to try to solve it afterwards. When constructing a questionnaire, you should take measures wherever possible to prevent questions from being skipped (such as a clear layout, clearly formulated questions and clear routes to other questions).

Finally, it is important to check whether the tendency to skip certain items is related to the topic of your research.

> For example:
> Individuals who frequently call in sick may tend to 'forget' to fill in the number of days they were absent during the last year more often than individuals who are rarely absent.

In this case, the relationship between completing or skipping a question, and the score on one or more important variables in your research can provide an answer. Of course, you hope that there is no link between skipping or completing questions and the important variables in your research.

■ 8.6 OVERVIEW OF STATISTICAL TECHNIQUES

8.6.1 Independence and dependence techniques

There are many statistical analysis techniques. Finding your way among all these techniques requires time and insight. Before you can make a choice, you must first clearly formulate exactly what it is you want to know.

If you only want to investigate whether there is a relationship between variables without making a distinction between dependent and independent variables (for example, if you want to determine whether there is a relationship between work satisfaction and work quality without knowing whether satisfaction leads to higher quality or higher quality leads to more satisfaction) then you should use *independence (symmetric) techniques.* Examples of these techniques are correlation analysis (8.6.4), factor analysis (8.6.5), cluster analysis (8.6.6), multidimensional scale analysis (8.6.7) and canonical correlation analysis (8.6.9).

If you want to explain or predict the relationship between two or more variables, then you should use the so-called *dependence (asymmetric) techniques.* These techniques require some sort of distinction between independent and dependent variables. One or more variables are explained by one or more other variables (for example, you can attempt to explain absenteeism as a result of work satisfaction or dissatisfaction). Examples of dependence techniques include regression analysis (8.6.8), path analysis (8.6.10), the t-test (8.6.11), analysis of variance (8.6.12) and discriminant analysis (8.6.13). Note that the distinction between dependent and independent variables is one that you make yourself. The statistical tests do not tell you whether this distinction is correct!

8.6.2 Combining the research question, the number and level of measurement of variables

The choice for a specific statistical analysis technique depends on the research question, the number of independent and dependent variables and the measurement levels of these variables (see Section 4.5). Generally speaking, there are three types of research questions:

1. Questions concerning the frequency of phenomena ('How frequently or to what degree do you ... ?')
2. Questions concerning the differences between two or more groups ('Is there a difference between ... and ... ?')
3. Questions concerning relationships between phenomena ('What is the relationship between ... and ... ?')

Table 8.1 provides a summary of a number of tests classified according to these three types of research question and shows the

Table 8.1 Summary of a number of analysis techniques and statistical tests combined with types of research questions and the measurement level of the variables (based on Huizingh, 1991)

Desired type of analysis/ Type of research question	Measurement level of the dependent variable		
	Nominal	Ordinal	Interval/ratio
1. Describe variable			
How much/how frequently does absenteeism occur in the company?	Frequency table Histogram		Indicators
Central tendency			
How many days are employees absent?	Mode	Median	Mean
Distribution tests			
Is there a normal distribution of absenteeism?	Chi-square		Kolmogorov– Smirnov
2. Describe groups			
What causes for absenteeism are given by employees at different departments?	Contingency table		Indicators (mean, variance)
Testing for differences between two groups			
Are purchasing staff more frequently sick than sales staff?	Chi-square	Sign test Mann-Whitney Kolmogorov– Smirnov	*t*-test
Testing for differences between more than two groups			
Are there differences in absenteeism between younger, middle-aged and older employees?	Chi-square	Kruskal–Wallis	*F*-test (univariate or multivariate analysis of variance)
3. Insight into possible relations			
Is there a relation between having a personal relationship and the absenteeism of male and female students?	Contingency table	Scatter diagram	
Testing correlations between two variables			
Is the correlation between work load and absenteeism positive?	Chi-square	Rank correlation (Spearman's rho or Kendall's tau)	Product–moment correlation (Pearson)
Testing relations between more than two variables			
Which factors affect absenteeism?	Log-linear analysis	Ordinal regression analysis	Regression analysis

measurement level and the number of variables. Generally speaking, more analyses may be conducted with variables at a higher measurement level, for example at the interval level, than with variables that are measured at a lower level, such as nominal variables. The reason for this is that all the statistics that can be calculated at a lower level, such as the mode or median, can also be calculated at a higher level, but the opposite is not allowed. For example, the mean score can be meaningfully calculated only at the interval level, not at the nominal or ordinal level (for example, there is no point in calculating the mean of the shirt numbers of football players). The formulae, implementations and setups can be found in the SPSS manuals.

FREQUENCIES

First calculate the descriptive statistics and draw graphs for the individual variables and the mutual relationships between the variables. This provides you with better understanding of your data, and you can use this understanding to check the assumptions of the analysis techniques described below. For example, you can discover possible *outliers* (see Figure 8.3). It is important to have insight into such aspects because most techniques, especially if you want to apply statistical tests, are based on a normal distribution of variables, linearity of relationships between variables and random measurement errors.

If your data do not satisfy these requirements, you may be able to conduct transformations to satisfy the demands for these analysis techniques, or you could use *non-parametric* techniques that are less demanding.

Table 8.1 shows that there are differences in frequency measurement between variables with different measurement levels. In fact, with nominal data you can only count how often the specific answer category is ticked (the *frequencies* and the accompanying percentages, for example, when respondents have ticked which illness they have

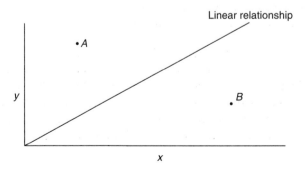

Figure 8.3 Example of a linear relationship between x and y and the outliers A and B.

had: flu, measles or headache). Besides the frequency (the number of research units per category, the number of times that a specific event has occurred, the number of organizations that have a specific property or fall in a specific category) the *relative frequency* is also calculated (also known as *proportion* or *fraction*). This is the frequency divided by the total number (research units or organizations). When you multiple this by 100, you obtain percentages.

The descriptive central tendency measure for nominal variables is the *mode*: this is the value that occurs most often.

> For example:
> We asked individuals to evaluate the general quality of the absenteeism supervision in their company on a five-point scale ranging from 1 (poor) to 5 (good). In a department of seven employees, we observed the values 3, 3, 3, 4, 4, 5, 5. The mode is therefore 3.

The mode is generally used if different values occur more frequently. In a histogram, if the number of observations for each possible value is used (in case of only one value being the mode, the distribution is called unimodal), the mode is the highest bar. A graph with two equally tall top bars is called bimodal (for example, the responses 'have a cold' and 'have a headache' may occur with equal frequency in answer to the question, 'What is your most important reason for calling in sick during the past year?'), and a graph with more than two tops is referred to as multimodal.

With ordinal data, the *median* is used as a central tendency measure this is the middle value of a series listed in order of magnitude (50 per cent of the measurements lie above the median and 50 per cent lie below).

> For example:
> We asked individuals to evaluate the general quality of the absenteeism supervision in their company on a five-point scale ranging from 1 (poor) to 5 (good). In a department of seven employees, we observed the values 3, 3, 3, 4, 4, 5, 5. In this case the median is 4.

If there is an even number of observations, there is obviously no middle observation. In this case, the mean value of the two observations closest to the middle is used. This shows that the median does not have to be an actual value or even a possible value. In contrast with the mean, the median is insensitive to outliers because it only takes account of the ranking of the scores, not their absolute values.

For variables that are measured at the interval or higher level, the mathematical *mean* and *variance* can be calculated. The mean is calculated by adding all scores and dividing by the total number of scores.

For example:
We asked individuals to evaluate the general quality of the absenteeism supervision in their company on a five-point scale ranging from 1 (poor) to 5 (good). In a department of seven employees, we observed the values 3, 3, 3, 4, 4, 5, 5. The mean is therefore 3.86.

The difference between the minimum and maximum value is the *range*. In the above example the range is 2. Since the range does not say anything about the structure of the values surrounding the mean, the *variance* indicates how the values surrounding the mean are distributed: it is the mean of the sum of the squared distances to the mean. In the above example, the variance is 0.69. The square root of the variance is the standard deviation. In the example the standard deviation is 0.83.

For a *normal distribution* (*Gaussian curve*), approximately two-thirds of the observed values lie between the mean minus one standard deviation and the mean plus one standard deviation (see Figure 8.4). The normal distribution is a continuous symmetrical curve where the top is both the mean score and the median.

Another type of distribution is the *skewed distribution* (see Figure 8.5). The skewness is an indication of how many extreme values there are. SPSS can calculate the skewness for you. There are left and right skewed distributions. In a skewed distribution, a relatively large number of people have a low score or a high score.

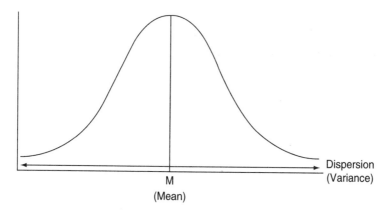

Figure 8.4 The normal distribution.

There are tests to determine whether a distribution is skewed to the left or to the right (generally speaking, you can assume that a skewness less than −1 or +1 indicates a distribution that deviates too much from a normal distribution) and whether a distribution is normal (see the Shapiro – Wilks test and the Kolmogorov – Smirnov test in SPSS).

The *kurtosis* is a measure of the flatness or peakedness of the distribution. A high kurtosis means that there is a tall peak, which usually indicates that there is little variance (see Figure 8.6).

The kurtosis of a perfect, normally distributed variable is zero. A rule of thumb is that the assumption of a normal distribution becomes suspect if the kurtosis is larger than +1 or smaller than −1. With such variables it is preferable to use *non-parametric techniques*. These techniques are also applicable to small samples ($N < 25$) when the measurement level of the variables is considered to be ordinal. You can also attempt to obtain a normal distribution of a variable by using transformations such as square roots or squares.

DIFFERENCES BETWEEN GROUPS

If you want to test the differences between groups (the groups are then assigned according to the nominal independent or classificatory vari-

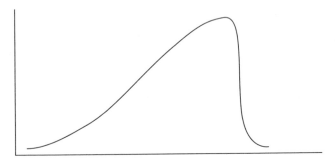

Figure 8.5 Example of a skewed distribution.

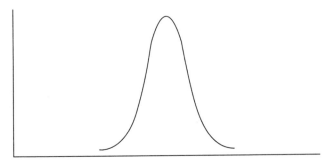

Figure 8.6 Example of a high kurtosis.

able) concerning an ordinal dependent variable, you can use the Mann – Whitney U-test for independent groups and the Wilcoxon – Matched-Pairs Signed Ranks test in the case of dependent samples.

> For example:
> We asked individuals to evaluate the general quality of the absenteeism supervision in their company on a five-point scale ranging from 1 (poor) to 5 (good). In the personnel department with seven employees, we observed the values 3, 3, 3, 4, 4, 5, 5 and in the marketing department with nine employees we observed the values 2, 2, 3, 3, 5, 5, 5, 5, 5. By using the Mann – Whitney U-test, it can be determined whether the personnel department generally produces lower scores than the marketing department.

When testing the differences between two groups (samples) with respect to a dependent variable, which is measured at the interval or ratio level, it is advisable to use the t-test for independent samples (for example, if you want to determine whether the mean absenteeism for male employees differs from that for female employees). The condition for using this test is that the samples are drawn independently and randomly from the population. With small samples, you must check whether the scores are normally distributed. There is a special formula (*t-test pairs*) for dependent samples (paired observations). Paired observations are, for example, observations conducted on the same research units at different times. As a result, the scores from the first measurement are related to those of the second measurement; in other words, the observations are correlated. The special testing method takes account of this fact (see also Section 8.6.11). With a comparison between more than two samples, *analysis of variance* is used. This concerns the differences between two or more groups (nominal independent variable) with respect to one or more dependent variables that are measured at the interval level (univariate versus multivariate analysis, see Section 8.6.12) (for example, you want to determine whether eight departments in the same company differ from each other regarding absenteeism). You then determine the effect of the nominal group assignment on the scores on the dependent interval variable.

You may also want to know how to assign the research units to groups so that these groups differ as much as possible concerning a specific variable.

> For example:
> You assign individuals to groups according to characteristics such as age, education, satisfaction with work and health, so that the groups differ as much as possible regarding mean absenteeism.

In this case, the aim is assigning research units to two or more groups such that these groups differ as much as possible on the independent variables. Use discriminant analysis in this instance (see Section 8.6.13). Discriminant analysis is therefore strongly explorative in nature.

RELATIONS

When studying the relationship (association) between nominal variables (also known as qualitative, categorical, non-metric or non-numeric variables), it is advisable to place all the values of two variables next to each other in a *contingency table* (also known as a *two-way table*).

> For example:
> You can determine the relationship between the nominal variables 'department' (such as the personnel and marketing departments) and 'sex' by using a contingency table to show how many male and female individuals work in the two departments.

A pie chart or circle diagram is frequently used to graph such a frequency distribution (see Figure 8.7).

By using the chi-square (χ^2) test, you can check whether there is a link between these two nominal variables. In the case of small samples, it is best to use Fisher's exact test with 2×2 tables.

It is preferable to use a *histogram* to graph a frequency distribution or probability distribution of numeric variables. By using the ranking coefficient or Pearson correlation coefficient you can test the degree of correlation between two ordinal or interval/ratio variables (see Section 8.6.4).

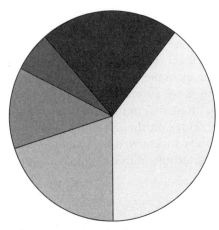

Figure 8.7 Example of a pie chart.

For example:
We asked individuals to evaluate the general quality of the absenteeism supervision at their company using a five-point scale ranging from 1 (poor) to 5 (good) and also to evaluate work satisfaction on a five-point scale. The rank correlation between both series of ordinal numbers can then be determined.

8.6.3   Example of a sequence of analysis techniques

Although every researcher uses analysis techniques that are suitable to the specific study based on the specific research questions and the number and measurement levels of the variables, a global application sequence for data analysis techniques is given below. First, this sequence will be described. Then the individual analysis techniques will be discussed more extensively.

First calculate the frequencies of all variables and the means and standard deviations of the items and the scales. During this process check whether coding errors have been made, for example, scores that are impossible (according to the codebook) for a specific variable. If possible, repair these errors. You can also use this output to evaluate whether the variables display sufficient variation.

For example:
If you want to study the difference between males and females regarding absenteeism, and the sample is entirely male (in other words, the variable of sex does not vary), then there is no point in continuing the study.

Then attempt to reduce the data, for example by using factor analysis (Section 8.6.5), cluster analysis (8.6.6) or multidimensional scale analysis (8.6.7). Your choice of analysis method depends, among other things, on the measurement level of the variables. Based on existing measurement instruments and/or your own ideas about the possible correlation of items that measure a specific underlying concept or construct, you can conduct a factor analysis on the items of scales which appear to have most in common. After this, for example, you can conduct reliability analyses (Section 4.6.1)

The next step is to calculate the correlation coefficients (Section 8.6.4) of all items and scales so that you can observe the mutual correlation in terms of logical direction, strength and significance. Then, depending on the measurement level and the research question, two main types of analyses are conducted: the analysis of differences between groups (t-test and variance analysis (multivariate or univariate, see Section 8.6.12)), or the analysis of relations between variables (regression analysis, see Section 8.6.8). By using regression analysis, the effects of a number of independent variables on a single dependent variable are studied. These variables are measured at the interval level or above. If there is more than one dependent interval variable (and multiple independent variables), then you can conduct canonical analysis (Section 8.6.9).

If there is more than one independent variable, you must first conduct a multivariate F-test for all independent variables together. Then continue with univariate tests for each independent variable if this multivariate F-test is significant. The reason for this is the phenomenon of *capitalization on chance*, where some tests always produce significant results purely on the basis of chance if a large enough number of tests are used. This can be prevented as much as possible by first conducting a protective (or general) multivariate test. However, such a test is more complex than univariate or bivariate tests. This complexity is caused by the possibility of *multicollinearity*; this is the case when the independent variables have a high mutual correlation.

8.6.4 Correlation analysis

> For example:
> If you want to know if there is a relationship between absenteeism and the level of income, then you can apply correlation analysis.

The degree of relationship between two variables, both of which are measured at the ordinal level or above, can be determined by using a rank correlation (Spearman's rho or Kendall's tau). To determine the correlation between a dichotomous variable (see Section 4.5) and a numeric variable, (point) bi-serial correlation can be used. To determine the relation between interval or ratio variables, you can calculate the Pearson product moment correlation coefficient (Pearson's r). Although there are even more measures for correlation concerning specific combinations of variables that are measured at different levels, the following section will deal primarily with Pearson's r.

To calculate correlations between variables, the observed values for the variables must have sufficient variance: there must be research units that score high or low, while the majority of the research units must score around the mean (a normal distribution).

You can acquire insight into the principle of a correlation by using a *scattergram*. It is customary to place the variable that you want to predict (the dependent variable, for example during a regression analysis, see next section) on the vertical y-axis. The other variable from which you want to make a prediction (the independent variable) is placed on the horizontal x-axis. By finding the scores for the independent (x-axis) and dependent (y-axis) variables, every research unit can be represented as a point on the $x - y$ axis system. A straight line can be fitted to these points that provides the best possible representation of these points. The correlation coefficient is an index for a linear correlation. This indicates to what extent the straight line represents the observed relationship between the two variables, that is to what extent the points (x, y) do not deviate from the line.

There are a number of possible patterns of correlations. Several of these are represented graphically in Figure 8.8 ('r' stands for correlation).

A perfect correlation ($r = 1.00$) means that all points lie exactly on a straight line; this virtually never occurs in organizational research. A relatively round scatter pattern ($r = .30$) indicates there is little correlation between the variables x and y. A large and positive correlation ($r = .80$) means that the high values for one variable are associated with high values on the other variable. The line goes from the left lower part of the graph to the right upper part of the graph. Finally, a large and negative correlation ($r = -.90$) means that high values for one variable correlate with low values on the other variable. The line runs from the upper left quadrant to the lower right quadrant.

The square of the correlation coefficient multiplied by 100 indicates the percentage of overlap in variance between both variables. This square indicates what percentage of the variance of one variable can be predicted or explained by the other variable.

The mutual correlations between a series of distinct variables can be shown in a correlation matrix. The values on the diagonal are all '1'; after all, the correlation between a variable and itself is 1. The matrix is

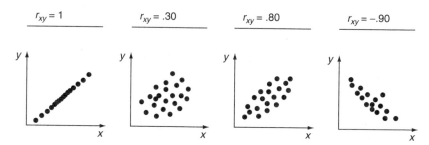

Figure 8.8 Example of different types of correlation

symmetrical: it is therefore sufficient to fill in only half of the matrix. This matrix is frequently used as input for other analysis techniques such as factor analysis.

8.6.5 Factor analysis

If you want to know how a number of variables are related to each other, the best approach is of course to first calculate the correlations between the variables. However, if there are many variables, it becomes difficult to ascertain a clear pattern in the correlations. In that case, *factor analysis* is the recommended analysis technique.

Factor analysis is a method where one or more new *factors* (or *dimensions*) are constructed based on a number of measured (collected, observed, manifest) variables. Consequently it is an interdependence method: no distinction is made between independent and dependent variables. The aim of the analysis is to acquire insight into the structure of the data by reducing the number of variables. This entails constructing a smaller number of new underlying (*latent*) variables (called 'factors') based on the correlations between a large number of variables. The question is then to what extent this large number of original variables is related to this smaller number of factors. The factors must represent the variables with the smallest possible information loss.

Generally speaking, there are two possibilities:

1. Let the analysis program decide about the number of factors and which variables are most heavily 'loaded' on these factors (*explorative* factor analysis).
2. Determine which variables you believe are loaded on which factors. The analysis program then determines to what extent the data fit the model you have provided (*confirmative* factor analysis). This second method is recommended if you have an idea beforehand about the factors that underlie the data, for example, based on your theory or on previous analyses.

The requirements for factor analysis are that the variables are measured on a metric scale and are more or less normally distributed. In addition, the sample must contain a minimum number of research units in both absolute terms and in relation to the number of variables that are included in the analysis. A rule of thumb is that you must have at least 10 times as many research units as variables (for example, if there are five variables, you must have at least 50 research units).

The basis of factor analysis is the correlation matrix of the measured variables. There are two methods: *Q analysis* and *R analysis*. With Q analysis, you analyse the correlation between the research units across the variables. The question is which research units are strongly similar to each other in view of the score pattern on the variables. The basis for this analysis is the correlation matrix between the research units. In R analysis, in contrast, you analyse the correlation between the variables across the research units. The question is which variables are strongly similar in view of their score pattern across the research units. In this case, the basis is the correlation matrix between the variables. In practice, R analysis is primarily used because there are usually many more research units than variables. The correlation between the variable and the factor is defined as the loading of the variable on the factor. A high loading means that the relevant factor is important for the variable: a minimum value of .30 is used and .40 or .50 is considered normal.

You can order the computer program to construct the various factors in such a way that they do not have any mutual correlation. In that case, the factors are said to be *orthogonal* (at right angles to each other, independent). There are various ways to determine the factors: the two most important are:

- the principle component (PC) model where all correlation is initially considered to be relevant;
- the factor model (principle axes) where a distinction is made between shared variance and unique (including unreliable) variance.

You would use the second method if you have some idea beforehand about which part of the total variance is shared between all variables and which part of the variance is only shared by a few variables.

You can consider the orthogonal factors as the *x*- and *y*-axes in a set of coordinates. By using the loadings the variables can be drawn on that set of coordinates. Frequently it is necessary to first rotate the factors (this means choosing other axes) in order to be able to interpret the figure. By using rotation, an attempt is made to provide a variable with a high loading on only a single factor and to provide a low loading, preferably zero, on the other factors. This makes it easier to interpret the factor. During rotation, there is no change to the fit of a factor solution, to the communalities (see below) or to the total explained variance. Roughly speaking, there are two possibilities: *varimax rotation*, where the orthogonality of the factors is conserved, and *oblimin rotation*, where oblique (slanted or skewed) rotation takes place. In the latter, the factors can still be distinguished from each other, but they are correlated: this situation often comes closer to reality, but is more difficult to interpret. Choose an oblique axis system if, on the basis of a theory, you have good reasons to assume that the factors are correlated.

Sometimes you take a following step by describing the research units for whom you have measured the variables in terms of the factors that are found. Then calculate the scores of the research units on the new factor: these are the *factor scores*. Since a factor is constructed from a specific combination of the variables, a factor score is the linear combination of the original variables. *Linear* means that the only operations that can take place are addition and subtraction – the values cannot be squared, for example. When adding or subtracting, every variable is given its own coefficient (weight), which indicates how heavily the variable should weigh when calculating the factor score. However, factor scores are seldom used because they are relatively unstable and unreliable. Instead, the variables with the highest loadings on a factor are compiled by simply calculating the average. During this process the weights of the variables are in fact zero and one.

> For example:
> According to a factor analysis, three items involving questions about work satisfaction result in a single factor:; the weights (the loadings: correlations between variable and factor) are .56, .83 and .67. For convenience sake, the factor score is calculated as the unweighted sum of the scores on the original three items. You then proceed as if all items have an equal loading on the factor.

More than one solution is almost always possible in factor analysis. The solution that is ultimately chosen depends partly on your own substantive interpretation capacity in addition to a number of statistical criteria. One suggestion is to look at the number of factors. Various criteria are available for this, such as the *eigenvalue* (the total variance explained by a factor; the larger the eigenvalue, the more important the factor), and the *elbow criterion* (there is a sudden change such as a sharp drop in the plot of the eigenvalues). The problem with this criterion is that the curve that illustrates the progression of the eigenvalue often has more than one bend. This happens especially if there are a large number of variables in combination with a relatively small sample size. You can then look at the content of the variables that have the highest loading on the factors. Try to interpret the factor by looking at the substantive common denominator of the variables that have a high loading on a factor and thereby give this factor a name.

For example:
If all items that have a high loading on the first factor are concerned in one way or another with questions about satisfaction with the work itself, and all items which have a high loading on a second factor concern questions about satisfaction with the results of the work, you can denote the first factor as 'intrinsic work satisfaction' and the second 'extrinsic work satisfaction'.

You can also look at the percentages of explained variance for each of the variables. This is the *communality*; it is the portion of the variance of a variable that can be attributed to all the common factors. The remaining variance that cannot be explained by the common factors is called *uniqueness* of that variable. This is partly systematic, but not common, and partly the result of chance. In addition you can also inspect the *matrix of residuals*: the differences between the observed and estimated correlations must not be too large.

Finally, the aim of your research determines what and how much information you include about factor analysis in your report. For example, if the topic of your research is instrument construction, you would discuss factor analysis more extensively than if your intention is to conduct additional substantive analysis on the basis of the new factors. In any case, your report must answer the following questions:

- Why have you decided to use factor analysis?
- Which method and which rotation method have you chosen?
- How many factors have been chosen according to which criterion?
- What are the eigenvalues of the factors?
- What is the total percentage of explained variance?
- What is your substantive interpretation of the factors?

Factor analysis is frequently used to construct item scales. First determine which variables together form a factor. Then calculate the internal consistency for the variables which have a high loading on the same factor (i.e. how strong is their mutual correlation, determined by using Cronbach's alpha coefficient – see Chapter 4). If this coefficient is high enough, then you know that the items are strongly correlated and that they also measure only one single factor.

8.6.6 Cluster analysis

Factor analysis is concerned with knowing which variables belong together. Cluster analysis is concerned with knowing which research units belong together. Cluster analysis is also used for data reduction. The large quantity of original data is reduced to a more orderly and conveniently arranged whole. However, during this process correlations are generally analysed between research units, not between variables (as is the case in factor analysis). Earlier this was referred to as Q analysis.

Cluster analysis is a multivariate technique. For each research unit, data are collected about different variables. The research units are grouped into classes (clusters) based on this data. The research units within a cluster must be as similar as possible regarding their data (scores on the variables) and must be as dissimilar as possible from the research units from other clusters. A similarity measure is calculated that indicates the strength of the average similarity within a cluster and the level of average similarity between clusters. Then the clusters (these are groups of research units) are chosen in such a way that the similarity within the cluster is as large as possible and the similarity between the clusters is as small as possible. Based on the results of the cluster analysis, you can determine how many clusters there are, which research units belong to which clusters and what the common characteristics are of the research units that belong to the same cluster. Because you instruct the computer program to calculate which research units belong together, cluster analysis, like explorative factor analysis, is an explorative technique. In contrast to factor analysis, however, your data do not have to satisfy strict requirements regarding the number of research units or the measurement level of the variables.

8.6.7 Multidimensional scaling

Besides factor and cluster analysis, there is also *multidimensional scale analysis* or *multidimensional scaling* (*MDS*). With this technique, there is a given similarity measure on the basis of which the variables are classified into groups. However, this measure is not a calculated correlation, but is often based on an estimation that the research units themselves are asked to make. So, research units produce similarity measures between the variables.

> For example:
> A respondent is repeatedly presented with a group of three different retail articles: e.g. coffee, chocolate and a laundry detergent. The respondent must repeatedly indicate the article that is least similar to the other two. During this process, the respondent may decide how he or she determines this similarity. The respondent is free to apply his/her own

choice criterion. By repeating this choice process many times with a large retail assortment, levels of similarity between the articles can be calculated (such as the relative frequency with which two articles tend to be chosen together). The market researcher now wants to know what are the underlying dimensions of this choice process. In other words, what does the 'choice space' of the respondent look like? Is he/she selecting the articles on the basis of price, type of use (breakfast food, cleaning agent, etc.) or on the basis of another criterion?

With MDS, the groups are determined afterwards. It is therefore an explorative technique. The difference with cluster analysis is that in MDS the variables are depicted as points in a so-called Euclidean space with one or more dimensions. In this respect, multidimensional scaling appears to be similar to factor analysis. However, instead of factors, there are now dimensions. In multidimensional scaling the aim is to chose the points in the space in such a way that the distance between the points provides a good representation of the similarity or dissimilarity between the variables that correspond with the points. This means that multidimensional scaling can be used on ordinal data.

The aim of multidimensional scaling is the following: if variable X appears to be more similar to variable Y than variable Y is to variable Z (the level of similarity between X and Y is therefore greater than the level of similarity between Y and Z), then the measured distance between the points X and Y in the space must be smaller than the distance between the points Y and Z.

Once again, multidimensional scaling is an interdependence method: no distinction is made between dependent and independent variables. Like factor analysis, the idea is to represent the patterns in the similarity data as much as possible as a function of the smallest number of new dimensions. The difference with factor analysis is that the only demand that is placed on the space is that the sequence of the distances between the points must correspond with the sequence (in terms of similarity) of the variables that correspond with the points.

> For example:
> If coffee and chocolate very often remain after a choice is made from three items, then the points of coffee and chocolate must lie very close to each other on the representation image. The graph can then be interpreted, for example by using other research concerning how consumers perceive products.

There are statistics to determine how well the representation in Euclidean space reflects the original data, i.e. how well the distances in the space are in accordance with the levels of similarity as indicated by the respondents. Depending on the level of this so-called *stress*, the researcher can decide to choose more dimensions (in case the stress level is poor) or fewer (in case the stress level is very low). In general, the following applies: as in factor analysis, the more dimensions or factors allowed, the better the program can find a solution that reflects the correlation or similarity patterns in the data.

8.6.8 Regression analysis

You should use regression analysis, for example, if you want to know if absenteeism is caused by work satisfaction. Regression analysis is a dependence method where, as with correlation analysis, you assume that all variables are measured on a metric scale. This also assumes a linear model, i.e. there are only linear combinations of variables. In contrast to factor analysis, a clear distinction is made within the group of variables between a single dependent variable (defined as the 'criterion') and one or more independent variables (the 'predictors').

> For example:
> If you intend to use regression analysis to explain absenteeism as a result of the sex of a employee, it makes a major difference when the sequence of the variables is reversed in the analysis: absenteeism can of course not explain the sex of an individual.

Although it was recently stated that an interval measurement level for all variables is required for regression analysis, this requirement is dealt with flexibly in practice. One solution is to conduct a separate regression analysis for the various values of a nominal variable.

> For example:
> First conduct a regression analysis concerning absenteeism as an effect with the possible cause being work satisfaction for the group of males, and then conduct a similar regression for females. By comparing the analysis results, you can determine whether the link between absenteeism and work satisfaction for men and women is different. Another example is to determine whether different factors determine absenteeism for different companies.

With simple regression analysis there is a single independent variable ('predictor'). Multiple regression analysis has more than one independent variable. The input for regression analysis is once again a correlation matrix between all independent and dependent variables. The correlations between the independent variables must not be too high due to the danger of *multicollinearity*, which makes it difficult to determine the unique contribution of each independent variable to the dependent variable. This is obvious: if two predictors measure almost the same thing, and therefore have an extremely high correlation, they also make the same contribution to the prediction of the dependent variable. The technique of regression analysis is structured statistically in such a way that when calculating the predictive power of the predictor, it repeatedly corrects for what the other predictors have already contributed. If two predictors have a high correlation, this means that in the regression the predictor with the highest observed correlation with the criterion, acquires a higher weight and the other a lower weight. One predictor outweighs another, as it were. However, these two strongly differing weights provide a distorted picture of the actual contribution of both individual predictors to the prediction of the dependent variable; this contribution is equally high since the predictors are virtually the same. For these reasons it is advisable in regression analysis to use only predictors that have a mutual correlation of less than .50 (for example, two possible causes of absenteeism can be collegiality and stress. A respondent who evaluates collegiality very positively will often have a low score on stress, and the reverse. The cause of this phenomenon is not important at this point. In this case, it is difficult to determine exactly whether a high absenteeism can be attributed to collegiality or to stress.). With respect to multicollinearity, there are a number of possible solutions. The distorting variable can be omitted, or the variables with a high mutual correlation can be combined to make a new variable.

In regression analysis, a regression equation is created. The equation for single regression appears as follows:

$$y = a + bx$$

This means: y (dependent variable) $= a$ (constant, this intercept indicates where the line intercepts the y-axis or the level of the dependent variable when the independent variable is zero) $+ b$ (regression coefficient or partial regression coefficient, regression weight or the slope of the regression line) times x (independent variable). This equation can be stated in words as follows: if the variable x increases by one unit of measurement, then the dependent variable y will increase by b units.

For example:

If the equation $y = 25 - 5x$ is found for the regression of absenteeism (y: number of days absent per year) on work satisfaction (x), this means that absenteeism declines as work satisfaction increases and that absenteeism is equal to 20 days if there is minimal satisfaction (if x is measured on a five-point scale, at minimal satisfaction, $x = 1$). For each point of increase on the scale of work satisfaction, absenteeism decreases by five days. If there is maximal work satisfaction ($x = 5$), absenteeism on an annual basis is 0 days.

By means of regression analysis you can determine to what extent the independent variables (individually and collectively) can explain the variance of the dependent variable, and consequently the total percentage of variance explained by the predictors. In addition, you can determine the degree to which changes in values of the independent variables (x) affect the values of the dependent variable (y). You should interpret the percentage of explained variance as follows: a percentage of 50 per cent, for example, means that for the group of research units as a whole, 50 per cent of the differences between the research units regarding the dependent variable can be explained from differences in the independent variable or variables.

It was previously stated that the link between two numerical variables is expressed in the correlation coefficient: the square of this correlation coefficient times 100 gives the percentage of variance for one variable which is explained by the other variable. In the same way, there is a multiple correlation between the criterion and all predictors in multiple regression. However, the multiple correlation is always larger than zero. Negative multiple correlation does not occur because the computer program simply inverts the regression weight of a predictor (makes it negative) so that the multiple correlation again becomes positive. In this case as well, the square of the multiple correlation gives the total variance in the criterion, which is explained by all predictors. As the explained variance increases in relation to the total variance, the prediction of the score of a research unit on the dependent variable improves if the scores of this unit on the independent variables are known. The unexplained variance of the dependent variable can be caused by chance (measurement errors) or by the lack of relevant variables in the model.

The (adjusted) squared correlation coefficient (R^2) is a measure of the actual fit of the best-fitting straight line. The R^2 falls between 1 (all points are situated on the straight line) and 0. If R^2 is equal to 0, this does not mean that there is no relationship at all; it only means that there is no linear relationship. The slope of the line (b or beta) is not related to R^2: both steep and less steep slopes can have a high R^2. The slope only indicates by how many units the dependent variable y rises with a single unit increase in the independent variable x. This is greatly affected by the scale on which x and y are measured. The slope of the line is therefore partly affected by the measurement unit of the variables. Variables can be measured on differing scales. For example, if a dependent variable is measured on a 10-point scale instead of a five-point one, then the slope of the line would increase, but the value of R^2 would not change. The value of R^2 also does not change if all scores on the variables are replaced by standard scores, but this does affect the slope of the line: the regression coefficient then has the same value as the correlation coefficient if there is a single independent variable. This is also why it is preferable to look at the betas rather than the bs if there is more than one independent variable. This is because the betas are standardized (this means that the mean is 0 and the standard deviation is 1). A standard score (or z score) indicates how many standard deviations a score lies above or below the mean. This standard score is calculated by subtracting the mean from the given score and dividing the result by the standard deviation. Standardization is essential if various measurement scales for the variables are used; otherwise the contributions of the variables are not comparable. Because the variables are assigned to the same measurement unit as part of the standardization process, it is easier to compare them.

If a multiple regression analysis indicates that R^2 is significantly larger than zero, then it is known that two or more than two independent variables together have a significant effect on the dependent variable. But you still do not know which predictors have an effect on the criterion. In order to find this out, the beta coefficients of the independent variable must be tested for significance using a t-test.

The use of regression analysis is based on the following assumptions:

1. The regression line is linear: the average values of the dependent variable for different values of the independent variable are situated on a straight line.
2. The residual scores are normally distributed. The residual score is that part of y that cannot be predicted by x: these are deviations from the regression line. It is assumed that these deviations or errors are the result of chance, i.e. no systematic pattern can be found in the deviations. It is known that random errors are normally distributed (for example, errors in measuring length are characterized by a normal distribution of deviations around the true length). In that

case the probability of an extreme deviation is much smaller than the probability of a small deviation.

3. There is no *heteroscedasticity*: this means that the variance of the residue scores is unrelated to the value of the dependent variable. As stated above, it is assumed that the residue scores are normally distributed around the regression line. Homoscedasticity means that the variance of this normal distribution is the same for every value of the predictor.

> For example:
> The deviation from the regression line is no greater for individuals with a high score on x than for individuals with a low score on x. The predictor x predicts with the same precision the criterion y for all values of x.

4. No auto-correlation (self-correlation) is present. This means that sequential measurements do not have any mutual relationship. Such a relationship is especially present in a time series where the same respondents are asked the same question at different times.

> For example:
> During a study about the progression of work satisfaction in time, it is entirely possible that the sequential measurements could affect each other, for example, because the respondent still remembers his/her previous score. In this case, there is an unintended artificial correlation in the data.

These conditions all concern testing the regression coefficient for significance. It is advisable to first make a plot to determine whether it is possible to draw a straight line. You can also analyse the residue scores and the assumptions of normality and heteroscedasticity. Although these assumptions are dealt with flexibly in practice, it is advisable to inspect the data and take the following actions if necessary:

1. Transformation of variables: an initially non-linear line is made to be linear.
2. Selection of research units: by finding outliers (individual observations that deviate strongly from the other observations, see Figure 8.3) and removing them only if they are uninteresting coding or input errors. You must be cautious about removal, since outliers could also be valid observations.

There are various methods for selecting independent variables for regression analysis. The most important basis for selection is formed by your own theoretical considerations. You should consider this aspect during data collection since it is impossible to include a variable in the regression analysis afterwards if there is no data for this variable. There are three statistical methods for selecting independent variables:

1. In the direct, *simple* method, all predictors are included directly in the equation. The program itself then calculates which predictors make the largest contribution. The disadvantage of this method is that there is a serious danger of multicollinearity. Differences in correlation between the predictor and the criterion and between the predictors themselves that are due to chance can have a major effect on the results of the analysis. In addition, you must not include too many variables since R^2 generally increases when a new variable is included. However, this does not make the prediction any better. In addition, the result is difficult to interpret.
2. Besides looking at variables, you can also apply the *hierarchical* method. This is where the independent variables are entered in a sequence that you determine yourself and/or which is determined by a theory. This is implemented by repeating the enter command in SPSS. During this process, the researcher determines which predictors are included first in the regression equation to predict the criterion and which predictors are then included as the second and third predictors.
3. *Selective analysis* has three variants: *forward inclusion, backward elimination* and *stepwise solution*. The program again determines the sequence. In forward inclusion, the first predictor that is selected is the one that produces the highest R^2 with the dependent variable. This is followed by the predictor that provides the highest significant increase (partial correlation) while taking account of the variable that is already included. In backward elimination, this process is reversed, while the stepwise variant is a combination of forward inclusion and backward elimination.

If you have a clear theory about which independent variables predict the criterion variables at which points in time, it is advisable to choose the second method. Then test your theory. If you do not have any idea and primarily want to know how much variance can be predicted by all the predictors together and which predictor provides the best relative prediction, use the first, more explorative method. The third method is an intermediate variant; it is less explorative than the first, but still more open and explorative than the second. For example, you may decide not to try all the independent variables using the second method, but only those which contribute to the prediction according to your theory. With the third method, repeat the process until the statistics indicate that nothing more can be predicted.

Finally, an important variant of regression analysis must be mentioned here: logistic regression. This analysis technique is used to study the correlation between nominal or ordinal variables. For example, you can use logistic regression to determine the relationship between sex, company size (coded as small, mid-sized and large), and absenteeism (coded as below average, average and above average). The basis for the analysis is the contingency table between all variables. In this table the cells contain the number of research units with the given scores on the variables (for example, the number of female individuals from a mid-sized company with above average absenteeism). The analysis uses the frequencies of the variables. For this purpose you can use association statistics such as Cramer's V, the contingency coefficient lambda, and the tau of Goodman and Kruskal. If the variables have been measured in a sample that was drawn randomly from the population, these statistics can be tested for significance (see Section 8.7).

8.6.9 Canonical analysis

Regression analysis calculates the correlation between a single dependent and multiple independent metric variables. There are two groups of variables, where one group comprises a single, dependent variable. If there are two groups of variables with more than one variable in each group, and it is unclear which variables are dependent and which are independent, canonical correlation analysis can be applied. Use canonical correlation analysis if you want to determine the relations between two groups of variables in one analysis.

> For example:
> You have measured variables that refer to work performance such as productivity, labour performance, output and sales, and variables that refer to work experience such as tendency to call in sick, involvement, satisfaction and stress. It is unclear which group of variables is the cause and which is the result. In this case, you can use canonical correlation analysis to determine if there is a strong correlation between both groups of variables and which underlying factor or factors in the groups of variables determine this correlation.

These factors are defined as canonical variates.

Canonical analysis is a multivariate technique with numerical variables. As stated above, it concerns the correlation of a group of variables with another group of variables. The question is: how and to what extent are the scores for one group of variables related to the scores for another group of variables? It is a sort of double principle component analysis: the canonical variates are comparable to principle components. The variables within every group are combined to form a new variable (canonical variate), which is a linear combination of the original variables. The canonical coefficients are comparable with factor loadings. It is impossible to directly determine how much every variable contributes individually. It is therefore advisable to look at the correlations of the canonical variates with the original variables. The disadvantage of this type of analysis is therefore that the results cannot always be clearly interpreted.

8.6.10   Path analysis

If there is a complex theoretical network of possible correlations between many variables, you can conduct a large number of individual regression analyses. However, it is better to combine these analyses in order to determine in a single operation whether your theoretical network is in accordance with the collected data.

Path analysis is made up of a large series of regression equations. A precondition for path analysis is *non-recursivity* (does not recur). A non-recursive path model means that the causal paths never return to a variable which previously occurred in the causal chain, not even through feedback via a third variable: only one-sided causal relationships occur. The reason for this non-recursivity requirement is that you do not want to have to explain a dependent variable from a complex network of other variables in which the variable you are trying to explain also appears at some point! This is course leads to a perfect, but meaningless, prediction. It is especially important to check for non-recursivity with complex network models between variables where there are many paths; but this is not a simple task.

With such network analysis, a distinction is made between *exogenous* (purely independent) and *endogenous* variables (which are always affected by other variables, they are therefore always dependent, but sometimes also function as the cause for other variables and are therefore sometimes partially independent as well).

For example, in the path:

$$X \rightarrow Y \rightarrow Z$$

X is exogenous and Y and Z are endogenous. An example of this path model is that a poor evaluation (X) leads to dissatisfaction (Y), which in turn leads to absenteeism (Z).

In normal regression analysis, there is only a single endogenous variable (the dependent variable). Every endogenous variable is not only determined by at least one other endogenous or exogenous variable, but also by otherwise unexplainable measurement errors. The assumption is that the latter terms do not correlate with each other or with other variables in the model. Otherwise they would be systematic sources of correlation, and that would distort the view of the actual theoretical relations in the network.

One way to assess such a network in a single analysis, where you try to separate the effects of measurement errors from the actual theoretical model, is by using *LISREL*. The 'LInear Structural RELations' program of Jöreskog and Sörbom was previously available only as a separate computer program, but it has been included in SPSS beginning with Version 6. LISREL is actually a combination of the characteristics of factor analysis and path analysis. There are two models: a measurement model and a structure model. In the measurement model you attempt to determine the magnitude of the measurement errors in the data (factor analysis). In the structure model, you then determine how these *latent variables* actually correlate after the measurement errors are removed. In the structure model, a path or regression analysis is conducted on the latent variables. The model then is used to generate the correlations between measured variables; these are compared with the actual correlations in the observed data. The discrepancy between them is expressed as a chi-square value. In addition, the *goodness of fit indices* indicate how well the structure model fits with the research data.

8.6.11 t-test

If you are interested in differences between two nominal groups on a dependent variable, use a t-test (for example, you want to know whether women call in sick less frequently on average than men).

A t-test is a test procedure for making statements about means of populations or statements about differences in means between two groups. There are three types of t-test:

1. A t-test for the mean of a single sample where the question is whether this originates from a population with a specific mean.

2. A t-test for the difference between two means from independent samples.
3. A t-test for the difference between two means for paired observations from the same samples.

A precondition for performing a t-test is that the variances in both groups are approximately equal. You can determine that by conducting *Levine's test*. SPSS often conducts this test automatically; the program then warns you if this precondition is not satisfied.

After this, a so-called *t-value* is calculated. This generally means that you divide the observed mean by the standard deviation of the scores. However, the exact calculation of the t-value depends on which of the three types of t-test has been performed. There is a theoretical distribution of probability for the t-value. By comparing the t-value from your own research with this theoretical t-distribution, you can evaluate the probability that the calculated t-value was obtained by chance.

Note that a t-test is actually a type of regression analysis. In this case, however, the independent variable is nominal (the classification into two groups). You investigate the effect of the group classification on a metric dependent variable. This also applies to the following method.

8.6.12 Analysis of variance

Analysis of variance is an expansion of the t-test to more than two groups.

> For example:
> You want to know if there is a difference in mean absenteeism between young men, middle-aged men and older men. You must then compare three means with each other. Instead of conducting a t-test three times, i.e.
>
> 1   comparing young men with middle-aged men
> 2   comparing young men with older men and
> 3   comparing middle-aged men with older men
>
> it is better to test the three means against each other in a single operation. Use variance analysis for this purpose.

Again, variance analysis has a lot in common with regression analysis. In both analysis techniques there are one or more independent variables of which the effect on the dependent variable is determined by ascertaining which part of the variance can be explained by the independent variable(s). The method of variance analysis comes from laboratory experimental research, where the research units are placed into various groups or 'conditions' (for example, styles of leadership), and then the effects of group membership on a number of dependent variables are studied (for example, performance and involvement). Regression analysis is used primarily with survey-based research.

In variance analysis, there is one metric dependent variable with multiple nominal independent variables; in regression analysis, the independent variables are metric. Although the name *variance analysis* may lead you to believe otherwise, it is actually a technique to simultaneously compare a number of group *means* with each other. You might think that variance analysis is unnecessary because all groups can be compared two-by-two using t-tests. However, due to the large number of individual tests that result, the unreliability of all tests together increases. In variance analysis, all means of all groups are tested in a single operation, so that the reliability can be ascertained.

Variance analysis is concerned not only with the difference between the means of the groups (which can be far apart), but also about whether the variances of the data from the groups overlap. For example, the means may differ a great deal, but the variance around the means (the *within-group variance*) may be very large, so that the groups overlap a great deal (Figure 8.9).

In that case, there are fewer reasons to assume that the groups differ in their scores on the dependent variable than when the variance of the means is small and the groups hardly overlap regarding their scores. In variance analysis, you must therefore take into account the relationship between the variance within the groups and the variance between the groups. If the variance is small, then the scores are situated close to the mean. There is a difference between the *between-groups* variance (this is in fact the difference in means) and the *within-groups* variance. In variance analysis, you evaluate the relationship between these two

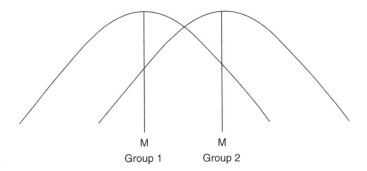

M   M
Group 1   Group 2

Figure 8.9 Example of two groups that strongly overlap

types of variance. The question is whether the variance between the groups is large enough with respect to the variance within the groups. The test takes place using an *F*-test (*Fisher test*). The F-test determines whether the means of the various groups are approximately equal. If *F* is larger than 1, this is an indication that the population means differ from each other. Like the t-distribution, it is a theoretical distribution of probability that is shown in tables in most statistics books.

A significant result in variance analysis indicates only that there are differences in group means, but does not indicate which differences are significant. You must determine the latter afterwards. The most commonly used method is to compare all means two-by-two, for example with the *Honestly Significant Difference (HSD) test of Tukey*.

Besides *main effects* (the influence or effect of every independent variable on the individual dependent variables), there are *interaction effects*. These are the effects of combinations of independent variables. This means that a combination of two variables (even if they have no mutual correlation!) can have an effect on the dependent variable. In other words, a relationship between two variables is not the same for all research units (or characteristics thereof). When no main effects occur in variance analysis, there may still be interaction effects. When there are main effects, an interaction effect can be seen as an exception to the rule of the main effect.

For example:
You are studying the effect of work satisfaction (three groups: satisfied, neutral, dissatisfied) and age (three groups: young, middle-aged, older) on absenteeism. Both independent variables have a significant effect on absenteeism. It turns out that absenteeism increases both with increasing dissatisfaction and increasing age.
(Please note that the latter is actually not the case!)

It is then interesting to determine whether both independent variables amplify each other. Assume the following:

—An individual who is satisfied is absent five days per year on average, an individual who is neutral is absent for 10 days, and an individual who is dissatisfied is absent for 15 days.
—A younger individual is absent three days per year on average, a middle-aged individual is absent for six days and an older individual for nine days.

If there is no interaction effect between work satisfaction and age, these independent variables simply add up. For example, if you want to know the average absenteeism of someone who is satisfied and is older, then the total absence is: 5 days (satisfied) + 9 days (older) = 14 days. The variables do not affect each other. However, there is an interaction effect if you discover that someone who is dissatisfied and is also older is not absent for 24 days (15 + 9) on average, but for 30 days, while someone who is satisfied and is also young is not absent for 8 days (5 + 3), but for only 4 days. The combination of 'dissatisfaction' with 'older' or 'satisfaction' with 'young' then has an extra effect on the independent variable.

The preconditions for variance analysis are the following. First, the research units in the various categories of the independent variable can be considered as samples that are independent from each other. Secondly, the samples are randomly assigned to various interventions or conditions. Thirdly, the dependent variable is normally distributed. Fourthly, the variance of the dependent variable is the same in every subpopulation (this can be determined by applying the Cochran test). The first two of these requirements can be controlled, the other two cannot be controlled. As explained in Section 5.3.3, it is customary in an experiment to establish the groups to be compared on a random basis: the research units are randomly assigned to the various experimental conditions. With randomized groups, possible differences before the experimental manipulation are the result of chance. However, it was also stated that in practice researchers often work with existing groups. With such existing groups, systematic differences before the treatment can occur. These distorting variables can be included afterwards in a *covariance analysis* (see Statistical Control, Chapter 4).

You can also use variance analysis if the independent variables are correlated and/or when the independent variables have not been measured at the nominal level. In these cases you can use covariance analysis. In this situation, the independent variables do not all have the same measurement level. There are one or more variables that have been measured at the nominal level (this is called the factor) and one or more at the interval level (this is called the covariate). The factors are in fact the independent variables: the covariate is the distorting variable. The effect of the factors on the dependent variable is corrected for the effect of the covariates. By using various options in the program, you can stipulate the sequence of how the variables are included in the analysis. The default situation is where first the covariate is included and then the factor. This is *statistical control* afterwards. A relationship between two variables is corrected for the effect of one or more distorting variables. For example, you can include the score on a pre-test as a covariate to study the effect of a specific intervention with the aim of eliminating initial differences between the groups.

8.6.13   *Discriminant analysis*

Discriminant analysis works in the opposite fashion to variance analysis; based on a number of numerical variables, it is predicted and consequently explained to which existing group a research unit belongs. In discriminant analysis, you want to predict which research units belong to a limited number of groups (for example, low absenteeism, average absenteeism, high absenteeism) based on scores on one or more metric independent variables (such as satisfaction and absenteeism tendency). In this way it is possible to make a maximum distinction (discrimination) between the groups (low, average and high absenteeism) on one or more independent metric variables (satisfaction and absenteeism tendency). There is a nominal dichotomous (for example, male/female) or polychotomous (such as high, middle, low) dependent variable. For example, a bank wants to evaluate companies in terms of their creditworthiness (creditworthy, possibly creditworthy, not creditworthy). The profit/equity capital ratio is calculated for the companies. On the basis of this ratio you want to predict whether the company will pay back the loan in the future.

▌ 8.7   STATISTICAL SIGNIFICANCE OF THE RESULTS

The computer then provides the results of the analysis techniques as *output*. It requires practise to read this output. Not everything is equally important and not everything must be reported. You can also indicate to the program beforehand, which output you want to have printed.

An important question is whether the results in the output actually show that there is really an effect or that the results are due to *chance*. You can determine this by using the *significance level* of a statistical test. If a specific result is statistically significant, this does not mean that the result is also of *practical* importance: statistical significance must therefore not be confused with importance or relevance. Statistical significance only indicates that the results are not due to chance.

The concept of 'significance' arises from the fact that during analysis one must take account of the fact that a random sample was drawn from a population. Consequently, the results are partially dependent on chance. If the entire population is studied, there is no reason to test for significance. Moreover, it is generally the case that the smaller a sample is in absolute terms, the less it can provide a good reflection of the population. With small samples, the role of all kinds of chance effects is therefore larger. If the sample is sufficiently large, all kinds of distorting chance effects generally add up to about zero – they virtually cancel each other out.

To further clarify the concept of significance, it is important to understand the distinction between the so-called alternative and null hypotheses. The *alternative hypothesis* is what you expect as a researcher. However, when testing hypotheses during data analysis, you use the *null hypothesis*. Usually this null hypothesis states that there is no difference between groups or that there is no correlation between variables. The null hypothesis states that there are no real effects. In the report, it is sufficient to discuss the alternative hypothesis, which is simply called 'the hypothesis'. The null hypothesis is tested during data analysis because it is infeasible to prove that a hypothesis or a theory is true (for example, all crows are black). It is much easier to show that something is not true with a specific degree of probability (for example, until now, a non-black crow has never been observed). In other words, it is better to try to reject the null hypothesis than to try to prove the alternative hypothesis (your own hypothesis) based on your theory. In the analysis it is determined whether the result deviates significantly from the value or values given in the null hypothesis.

> For example:
> If you expect that the absenteeism of sales staff differs from that of personnel advisors, test the null hypothesis that the absenteeism of sales staff does not differ from that of personnel advisors. By rejecting the null hypothesis, you may assume – although strictly speaking you have not proven – that personnel advisors differ in terms of absenteeism from sales staff.

The region of results that leads to the rejection of the null hypothesis is called the *rejection* area. The size of this region is the *significance level:* the total chance that observations fall in this area given the null hypothesis. If you find a result in the rejection region, then this is called a significant result.

Figure 8.10 shows an example of two groups that differ from each other.

You must define this region beforehand. It can never be changed afterwards (after the results have been obtained). The statistical significance is expressed by computer programs as a *p*-value (probability value). Every statistical test provides a *p*-value. In organizational research, it is customary to say the effect is significant if the *p*-value is less

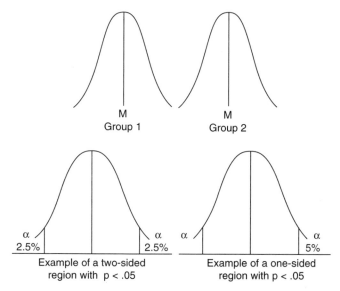

M
Group 1

M
Group 2

α
2.5%

α
2.5%

α

α
5%

Example of a two-sided
region with p < .05

Example of a one-sided
region with p < .05

Figure 8.10 Example of two groups that differ from each other

than .05. This means that the probability that the effect is the result of chance is less than 5 per cent. The reasoning is as follows. If the probability of a result under the null hypothesis is small (less than .05) and the result is still found, then the null hypotheses itself must be untenable so that we can reject it (for example, the probability that three-quarters of the students will get a perfect score if they take a well-constructed examination without cheating is very small. If this still happens, there is reason to doubt the construction of the examination or the course of affairs during the examination). When conducting tests in data analysis, two types of errors can be made:

1. Type I error is where the null hypothesis is incorrectly rejected. The probability of a type I error is known as alpha (α). This probability is known because you choose it yourself (for example, .05).
2. Type II error is where the null hypothesis is not rejected when it should be. The probability of a type II error is known as beta (β). This probability is not known, but can be estimated. Calculation procedures and tables are available for this purpose.

These two types of errors are related: if you decrease the risk of making one type of error, then you increase the risk of making the other. With an α of .05, the null hypothesis is only rejected if there are very strong indications for this in the data; you are then virtually certain that the alternative hypothesis is tenable. In any case, you can keep the probability of a type I error as low as possible.

The probability that an untenable null hypothesis is indeed rejected $(1-\beta)$ is called the *power* (discriminative capacity) of a statistical test. The power must of course be as high as possible; it is determined, among other things, by the sample size. A sample that is too small often leads to a low power. As previously stated, deviations that are due to chance have a larger effect on the result with a small sample than with a large sample.

> For example:
> If you want to be certain that a dice has not been tampered with (by for example, putting extra weight on the side opposite the six so that the six is thrown more frequently), then you must throw the dice often.
>
> If you throw twice and get a six both times, that is still acceptable, but if you throw 100 times and get a six 85 times, then there is reason to doubt the reliability of the dice.

With a small sample, chance can have a larger effect in all kinds of ways. With a sufficiently large sample, the distorting effects that are due to chance usually add up to approximately zero (they virtually cancel each other out). This is because you can assume that such errors are random: one measurement may be too high, the next measurement may be too low, but there is no systematic preference for excessively high or low values.

The concept of one-sided and two-sided hypotheses was discussed previously. *Two-sided* means that you do not have a clear idea about the direction of the possible relationship or difference. The relationship can be negative or positive, or one group may score higher or lower than the other group (for example, men and women score differently). The rejection region is therefore located on both sides of the mean (see Figure 8.10). The region can also be *one-sided*. This is determined by the alternative hypothesis. If this hypothesis clearly specifies a specific direction (for example, men score higher than women), then one-sided tests can be used. The rejection region then lies only on one side, either the right or the left side. Generally speaking, the more conservative or strict method of two-sided testing is recommended. Conservative means that the test is slower to produce a significant result. The default setting for most statistical analysis programs is also two-sided testing. If you prefer to use one-sided testing, you can sometimes instruct the program to do this. To manually convert from two-sided to one-sided testing, the *p*-value must be multiplied by two.

To go from one-sided to two-sided testing, the p-value must be divided by two.

The notation of the results of analysis techniques in the research report is as follows: name of the test (number of degrees of freedom) = value, significance level (for example, $F(3, 34) = 1.96$, $p < .05$, which means 'this F-test, under 3 and 34 degrees of freedom, provides the value of 1.96, and the probability for obtaining this value under the null hypothesis is less than 5 per cent'). Sometimes the exact p-value is recorded. The scientific notation is then $F(3, 34) = 1.96$, $p = .034$ (the probability of obtaining an F-value of 1.96 if the null hypothesis is tenable is 3.4 per cent). If no significant differences are ascertained, this is generally indicated by using the abbreviation 'n.s.' (not significant).

With a number of tests, such as the F-test, the concept of degrees of freedom is important. This is indicated with the Greek letter ν (pronounced 'nu'). The number of degrees of freedom indicates how much freedom the observations have for deviating from the model. This can be explained as followed.

For example:
You expect that the variables x (for example, dissatisfaction), and y (for example, absenteeism tendency) correlate with each other according to the model of a straight line. They therefore have a linear correlation:

$y = ax + b$

This formula comprises two unknowns: the slope a and the intercept b. These must be estimated from the data. If the two unknowns (parameters) a and b are estimated from the data, this means in turn that the data have somewhat less freedom to deviate from the model. Because two parameters are being estimated, you would therefore say that there is a loss of two degrees of freedom. If you have chosen a quadratic model:

$y = ax^2 + bx + c$

then three unknowns (a, b and c) must be estimated, and three degrees of freedom are lost. The quadratic model results in the loss of more degrees of freedom.

The number of degrees of freedom is equal to the number of independent observations minus the number of parameters that are estimated from these observations. The number of degrees of freedom indicates not only the freedom with which the data can deviate from the theory, but also the degree with which the theory limits the data. It is important to know that more degrees of freedom are better: if the model contains fewer parameters, then it is less complex and is therefore a better model. This is an expression of the scientific demands of simplicity and elegance (see Chapter 1). You encounter the concept of degrees of freedom when applying statistical tests such as the chi-squared and the F-test and when using the LISREL program.

Part III

REPORTING THE RESEARCH PROJECT

Chapter 9

THE RESEARCH REPORT

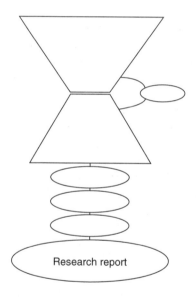

▌ 9.1 INTRODUCTION

The previous chapter focused on the analysis of the data that emerged from the empirical research. After completing the data analysis, you must combine these results with all the previous parts, such as the initial research question and the hypotheses that were formulated from the literature, into a coherent whole. This is done by writing a research report. You must describe all the phases of the research and the choices made during this process in a way that is understandable to the reader. In addition, you must draw conclusions correctly from your research.

Writing a research paper has the primary aim of informing others about the results and conclusions from the literature and the empirical study. In addition, a well-organized and clearly written report makes it possible for others to critically evaluate the research. As previously stated, other researchers must be able to monitor all steps in your research and replicate your study on this basis. Moreover, you must clearly describe and justify all the choices made before and during the research.

▌ 9.2 PLANNING

It requires a great deal of time to write a research report. Explaining all the choices that you have made during the research is especially time consuming. You must also take account of the time that your supervisor will require to evaluate the research design before you begin your empirical research and to check the draft and final versions of the report after your research is completed. You must take the initiative to make sure this process stays on schedule. You are responsible for planning and conducting your research and for writing the research report. While doing so, you must take account of the absence of supervisors due to holiday periods and attendance at conferences. Moreover, it is advisable to occasionally distance yourself from the written material – this enables you to see possible shortcomings. The best way to do this is to write a research proposal and a draft chapter that you temporarily set aside and/or allow another individual to read. After this, you can complete the definitive version of the chapter.

Although everyone has his or her own strategies or methods for writing, a number of general suggestions are included here. It is a good idea to first make a tentative table of contents with the titles of chapters and sections and then draw up a schedule. The best way to do this is to work backwards in time: what is the deadline, when must the final report be submitted? Then you can estimate how much time is required for each section. Make sure you also reserve extra time to put all the sections together to make a consistent and smooth line of reasoning. In a well-structured report, the reader does not become puzzled about why a specific passage has been included. In every paragraph, the reader must have a clear idea about where he or she is located in the line of reasoning, what the connection is with the preceding section and what will follow in general terms. Based on the tentative table of contents, the report can gradually be filled in to the required level of detail. This method ensures a properly structured text with a clear line of reasoning. It also gives you a plan of action. If you discover new literature or acquire new results, you can then place this information in the chapter or section where it belongs.

When writing the report, you do not always have to start with the introduction and end with the conclusion and discussion. The preface, the introduction and the abstract are often written at the end. For example, you can begin with the parts that are relatively easy to write, such as the methods chapter, in which you describe in detail which steps were taken in the empirical research and why. It is also a good idea to write a first draft of your theory chapter (or chapters) at an early stage. The process of writing the report therefore does not always follow the actual research process exactly. In the report, it appears as if you began with establishing the aim and the research question, then you collected the literature, formulated a research model with hypotheses, made a research design, drew a sample from a population, and collected, analysed and interpreted the data. In reality, however, these phases partially overlapped each other.

▌ 9.3 TARGET GROUP

While writing the report, you must keep the target group in mind: this is the group who will ultimately read your report. If it is written for a broad group of people from various levels of society, avoid using jargon as much as possible; generally speaking, you would also provide more information when writing for a broad target group. One option is to include the jargon in a separate terminology list; this allows you to write in a compact fashion for professional colleagues and others in your field while those outside the field can use the list to understand the report.

Sometimes it may be necessary to write multiple reports, for example, one report for the client, a different report for the respondents and yet another for the supervisor. The content of the report should have a different emphasis for each of these target groups. For example, for a target group of the client and the respondents, it is especially the main themes, the results and the recommendations for practice that are important. For scientific colleagues with whom you communicate via articles in (inter)national journals, it is not only the results that are important, but also the theoretical framework and the explanation of the data collection method. Before you begin writing the report, check any agreements you have made with other individuals, such as the respondents or the client. Have any agreements been made about the level of anonymity or about using the research data for other purposes (not only a company report, but also a scientific article)? Sometimes the viewpoints concerning these agreements have altered during the course of the research. This can be caused by changes in management at the client company or if the client does not like the results.

It is essential that you invest a great deal of time and energy in writing the report: after all, you are 'selling' your message. Sometimes it may even be advisable to approach a public relations advisor or scientific journalist. To publicize your research, you may want to consider publishing a press release, holding a press conference, writing a summary for the staff newsletter, or organizing a workshop. Before you begin writing the report, make agreements with a publisher, for example about how the report will be duplicated. With an eye towards distributing the report after it is duplicated, make sure you have a suitable address list and the correct envelopes and postage.

▌ 9.4 STRUCTURE OF THE RESEARCH REPORT

Although the detailed structure of the report depends on the topic, the type of research (literature research and/or empirical research) and the target group, the general structure of a scientific report is discussed below. There is one exception to this general structure, however. If you are writing a company report, do not begin with a theoretical chapter on the basis of which you attempt to answer the research question using a literature study. Instead, begin with a description of the organization. In a scientific research report, this description usually does not appear until the chapter about the research method.

9.4.1 The cover

The cover is the showpiece of the report. You should therefore give plenty of attention to its appearance. The following information must be included on the cover:

- the title of the report;
- the name(s) the author(s);
- the date;

- the framework in which the report has been written (as a thesis, report for a client etc.);
- the names of the client and/or supervisor.

The title must be brief and should precisely summarize the research question and the answer provided by the research in no more than 10 words. Make sure that the title attracts attention and covers the actual content of the report. If necessary, you can add a subtitle for explanatory purposes. This has the benefit of ensuring that the terms used in the subtitle are also included as keywords in library information systems.

For example:
The Effect of Personal Characteristics on Absenteeism. A Study among Nurses.

If there is more than one author, then the last names of the authors must be listed either in alphabetical order or the order of the significance of their contribution. In the latter case, the first author listed is often the main author, and the co-authors are listed in declining order of their contribution to the report.

9.4.2 Preface

The preface is not a mandatory part of a report. It usually includes a personal note from the author such as his or her personal involvement with the topic, how the research came about and in what framework the research has been conducted. People who have helped with the report can also be acknowledged. The preface should contain nothing about the actual content of the research. This information should be part of the introduction. This is because the introduction is part of the report itself, while the preface is not.

9.4.3 Contents

Give every paragraph and every section and subsection a distinct number and a title that adequately reflects the content. Avoid using more than three figures for numbering the sections or subsections (for example, do not use a number such as 9.4.3.1). The summary, introduction, reference list and appendices are not assigned chapter numbers, but they are given page numbers. Moreover, you should not give these parts of the report any title besides 'Introduction' or

'Abstract'. Theoretical chapters, however, are given a specific title (for example, 2.1 The social comparison theory).

Present these numbers and titles, with the relevant page numbers, in a detailed and logically constructed table of contents. This can be done automatically. The essential theme of the report can then quickly be seen in the table of contents. This thematic organization is also benefited by a logical layout, for example, by using different indents for sections and subsections.

9.4.4 Abstract

In English publications, two terms are used for this part of the report: 'Summary' and 'Abstract'. A *summary* is part of the report itself; as a result, it is assigned its own chapter or section number. An *abstract* is not part of the report itself, but can be read separately from it. The latter is generally characterized by a different font than the report, no section or chapter number, and it is usually placed before the introduction. In the present book, we will refer primarily to the abstract. In terms of content, the summary and the abstract are virtually identical. Both contain a concise presentation of the main issues, lines of argument and results in the report.

The aim of the abstract is to enable the reader to quickly acquire insight into the topic of the research and the content of the report; in this way the reader can decide if it is interesting to read the report itself. When you look for literature yourself, you realize the importance of a good abstract. Therefore invest sufficient time in writing an abstract of your report.

The abstract can be placed at the very beginning (or at the very end) of the report: it is not part of the report itself. The reader must be able to read the abstract as a separate document; it must be clearly written and must not present any new information besides that contained in the report. The abstract usually follows the same sequence as the report. The basic elements of an abstract are short answers (only a few sentences) to the following questions:

1. What is the research topic and research question, and why did you make this choice?
2. How did you conduct the research? Describe the type of respondents, the number of respondents, the research design, the measurement instruments and the analysis techniques.
3. What are the results and conclusions and why are they important?

The difference between the abstract and the introduction is that the introduction acts as a guide to the text and does not refer to the conclusions, while the conclusions are part of the abstract. The abstract must not contain any arguments in favour of the research question, background information, details of the method or the statistical processing or description of practical problems that were encountered. The length of the abstract must be in proportion to the length of the entire report – the most common length is 100 to 175 words.

Frequently, an executive summary or *Management Summary* is included in an organizational report. This is often printed on coloured paper. This summary contains little or no information about the methodology of the research and does not discuss any qualifications concerning the results. It briefly reports the concrete result of the research and the recommendations for practice that emerged from the research. It is in fact a 'short summary', which can be used immediately in practice by the management.

9.4.5 Introduction

The actual report begins with an introduction. The introduction is usually not assigned a chapter number and may not even be titled as the 'Introduction'. The central aim of an introduction is twofold: to motivate the reader to continue reading the report and to describe how the report is structured. The introduction is intended to inform the reader about the framework of the research, its background and what led to the research. Provide a brief description of the research topic and a brief summary of the previous studies that are relevant to the current research. Do not extensively discuss the research, or provide a summary of the conclusions of the report.

The introduction proceeds in a logical fashion to the research question. The research question therefore does not suddenly appear; it is presented in the context of previous studies from the literature. The introduction proceeds from general information to specific information and can therefore be compared to a funnel; beginning with a broadly structured, but briefly summarized, discussion of the relevant literature, it should end with a specific research aim, research question and sub-questions (see Chapter 2). After this there is a brief description of how the problem will be delineated (which aspects will actually be studied in which population), and which theory or theories will be used for answering the research question.

For example:
'The research was concerned only with short-term absenteeism, especially the difference in absenteeism between the sales and purchasing departments'. Or, 'This paper will use the social comparison theory (...)'. Or, 'Only companies with their headquarters in the UK will be studied'. Or, 'The research is limited to the behaviour of managers at the highest level'.

The most important concepts can also be defined in the introduction.

For example:
'In this report, absenteeism will be defined as (...)'.

The introduction ends with a summary of the content and structure of the report. The structure usually follows the sequence of the subquestions that are derived from the main research question.

For example:
'The first two chapters of the report will address the four most important theories concerning absenteeism. The third chapter will discuss the empirical research method. After this, the respondents and the measurement instrument will be discussed. Then the results of the research will be presented in Chapter 4. Finally, the conclusions will be presented and discussed in Chapter 5'.

9.4.6 Theory

In contrast to the introduction, the theory section of the report contains an extensive discussion of the relevant literature on the topic and the groups to be studied in the research. This chapter can also address the results from previous empirical research on the topic. Sometimes this part of the report comprises multiple chapters, each of which treats a different aspect of the problem or addresses different theories.

In the theory portion of the report, you answer the following questions:

- What is the current state of knowledge about the topic?
- On which points do authors agree and disagree?
- What are the possible causes of these agreements or disagreements?
- What is still unknown or unclear?
- How does this report contribute to the body of existing knowledge?

Although it depends on the type of research question and the phase of the research, this part of the report should preferably end with a discussion of the results that are expected from the empirical research. These hypotheses must be stated explicitly since they must be confirmed or rejected by the empirical research. Make sure that the hypotheses are well supported by relevant theory (see Chapter 4).

> For example:
> 'In accordance with the social comparison theory, the hypothesis/expectation is that purchasing staff call in sick more frequently than sales staff at the same company. After all, because sales staff ... they will ...'.

9.4.7 Method

The method section provides a detailed description of how the research was conducted so that the reader is theoretically capable of repeating the research. In this way you satisfy the requirement of replicability of scientific research (see Chapter 1). In addition, the reader can critically evaluate the correctness of the method and therewith the reliability of the results (How have the results been attained? Are the results possibly due to the specific method that has been used?). Therefore discuss the research design and implementation in detail. Do not write in a defensive manner: use a factual style instead. It is only later on, in the discussion part of the report, that you can address less fortunate circumstances or choices in the research and describe the effects these could have had on the results attained (or the failure to acquire results). This part of the report is usually divided into the following subsections: 'Organization and Respondents', 'Measurement Instruments' and 'Procedures'.

ORGANIZATION AND RESPONDENTS

Properly define the research population and explain the size and choice of the sample (if any) from this population (for example, how did you draw your sample and which criteria did you use for drawing the sample?). Describe several characteristics of the company, the departments, the jobs of employees and the employers that you investigated. For example, list the number of participants in the research, the average age and the percentages of males and females. However, it is important that the participants in the research remain anonymous. Only report names if you have explicit permission to do so from the company and the respondents.

For example:
'Sixty department heads of a medium-sized clothing company, 80 per cent male with a mean age of 42'.

Also describe how the company/respondents were approached, for example, with a letter or by telephone. If specific respondents refused to participate in any of the research (general non-response) or only participated in part of the research (partial non-response), then you must report this. You must also include the possible reasons for this non-response and the consequences it has on the interpretation of the research results.

For example:
'As part of a study of absenteeism, if the individuals responding to the request for research participation are only those who are virtually never sick or those who are frequently sick, you obtain a positively or negatively distorted picture'.

MEASUREMENT INSTRUMENTS

The measurement instruments (these are questions in an interview or questionnaire or tools that are used in an experiment, for example) must be described in detail. Explain how the various concepts have been measured, which scales have been used and how many items and which items have been used in the scales. Make sure you correctly acknowledge any literature sources. Include a few questions taken directly from the instruments as examples.

For example:
'Voluntary absenteeism is measured with the question "How often are you absent from your work without a good reason?" where the respondent answers on a five-point scale ranging from "1 = never" to "5 = very often".'

An appendix to the report should include the complete questionnaire and/or the codebook with all questions, all answer possibilities (in numbers and words), the way in which these were coded (if applicable) and how the total scores of the various items for the scales were calculated. Also provide information concerning the validity and the reliability of the measurement instruments (see Chapters 4 and 8).

PROCEDURE

On a step-by-step basis, describe which data was collected, and how, where and during which periods it was collected.

For example:
'In 2003, 12 trained interviewers in Amsterdam conducted interviews
with the entire sample of 100 department heads using the questionnaire.
The interviews lasted one hour on average'.

Describe which statistical analysis procedures were used and why they
were chosen. Clearly explain how the data satisfied the preconditions
for using these techniques. State how the hypotheses were tested and
which criteria were used for this testing.

For example:
'The question of whether the mean score on the item differed significantly between purchasing and sales groups was analysed using a t-test
for two independent samples where $p < .05$ was used as a significance
criterion'.

9.4.8 Results

This chapter begins with an objective discussion of the research results.
These results will not be interpreted until the following chapter (Conclusions and Discussion).

Briefly describe how you tested the hypotheses and state whether the
hypotheses were rejected. Do this in the same sequence as the sequence
in which the hypotheses were established. List the statistical tests that
were used, the test statistic (such as a t-value or F-value) and state
whether the results were significant or not (using a probability level or
p-value). It is customary to also report the number of degrees of freedom
(see Chapter 8) – DF is an abbreviation for *degrees of freedom*. You cannot
attribute any importance to results for which the p-value is above the
previously chosen significance value, even if it is very close to this value.
These results must be viewed as being due to chance and reported as
such. If the test result is not significant, then you report this without
stating the exact p-value. It is enough to simply state 'ns' (*not significant*).

Another way to report the significance level of test results is by using
stars next to the value of a test. The following format is generally used:
* $(p < .05)$; ** $(p < .01)$ and *** $(p < .001)$. However, you must always
explain the meaning of the stars. It is quite possible that other researchers use different significance levels.

For example:
'Purchasing staff score higher on question 3 than sales staff ($t = 3.96$,
$p < .001$), which supports hypothesis 1'.

Do not confront the reader with large quantities of 'raw' data, such as the output from a computer. You must organize this data and indicate the important findings. For example, do not report individual scores, use means, group means, minimum and maximum scores and frequencies instead.

> For example:
> 'Purchasing staff have a mean score of 5.17 on question 3 on a scale that ranges from 1 (disagree completely) to 7 (agree completely)'.

You can present your results in tables and figures. It is best to use figures (usually graphs) for presenting qualitative results, while tables are best for showing quantitative results. Use the correct type of graph. If you want your results to add up to 100 per cent, it is best to use a pie chart. Line graphs are most suitable for showing a trend. If you want to compare various aspects, a histogram is the best choice. Use tables and figures only if you actually want to clarify or illustrate something. Therefore do not automatically include a table or figure for every analysis that you have conducted.

It is important to present the results correctly and clearly. The patterns and exceptions in the data must be clear without requiring further explanation in the text. You should therefore think carefully beforehand about which data you will include in the rows and columns (or on the X-axis or Y-axis). With graphs, the dependent variable is generally placed on the Y-axis and the independent variable on the X-axis. If a second independent variable (in the form of an interaction effect) is involved, then show this on the graph.

Tables and figures must be numbered in separate sequences on a chapter-by-chapter basis (for example, Table 2.1 and Figure 2.1 are the numbers of the first table and the first figure that appear in the second chapter).

All tables and figures must be given a title. The title is placed above a table and below a figure. A table should have only horizontal lines (no vertical lines). Numbers in the columns must be placed directly under each other. Line up the decimal points and never centre the contents of a table cell. Percentages must be rounded off to whole numbers. Generally speaking, no more than two decimals are used. More exact results can always be included in the appendices. Statistical processing gives the reader the impression that there is a degree of precision that is actually unattainable: the results of statistical processing can never be more precise than the data used in the analysis. This once again shows

Table 9.1 Results of three *t*-tests. Differences between purchasing staff ($N = 234$) and sales staff ($N = 356$) regarding the frequency, duration and seriousness of illness during the past year

	Sales staff M (sd)	Purchasing staff M (sd)	t
Frequency of absences per year	5 (1.35)	2 (0.95)	1.96
Average length of absence	2 (0.53)	10 (1.95)	5.35**
Seriousness of illness	1.50 (0.67)	2.75 (0.99)	4.59*

Note: * $= p < .05;$ ** $= p < .01.$

the importance of discussing the reliability and validity of the measurement instruments when interpreting the results.

An explicit reference to the table or figure must be included in the accompanying text. This is usually done by including the reference between parentheses in the body of the text. Tables should also be discussed thoroughly. First discuss the general picture shown by the table. Then discuss the specific findings. Finally, make a conclusion regarding the results from the table.

For example:
'Table 9.1 shows the results of three *t*-tests that were used to determine whether purchasing and sales staff differ in terms of the number of times they have called in sick during the past year, the average length of absence and the seriousness of the illness'.

'Table 9.1 shows that the two groups indeed differ regarding two of the three variables. It appears that sales staff are absent for significantly shorter periods and are less seriously ill than purchasing staff. In addition ... It can be concluded on the basis of the data from Table 9.1 that, in accordance with the expectation, purchasing staff are absent more frequently than sales staff'.

If a figure from another publication is used, you must provide an adequate acknowledgement of the source by placing the acknowledgement below the title of the figure, for example (From: Jensen, 1997).

9.4.9 Conclusions and discussion

This last part of the report is broader in organization than the Results chapter. As in the introduction, the *funnel model* is used in the conclusions and discussions chapter, but it is reversed: the discussion expands from the narrow focus of answering the specific research question to include the theories and other studies on which the research question is based. The structure of the entire report is therefore analogous to two funnels with their narrow ends touching.

This chapter focuses primarily on interpreting the relationships that emerged from the results. In this part of the report, more than in the other chapters, you are expected to discuss your own opinion regarding the topic. Make sure that this opinion is well supported with appropriate arguments. Begin this chapter with a brief review of the research question and the answer to this question that was expected on the basis of theory (the hypotheses). Then explain what was found in the empirical research and attempt to answer the research question with this information. *Important note:* if you ascertain that the results of the research do not contribute to the solution of the problem, then this is also a conclusion. Negative findings must also be reported.

> For example:
> 'Based on the theory, it was expected that purchasing staff would be absent less often than their colleagues in the sales department. This expectation was not supported in the research: purchasing staff scored higher on their answers to questions about the average length of absence than sales staff'.

The next step is to compare the results with those from other studies: what are the similarities and differences? Place the results of your research next to that which is already known about the topic. At this point you must also return to the theories discussed in the introduction: which theories or aspects of these theories are supported or unsupported by the results of the research? The conclusions must follow logically from the introduction and must be based on the results. In any case, the conclusion cannot simply appear by itself.

In this chapter you should also consider possible alternative explanations for the results and discuss these. You may have attained certain results, but could they possibly be explained by other factors? For example, could the explanation be related to the specific company or problems with the research method or the questionnaire?

Take a critical view of your own research and describe its shortcomings. Discuss the extent to which the results can be generalized. In other words, do the results also apply to other populations (for example, to all companies or only to specific types of companies; to all staff, or only to supervisors) and why (or why not)? Explore the possibility of there being distorting factors that have affected the results and consider the possible strength of such factors (for example, was there a relatively high non-response from a specific subgroup of respondents which could have distorted the results? Or were the respondents asked only about their subjective opinions without making any objective measurements?). Describe the most important theoretical and practical implications of the results.

Finally, this chapter also contains recommendations for practice, theory and future research. For example, the importance of the results for practice could be formulated as follows:

'The research showed that a people-oriented style of leadership reduces absenteeism. To prevent absenteeism, the company could pay more attention to the style of leadership of its managers'.

Regarding recommendations for theory, if the hypotheses (or specific aspects thereof) have not been confirmed, you might conclude that the theory on which they are based should be modified. Try to describe this as thoroughly and carefully as possible.

Regarding recommendations for future research, you can determine what areas have remained under-illuminated or what problems have occurred (concerning the sample or the measurement instrument, for example) so that future research can focus on these areas. You can also formulate new hypotheses. In that case, try to indicate as concretely and precisely as possible how future research could be structured and implemented. Other authors can then make use of these specific recommendations and expand on this knowledge. In the same way, you made use of these aspects of articles that you studied when conducting your literature research (see Chapter 3).

Make a clear distinction between conclusions and recommendations. Conclusions are an opinion of the author based on the results of the *present* research; recommendations are suggestions made by the author for the *future*.

9.4.10 Reference list

The reference list is located at the end of the report. It must list the bibliographic data for all references in the report, but should not include any other publications. Therefore do not include a publication that you read but did not use when writing the report. Literature references in the text must of course exactly match the data in the reference list. Therefore check references in the text against the reference list and check the reference list against the references in the text to make sure they are exactly the same.

If there is literature that you feel is important, but which you have not used when writing the report, you can optionally include this in a separate list, for example under the heading 'Further reading' or 'Literature consulted'. The reference list should not be subdivided in any other way. For example, you should not make any distinction between books and articles published in English and other languages. Regarding the format of the bibliographical entries, you can refer to the guidelines from the *Publication Manual* of the *American Psychological Association (APA)*. The references in the reference list are listed in alphabetical order according to the last name of the first author. Do not list any first names, gender indications or academic titles in the reference list.

Books, chapters from books and articles from journals are indicated with different typography (plain text, underlining/italics), as shown below:

1. Book: surname of author, initials (year of publication). *Title*. Location of publisher: name of publisher.

   For example:
   Bass, B.M. (1981). *Stogdill's Handbook of Leadership*. New York: Free Press.

2. Chapter from a book: surname of author, initials (year of publication). Title of chapter. In: initials and name of editor (ed.) or editors (eds), *title of book*, page numbers of the chapter. Location of publisher: name of publisher.

   For example:
   Luthans, F. and Lockwood, D.L. (1984). Toward an observation system for measuring leader behavior in natural settings. In: J.G. Hunt, D. Hosking, C. Schriesheim and R. Stewart (eds), *Leaders and Managers*. New York: Pergamon Press.

3. Article in a journal: surname of author, initials (year of publication). Title of article. *Name of journal, volume number*, page numbers.

   For example:
   Hales, C.P. (1986). What do managers do? A critical review of the evidence. *Journal of Management Studies, 23*, 88–115.

4. If there is literature for which the author is unknown, list this according to the name of the institution or organization (for

example, Statistics Bureau) or the name of the newspaper or periodical from which you have obtained the information (for example, *The Times*).

5. Unpublished manuscripts, such as theses, papers for a congress or internal reports, can be listed in the reference list as shown below.

> For example:
> Peters, C. (1999). *The Effect of Organizational Culture on the Satisfaction of Employees with their Wages.* Unpublished doctoral thesis, Stoakdale University.

> For example:
> Van der Velde, E.G. (2001). *Employment Socialization among Young Adults.* Paper presented at the Second European Conference for Employment and Organizational Psychology, Amsterdam.

> For example:
> Jensen, A.F. (1998). *Declining Scores on Intelligence Tests for Very Young Children.* Unpublished report. New York: Institute for Test Psychology.

9.4.11 Appendices

In the appendices you can include tables, figures, illustrations, questionnaires, codebooks, correspondence and a summary of technical terminology if these items are too long to place in the report itself, but which you still feel should be available to the reader. Including such information is important because it also enables others to critically evaluate and replicate your research. If parts of these appendices have been taken from previously published literature, then there must be a clear reference to the source (for example, 'From: Pipers (1993). *Organizational Behavior.* New York: Prentice Hall, p. 183'). In the report itself, you should refer to the information in these appendices where this is appropriate. However, the reader must be able to read and understand the text without consulting the appendices and the reverse. The page numbering continues through in the appendices. Besides the keyword list or terminology list mentioned earlier, you may also want to include a name index of individuals and/or an address list.

■ 9.5 WRITING STYLE AND LAYOUT OF THE REPORT

If you want the report to make a good general impression, you should pay attention to its appearance. It must appear well organized and be inviting to read. The following points are important aspects of the appearance:

- Make sure the report has a clear structure. You can check this by doing the following. Read the research question, see whether the question is indeed answered in the conclusions chapter and then evaluate the content in between the research questions and the conclusions: are the steps that lead from the research question to the conclusions logically connected with each other?
- At the beginning of the report, define the concepts that will be used in the report and use these concepts consistently. Therefore use as few synonyms as possible.
- Make sure that the propositions, hypotheses and arguments are adequately supported and explained. Do not provide any summaries or lists of authors or theories for example, but provide a concise argument in which you make choices and explain these choices. For every aspect of your discussion, explain its function in the line of reasoning and in the research itself. Tell the reader what is going to happen (or will not happen) with these aspects and why you have made this choice.
- Make sure there is a good distinction between central issues and subsidiary issues.
- Make sure there are good cross-references to other chapters, sections and possibly to pages in the text.
- Make sure the layout is logical and consistent. For example, print all chapter titles in upper case bold and all section titles in lower case bold. Subheadings can then be printed in italics.
- Pay attention to the correct use of paragraphs and white space. Both have the aim of improving the readability and organization of a report. Paragraphs are a coherent set of sentences with a unifying aspect such as a specific subtopic, a comparison and contrast structure, a reference to a specific time period or an example or analogy that interrupts a line of argument. White space is used to group several paragraphs together on a page, there are usually four or five paragraphs on each page. Therefore avoid writing very short paragraphs (with only one or two sentences) or very long ones (10 sentences is usually too long). Either indent the paragraphs or start new paragraphs by skipping a line. Do not allow a single line of a paragraph to be printed separately from the rest of the paragraph on a different page.
- The length of a text must have a proper relationship to the depth of the topic that is being treated. For a Master's thesis, a length of

between 40 and 80 pages (not including tables and figures and with a normal font and line spacing, see below) is sufficient. When structuring chapters and paragraphs, also pay attention to the length of the text. A two-page chapter is too short, while a 25-page chapter is often too long.

- Generally speaking, you should number the pages of the preface and the introduction in small Roman numerals, while Arabic numerals are used for the body of the report. As previously stated, the pages for appendices are numbered continuously.

- If the various sections of the report are numbered (note that this does not refer to page numbers!), then the following rules apply. The preface, abstract and introduction are not numbered. The individual chapters are numbered in sequence (for example, Chapter 1: Theoretical framework). The appendices are numbered independently from the chapters and begin with Appendix 1. In a report, every chapter begins on a new page, usually an odd numbered right-hand page.

- Use consistently either UK or US spellings. When writing in English, you can choose either the American *Webster* dictionary or the British *Oxford English* dictionary. In any case, make sure you consistently continue with one of these choices. For example, do not use spelling such as 'behavior/behaviour' or 'organisation/organization' mixed together.

- Use abbreviations such as i.e. or etc. as little as possible. They should be used only if they improve the readability. If you want to use abbreviations (of jargon for example), then spell out the term the first time, followed by the abbreviation in parentheses.

    For example:
    'With respect to business finance (BF) the following applies.... In BF one often encounters....'.

- Make a consistent choice for using either the present tense or the past tense. A scientific report is often written in the past tense, with the exception of generally applicable statements or definitions.

- Use as few footnotes as possible. Excessive use of footnotes disturbs the line of reasoning. If a remark is sufficiently important, simply include it in the text itself.

- When you use demonstrative pronouns, make sure it is clear what they refer to (for example, if you write, 'This makes it clear that ...' it must be completely clear what 'this' refers to).

- Try to alternate short and long sentences, and avoid sentences longer than 40 words. Try to limit the use of jargon. Translate foreign terms wherever possible, optionally placing the term in the original language in italics in parentheses next to the translated term.

- Avoid vague and incomplete expressions, double negatives, authority-based arguments and arrogant or condescending remarks about other authors. Examples of such statements are, 'It is not clear that...' or 'Many would agree with me that...' or 'The renowned management authority Porter would agree with me that...'.
- Do not use popular, difficult, superlative or emphatic language. Such language does not belong in a scientific paper. This does not mean that a scientific paper has to be boring. Quite the contrary, the reader's interest must be stimulated primarily by the content of the report and not by the language in which it is written.
- Use businesslike language. For example, avoid 'I believe...' or 'In my opinion...' or 'One could say that...' Instead, use formulations such as 'However, the following arguments could counter this proposition...' or 'It could be concluded that...' The reader then knows that this is the opinion of the author.
- Use a single standard font between 10 and 12 points in size.
- Try to use as little italic, bold or underlined text as possible.
- The line spacing is usually 1 or 1.5 lines. For articles that are being submitted to a journal, double-line spacing is usually required.
- Use broad margins to achieve a pleasant page appearance.
- A report must be typed and printed on one side of the paper.

Chapter 10

PRESENTATION

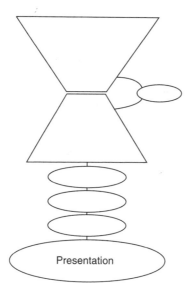

10.1 INTRODUCTION

Giving a presentation is not an art, but a professional task. You can learn this through frequent practice. This chapter provides a number of suggestions for giving a successful presentation. With this goal in mind, a number of steps should be taken. The first step is making good preparations (Section 10.2). Your presentation will succeed or fail based on the preparations you make. To hold the interest of the listener, you must apply a clear structure to your presentation. This is discussed in Section 10.3. After that, the presentation itself is discussed in Section 10.4, and Section 10.5 covers several audio-visual aids that can be used to support your presentation. Finally, Section 10.6 addresses a number of methods you can use to acquire and hold the attention of your audience.

▌ 10.2 PREPARING THE PRESENTATION

Collect as much information as possible about your audience: what do they know, what do they not know and what do they want to know? Before the presentation, orient yourself to the level of the listeners: can you use jargon, or should you explain the terminology? There will be a clear difference between a research presentation aimed at professional or academic colleagues and one for a client from the business community. In short, try to imagine yourself as a member of the audience. Give them the information they are interested in using language and methods they can understand.

Before you begin, decide what you want to achieve with the presentation. This will be the focus of your preparations for the presentation and must be explicitly stated at the beginning of the presentation. At the end of the presentation, you will return to this point: have you reached your goal?

The preparations for a presentation begin with making an inventory of the topics. Collect as many points and facts that could be of importance to the argument as possible. You can group this information into themes or clusters. After this, the clusters are placed in a logical sequence in such a way that each cluster:

● forms a complete whole;
● signifies that a step has been taken in the line of reasoning;
● can be understood by the listener.

When making a presentation about a report that has been distributed beforehand (where the listeners are already acquainted with the topic), it is advisable to limit yourself to the main issues. For example, describe the research question ('What is the report about?') and the results ('What emerged from the research and what can you do with it?'). A common misunderstanding is that you have to say something entirely new when presenting a report. If you do say something new that is not in the report, people often lose track of your argument. However, you can answer the questions of the listeners about matters that have perhaps remained unclear and therefore require further explanation.

Make suitable notes: write down keywords, use felt-tip pens and make 'crib sheets'. You can also use the printed version of the overhead slides as an aid for making notes. This ensures that your oral presentation is synchronized with the visual aids.

If you want to write out a presentation and then memorize it, it is advisable to have a number of well-conceived introductory sentences for each section on paper. These act as a memory aid in case you forget your lines. Underline or highlight the parts that you want to emphasize, and place parts that you can leave out (if you have too little time) between parentheses. Do not tell the listeners that you are skipping a section, however, because this is not informative. Moreover, if your presentation is written out entirely, you should not simply read it from the page.

Memorizing a presentation has advantages and disadvantages. One advantage is that you are then certain that you know what you are going to say. You will also know exactly how long the presentation will last and when to use visual aids. One disadvantage of memorization is that it is difficult to deviate from the planned sequence of the presentation. This makes it more difficult to deal with unexpected events, such as questions or remarks from the audience. Of course, the choice between memorizing and not memorizing depends on the aim of the presentation (for example, is the aim one-sided instruction or to interact with the listeners) and the personal preference of the speaker. Some speakers are worried about having a 'blackout' if they are interrupted by a question from the audience.

Practise the presentation. Time how long it takes – make especially sure it is not too long. Does it contain all the important facts? Should questions be allowed during the presentation or only afterwards? Make this aspect clear beforehand to the audience and take account of this aspect when planning the presentation. It is also advisable to:

- practise the entire presentation (or parts thereof) out loud; record it on a cassette tape if possible and then listen to the tape;
- practise difficult phrasings, difficult words and anecdotes;
- check your facial expressions and gestures by having them observed by others or do it yourself by using a mirror or make a video recording.

If possible, practise at the location where you will actually be giving the presentation: note the size of the room, the seating arrangement (for example, interactive work requires a different seating arrangement than an instructional presentation) and the important physical aspects of the room (for example, where are the switches for the lights and other equipment?). Every listener must be able to see and hear the speaker. This means that the acoustics should be tested beforehand. The visual aids must be prepared in advance, for example, the chalkboard (is there enough chalk?), the projector and/or the video apparatus (how does it operate?). When using audio-visual equipment, it is especially important that you understand exactly how it operates (see Section 10.5).

▮ 10.3 STRUCTURE OF THE PRESENTATION

The presentation begins with a brief introduction of the speaker or speakers, the aim of the presentation, the topic and subtopics, the structure and duration (the breaks and closing). The best way to do this is to write this information on a chalkboard or have it printed on an overhead slide that you can show to the audience (see Section 10.5). During the presentation, return to this outline several times to show where you are.

It is advisable to have a summary of the presentation on paper or on overhead sheets. This acts as a memory support for the participants as you proceed with your oral presentation and can also serve as a basis for the discussion. Consider whether it might be useful to distribute such a handout before or after your presentation. The disadvantage of distributing it beforehand is that the listeners will begin thumbing through the handout and reading it instead of listening to your presentation. Therefore, it is usually preferable to distribute the handout afterwards. However, you should announce this clearly at the beginning of the presentation to prevent the audience from taking notes instead of listening.

A good rule of thumb when making a presentation is to state your message three times. First, what you are going to say, then say it, and finally summarize what you have said. You can ensure a well-structured presentation by providing introductions to new parts and by reviewing and summarizing parts as they are completed. Moreover, this allows listeners to reorient themselves to the discussion as it proceeds (for example, 'I have just shown that ... The following point I want to make is ...').

The structure of the presentation must be clear throughout. You can do this by literally indicating the transitions in the line of reasoning (for example, 'Firstly ..., secondly ..., and finally ...' Or, 'Now that this topic is completed I will begin with the next aspect, which is ...').

In the closing section of your presentation you should make a brief summary and outline the primary conclusions (for example, 'What was the aim of the presentation?'). No new facts are presented during the closing section.

Formulate appropriate examples which make the presentation clearer and more interesting for the audience and also provide support for your memory. However, examples must never be used as an argument in a line of reasoning.

To create more structure in the presentation you can also:

- place the presentation in a bigger context: larger events concerning the topic;
- continually make links with practice by using examples, illustrations, applications and anecdotes;
- present the data in contrasting terms, where you also give your own opinion, however, make a clear distinction between the facts and your own opinion;
- ask rhetorical questions in the form of questions which you answer and which cause your listeners to think (for example, 'What is the core of this argument?'). You can also use a rhetorical question to introduce the next point of your presentation (for example, 'What are the fundamental causes of this phenomenon?').

■ 10.4 THE PRESENTATION: SOME RULES OF THUMB

Speaking in front of a group is something that becomes easier with practise. Here are a number of suggestions:

- Speak clearly with good articulation. Speak somewhat slower and more emphatically than you normally would. Try to avoid using stop-gap words (such as 'you know').
- Make eye contact with the audience. Look at all the people, not just at a single person, the window or the ceiling.
- Avoid the use of abbreviations and specialized terminology (jargon) unless the audience is familiar with them. At the beginning of the presentation, make a brief query about this (for example, 'Are you familiar with these terms, or shall I explain them in more detail?').
- Use simple words and short sentences.

- The tempo must be just right – certainly not too fast, but also not too slow.
- Every good presentation has a number of silences. Natural breaks can serve, for example, to close one part of the presentation before moving on to the next topic. A brief silence allows the audience to absorb the information that has just been provided and enables the speaker to concentrate on the next part of the presentation.
- Good body language is important when giving a presentation. Use hand and arm gestures to prevent the presentation from becoming too static. Of course, do not exaggerate these gestures. Many people are nervous when speaking in public and do not know what do with their hands. In that case, holding a pen can provide you with a literal handhold. Moreover, the pen can be used to point to the next item on an overhead sheet. However, make sure you do not play with the pen too much.
- A presentation must never be too long, not even one minute too long. A presentation that is too short is always better than one that is too long. Do not tell the audience everything you know about the topic, do not provide more details, but try to limit the presentation to the main issues.

▮ 10.5 TOOLS

Various media can be used as audio-visual aids during the presentation. Take the words 'audio-visual aids' literally – these tools are not an end in themselves, but are intended to clarify the presentation and make it more lively. A cartoon is an example of a visual aid that makes a presentation more lively. You can encourage your audience to listen by alternating a verbal message with various media. A good combination of words, images and tables is the best way to present your message. A number of suggestions are given below for using a chalkboard, flipchart, the overhead projector, the transview, videos and the microphone.

10.5.1 Blackboard or flipchart

One advantage of using these visual aids is that they are easy and inexpensive to arrange, since they are already present in many meeting rooms or lecture halls. Another advantage is that it is possible to improvise during the presentation itself and to make notes as you go.

The blackboard is especially suitable for making explanations, such as explaining a formula or the structure of a research model.

A disadvantage of these methods is that it is difficult for most people to write clearly on a chalkboard or flipchart: it is difficult to write consistently in letters that are not too small. You can learn how to do this by practising beforehand. Another disadvantage is that you must turn away from the audience to write on the board or flipchart during the presentation. As a result, you lose contact with the audience and therefore lose your grip on the events. You can prevent this by writing the relevant notes on the chalkboard or flipchart before the presentation. However, this means that you can no longer improvise during the presentation.

The following are some general suggestions for using chalkboards and flipcharts:

- If you intend to use a chalkboard or flipchart, it is useful to decide beforehand exactly what you are going to write.
- Use letters that are the correct size and are evenly spaced: everyone in the room must be able to read the board or flipchart.
- Emphasize main issues and subsidiary issues by using a structure, for example, underlining important parts and using arrows.

10.5.2 Transparencies/slides

Generally speaking, the overhead projector is an excellent visual aid for providing structure to your presentation. Using the overhead projector has the same goal as using the chalkboard, and the sheets must also meet the same requirements concerning readability. An advantage of the overhead projector over the chalkboard is that you can establish the structure of the argument beforehand. As a result, you can pay more attention to the presentation itself. The line of reasoning is already summarized by the items on the sheet. In addition, you can clearly present your important results and conclusions and provide an accompanying story without there being an excess of information and without running the risk that your listeners will lose the thread of the story.

An overhead sheet must be structured in such a way that it does not present too much information simultaneously. This can also be achieved by covering part of the text on the sheet with a piece of paper. As a rule of thumb, you should not have more than five items on a sheet. To prevent excessive amounts of information, it is advisable to use keywords instead of entire sentences. You can also use various colours. However, make sure the colours are not too light. The letters on the sheet must be at least half a centimetre in height. You can check the correct size by laying a sheet on the floor and seeing if you can read it while standing over it.

10.5.3 Slides

Slides are good for showing pictures. Using specially created slides is significantly more expensive than sheets on an overhead projector.

10.5.4 Transview

This allows you to show images on a computer screen to a large audience by means of overhead projection. This is especially useful if you want to show how a specific software program operates.

10.5.5 Video

Videos should be used only if this is an essential part of the presentation. Since a video comprises moving pictures and sound, you run the risk of the audience paying more attention to the video than to you. Make sure that you still provide the most important information yourself. If you decide to use a video, the best time to do this is at the beginning or end of the presentation. Make sure you place the video clearly in the context of your presentation.

10.5.6 Microphone

Use a microphone only if there is a large group or if the acoustics in the room are poor. When using a microphone, make sure to keep it at the proper distance from your mouth when you are moving around and/ or looking at the chalkboard or overhead projector. Otherwise the audience may be unable to hear some parts of the presentation, and other parts may be too loud.

▌ 10.6 THE AUDIENCE

Generally speaking, people are prepared to listen, but they require regular opportunities to relax or escape. Moreover, people like to laugh. If a presentation lasts longer than 30 minutes, you often lose the attention of the audience. Therefore, take note of non-verbal signals from the audience while you are speaking, such as surprised, irritated or approving expressions. Also ask the audience periodically whether they are still following the presentation. Repeat the questions that are asked during the discussion to make sure you understand them yourself and that they are understood by everyone in the room. Don't worry if you are unable to answer all the questions in the time allowed. You can return to the unanswered questions after the presentation if necessary. However, to speed things up it is a good idea to formulate as many potential questions and answers beforehand as possible.

There are a number of ways to acquire and hold the attention of the audience:

- Make a joke. However, the joke must be within the frame of reference of the audience and the topic.
- Refer to a previous speaker ('As Mr Jensen previously stated ... ').
- Refer to the location ('It was at this university where the very first ... ').
- Refer to the time period ('It has been nearly 10 years since ... ').
- Refer to a current event ('Yesterday you probably read the article in the newspaper about... ').
- Finally, you can refer to the importance of the meeting ('Today we are faced with the important task of ... ').

Chapter 11

CASE STUDY – THE TRANSPOST CASE

▌ 11.1 INTRODUCTION

Transpost is an organization that specializes in the collection, transport and distribution of documents and goods. Approximately 20 000 people work at Transpost in various business units. These business units are subdivided according to the core tasks of collection, sorting, distribution and delivery of goods. Transpost does not bring every object individually from the sender to the destination. The transport of goods is combined wherever possible, so that flows of goods join and divide at many locations in the country. In this way, the company creates a network that begins with small flows of goods, moves to larger flows and main flows, and then branches out again into smaller and smaller flows. Each time the goods are divided, they must also be sorted.

The company has recently been experiencing several problems: a sharp increase in complaints about deliveries; a continuing increase in costs caused by incorrect deliveries; and a dramatic increase in absenteeism. The management of Transpost decided to commission a study into the causes of these problems. For this purpose, an external researcher was hired. The first discussions indicated that one cause of declining quality could be the lack of 'cooperation' at the department level, i.e. the social climate.

There are two parts to this case study. It initially concerns the construction of an instrument for measuring the social climate. The second part concerns a study of the relationship between social climate, absenteeism and the quality of the delivery service.

11.1.1 Methodological requirements

The aim of the research is to find a solution to a concrete problem instead of acquiring more general knowledge. The researcher therefore did not accept this assignment to satisfy his own curiosity, but to solve the client's problem. The researcher will proceed with his task by initiating discussions, studying written material and conducting interviews. In any case, it has become clear to him that this study will involve the characteristics of precision (the results will form the basis for action), specificity (the research focuses only on Transpost) and complexity (many issues play a role).

The research is intended not only to find the causes of the problems, but also to provide feasible suggestions for improvement. However, this brings up two important questions: which problem should be studied, and who is the client? The latter question is closely related to two of the methodological requirements: the public access to the information and ethical responsibility. Within the organization, information about the social climate, absenteeism and productivity can be very sensitive.

What does the management expect of the reporting? Does it expect general reporting (which is more anonymous) or very detailed reporting (which entails a risk of tracing to specific respondents)? And what do the employees expect? Investigating the social climate in the company requires the cooperation of employees, and they may expect that measures will actually be taken as a result of the research. Is the research really aimed at improvements, or is it just intended as a pacifier?

11.1.2 Clients and other discussion partners

In order to deal with the ethical responsibility and public nature of the information, it is important to be clear about two questions: who exactly is the research client and what exactly does the assignment entail? In addition, the researcher must determine if there are any other interested parties and define their interests.

Transpost's management commissioned the study. The exact formulation of the assignment took place following a series of discussions. It initially appeared that the study would focus on the relationship between absenteeism and the number of complaints about delivery. The problem with this research focus was that no areas were identified that could feasibly be improved. On the other hand, social characteristics, such as the manner of communication, management style and the atmosphere in the department, are areas that can be influenced and that may affect both absenteeism and productivity. The question is then: *what* will be (or can be) investigated with respect to these social characteristics?

It is now clear that there are a number of parties who are interested in the research and in the results. The middle management of the company is directly interested in the research. The behaviour of the departmental managers has a significant effect on the atmosphere in the department. The managers may experience a study of their management style as a type of personal assessment. The researcher must make it clear to this group that that the conclusions will not be used as a personal assessment, but will be used to improve policy where possible, and that the research will benefit them.

The Employees' Work Council represents the employees. The Council has the legal obligation of ensuring the well-being of the employees and the organization. All policies concerning personnel or the operational methods within the company must be submitted to the Council for its approval or recommendations. Of course, the Work Council needs accurate information in order to aid its decision making. Transpost's employee participation structure involves subcommittees at the department level and five regionally organized Work Councils. The general Work Council represents these.

Another party who is interested in the results of the research, especially regarding the social climate and absenteeism, is the Trade Union. Support from the Work Council and Trade Union can positively influence such research. In return for their support, they expect to be informed about the conclusions of the research.

Other interested parties can be found in a totally different area. Besides its organizational management value, this research has academic and commercial significance. An instrument for measuring the social climate must be created for this study. For academics, it is extremely interesting to determine the extent to which this instrument measures what it is supposed to measure and to unravel the possible relationship between absenteeism, quality of service (deliveries) and social climate. Academics require more data and very detailed analyses, but these aspects are not equally important to all interested parties.

The commercial value of the research is represented by the enormous costs incurred by high absenteeism and poor quality of service. The methodology and the company-specific recommendations could also be used by other organizations.

Agreements with management must be made about a number of issues:

- What is the status of the research (the start of a genuine process of change or a 'pacifier')?

- What exactly will be studied?
- How will the information be reported to the client (anonymity)?
- What will be reported (level of scientific detail)?
- Who is the owner of the assessment method?
- What is the position of the employee participation bodies and the Trade Union?

11.2 PROBLEM ORIENTATION

11.2.1 Aim and problem definition

The management asked the researcher to look for ways to improve cooperation and the quality of deliveries.
The aim of the research is therefore:

To obtain insight into the relationship between social aspects of work/absenteeism and the quality of deliveries.

Since the researcher already suspects that such a relationship exists, the research is concerned with hypothesis testing. This leads to the following preliminary problem definition: is there a significant relationship between social aspects of work/absenteeism and the quality of deliveries?
The problem must be delineated further to allow the researcher to arrive at a final definition. But which objects will the researcher investigate (i.e. what domain will the research cover)? Will he study goods, employees, distribution systems or departments? The researcher decided on the following delineation:

- *Domain:* departments. The object to be studied or the research unit is therefore the department.
- *Variables:* the characteristics of a department. These include both objective characteristics such as absenteeism and productivity and more subjective characteristics such as communication, collegiality and management style.

The final problem definition is:

What is the relationship between the social characteristics of a department and efficiency characteristics such as absenteeism and productivity?

11.2.2 Subsidiary questions

The final definition of the problem leads to a number of subsidiary questions. The most important are:

- What are relevant social characteristics?
- What is absenteeism?
- What is productivity?
- What are the differences between the departments concerning the characteristics to be investigated?
- What is the relationship between social characteristics and absenteeism?
- What is the relationship between social characteristics and productivity?

Other subsidiary questions are certainly possible.

■ 11.3 RESEARCH MODEL AND VARIABLES

11.3.1 Research model

The starting point of the research was to establish the social causes for the differences in productivity between different Transpost departments. Considering that their formal structure and functional responsibilities are the same, the researcher decided to concentrate on operational and cooperation aspects. This decision was supported by the fact that there are major differences between the departments, not only in productivity but also in absenteeism. The researcher therefore suspected that the cooperation behaviour could be a determining factor in the differences in productivity. The initial, preliminary research model will therefore be:

Cooperation behaviour $\longrightarrow$ Productivity and absenteeism

On the basis of desk research and meetings with managers and employees, the researcher arrived at the following definition of 'cooperation' in this context. Transpost works with quality improving teams. These teams are characterized by cooperation and teamwork while searching for solutions to problems. Good mutual understanding appears to be essential. This applies not only to participants in the quality improvement teams, but also to the relationship between participants and non-participants. The concept of 'collegiality' therefore quickly emerged during the discussions between the researcher and the employees. Employees appeared to consider this an important topic, particularly in relation to the following problems:

- Lack of interest (or assumed lack of interest) of non-participants in the quality improvement teams.
- Lack of communication about the activities within the quality improvement teams (confusion about the actual work of the team, suggestions from non-participants are not taken into account).
- Accusations from non-participants that the quality improvement team participants were happily drinking coffee while the others were working.

The researcher therefore decided to investigate the following aspects of cooperation:

- communication;
- collegiality.

Communication and cooperation are attributes of the department. Moreover, the effect of both departmental attributes on productivity and absenteeism appears to be influenced by the departmental manager's style. Departments with a 'coaching' manager appear to have a stronger link between collegiality and communication on the one hand, and higher productivity and reduced absenteeism on the other. Formulated in a negative fashion, if the department manager is strongly supportive (coaching, people-oriented), the productivity and absenteeism will be less negatively influenced by poor communication and lack of collegiality. The manager then operates as a kind of buffer against the negative influence of poor cooperation within the department on the output of the department. The researcher therefore incorporated the variable 'management style' (also a departmental attribute!) as a moderating variable.

The final research model then appears as follows:

Collegiality, Communication $\longrightarrow$ Productivity, Absenteeism

$\uparrow$

Management style

11.3.2 Hypotheses

The researcher was then able to quickly derive the following hypotheses from this research model:

1. Departments with high levels of collegiality have low absenteeism and high productivity.
2. Departments with good internal communication have low absenteeism and high productivity.
3. A strongly supportive management style strengthens the effect of collegiality and communication on productivity and absenteeism.

11.3.3 Operationalization

The researcher decided to operationalize the independent variables 'collegiality' and 'communication' and the intervening variable 'management style' via a *Social Climate* survey. Employees will be asked to assess their department (concerning the variables collegiality and communication) by means of a large number of related questions from the *Social Climate* survey (e.g. 'I get on well with my colleagues' or 'If we make an agreement, we keep it'). And they will be asked to assess their manager concerning the management style variable.

As a measurement of collegiality, communication and management style, the researcher used the total score of the items that measure the variable concerned. The researcher assumed that collegiality, communication and management style would be measured on an interval scale.

Productivity will be measured using the transit time of test goods that are dispatched at set times. The time in transit will be figured in minutes, and will therefore be measured on a ratio scale. The same applies to absenteeism.

11.3.4 Reliability and validity

The researcher was not concerned about the reliability of the two dependent variables. After all, they are reasonably objective measurements. He did evaluate the reliability of the three other instruments (questionnaires) from the *Social Climate* survey in two ways. The first was to submit the questionnaires to the same group on two different occasions, separated by a one-week interval (the test–retest method). The second was to measure the internal consistency (Cronbach's alpha). Both methods indicated adequate reliability for the three questionnaires from the *Social Climate* survey. The researcher consequently assumed that the questionnaires measure systematically and that the proportion of measuring errors in the scores will therefore be relatively small in relation to the systematic part.

To assure the acceptance of the survey, the researcher considered it important that the questionnaires from the *Social Climate* survey actually measure that which was experienced as being problematic within the relevant department. He checked this face validity by presenting the items to a limited, representative group of individuals from the target group. He asked two questions about the items: (1) could they identify with the items? (2) Did the items concern issues that are indeed relevant to them? It is also important that the items actually measure the constructs (collegiality, communication, management style) that are intended. Is the questionnaire for 'communication' from the *Social Climate* survey actually a good operationalization of the theoretical construct 'Communication within the department' that cannot otherwise be observed? This instrumental validity was checked by means of factor analysis (see 11.9.2). Finally, the researcher checked the validity of the contents of the items by submitting them to a colleague researcher with expertise in this area. He asked the colleague two questions: (1) do the items properly represent the collegiality construct? (2) In this respect, are the items related?

11.3.5 Population and sample

Finally, the researcher decided on the sample. In principle, he wanted to include every Transpost department in the research. He therefore counted the total population of departments in the company. Due to efficiency considerations, however, he submitted the survey to a smaller, random sample of employees. Because he believed that the results might vary according to gender and duration period of employment, and because there are relatively few female and young employees at Transpost, he decided to stratify the sample within each department by sex and age.

▮ 11.4 RESEARCH STRATEGY

The researcher has focused on a specific research problem at a specific company. The problem is: why are certain departments not as productive as others? On the basis of the answer to this question, the researcher then makes proposals for specific measures to be made. In this respect, it is clearly applied research. The aim is not to contribute to scientific knowledge, but to solve an existing, concrete problem. The researcher wants to arrive at specific conclusions, and is not aiming at generally applicable knowledge.

The researcher does, however, intend to generate knowledge. He must find out what is happening. Although the generated knowledge will be specific to the relevant parts of the company being studied, it will still apply to the entire company. The researcher wants to reach general conclusions about Transpost that apply to all departments and employees. Moreover, he would like to repeat this study annually. Only then will he be able to make intervention plans.

In conclusion, even though the researcher ultimately wants to make proposals for intervention, the research itself must not be too invasive. After all, he should not conduct experiments on a company that is functioning normally.

11.4.1 Steps in the study

The preceding sections make it clear that various research strategies will be used at various times in the project.

1. Initially, the researcher must listen carefully so he can get an idea of what is really happening. In this case, he must intervene as little as possible, but explore as much as possible. The preliminary research will not be structured. The researcher will limit this phase to minimize costs and complete the project in a reasonable time.
2. To understand what is important, the researcher will investigate what is already known from earlier studies into these issues. The researcher therefore decides in any case to use theoretical research as a general, non-intrusive research strategy. He plans to read extensively to arrive at some preliminary ideas about the hypotheses. He also expects to come up with ideas and find examples of a relevant questionnaire in the literature.
3. After completing strategies 1 and 2, the researcher will construct a questionnaire. In this case, he believes a questionnaire is the best way to make general conclusions about the company without incurring excessive costs. General conclusions are conclusions that apply to all departments. In addition, a questionnaire is a fairly non-intrusive strategy. The researcher is aware that completing a

questionnaire about themes such as collegiality, communication and management style may start employees thinking. In this regard, the questionnaire strategy can be considered intrusive, but he is not worried about this. He will impress on the management that the questionnaire is a deliberate choice for an initial, cautious intervention.

4. Finally, the researcher will come to the point where he is able to make recommendations about concrete interventions. In some cases, these recommendations may concern invasive measures. The researcher is considering interventions such as reorganizations, management changes and the implementation of various measures for the prevention of absenteeism. But the nature of these interventions will depend on what is revealed by the research. In this case, specific, even drastic strategies are a possibility. At this point, the strategies will not focus on the development of knowledge, but on change. However, if the researcher systematically observes the effects of the interventions, this would actually be a field experiment.

Note that we have not mentioned the strategy of the case study here. Even though it clearly involves a single company, it does involve multiple cases, namely departments. The unit of analysis is not the company, but the department. Moreover, only a limited number of aspects of these units will be studied. Only the first phase of the unstructured preliminary study could be called (at most) a case study.

11.4.2 Causality

What is the situation here with respect to causality? For example, how does the researcher know that poor collegiality is really the cause of poor productivity instead of the other way around? The researcher carries out the following actions in order to be as certain as possible about this issue:

- He attempts to correct for other hidden causes, such as management style. He verifies whether other variables might interfere with, contaminate or influence the results.
- In principle, he attempts to make a longitudinal research in which the individual variables are repeatedly measured. In this way he can compute the effect of specific interventions more precisely. This strategy will certainly prove that an intervention precedes an effect.

- He minimizes the test effect by repeating the questionnaire after a period of at least one year using different samples from the departments. In this way, not everyone will participate in the same survey each year.
- He makes sure that employees who have been ill for long periods or who have resigned recently also take part in the survey. They may well have a more negative opinion about collegiality.

▍ 11.5   COLLECTING EXISTING DATA

11.5.1   Existing material to be collected

Earlier, it became clear that the researcher is planning to use several methods for data collection during the various phases of the study. He will therefore conduct observations, hold interviews and carry out a survey. For his theoretical model, the researcher also used findings from scientific meta-analyses involving a large number of investigations into the determinants of absenteeism.

The company commissioned the researcher because of disappointing scores for productivity and absenteeism. The researcher will therefore request these figures and study them. He also wants to investigate the background of these figures and see if there is a temporal trend. After all, it is important to know exactly how productivity and absenteeism are measured: these are indicators for symptoms that have been chosen and constructed in a specific manner. The researcher will carry out both vertical and horizontal analyses.

In a *vertical analysis*, the researcher chooses a specific time period (for example, the previous year). He investigates existing data for this period *in as much detail as possible*. He not only investigates productivity (measured as duration of goods in transit) and absenteeism, but also other data that relate to the period. Examples could be customer surveys, complaints about incorrect deliveries, and results of job performance evaluations, internal company reports and summaries of company costs. However, he is aware that these types of data are often collected incidentally and could therefore provide a distorted picture of the actual situation. For example, a comprehensive customer survey is often implemented when there has been an exceptional number of complaints; this means that the results of that research provide a more negative picture than that which is shown by the customers in normal circumstances.

In a *horizontal analysis* the researcher is concerned only with the figures for productivity and absenteeism during the previous five years. In this way he can see if there are any trends. Is the prior period atypical in any way, were there unusually high or low figures, or was there a steadily declining trend (production) or a rising one (absenteeism)? He checks to see if data are available about companies that are active in the same sector. For example, national absenteeism figures for various organizational sectors might be available.

11.5.2 Existing databases

Although the researcher checks if he can partly answer his question by making new analyses of previously collected data, he realizes that the chance of success is small. Company staff previously participated in a study about the sector (at that time there was a national survey), but the number of participants is too small to draw conclusions about the current company. Recently, however, some employees of the company have written reports on their experiences, but this was not a systematic data collection process.

11.5.3 Observations

The researcher wants to obtain a good picture of what is going on inside the company. To acquire an impression of the type of cooperation and the management style, he decides to measure the variables not only by conducting a written survey, but also by making direct observations based on a number of indicators. He decides to make his identity as a researcher known, thereby deciding against participatory observation in which he would hide his identity. In view of the aim of the research, he believes it is unwise to 'spy' as an accomplice of management. However, to avoid obtaining an exaggeratedly positive impression (because everyone may put their best foot forward when the researcher is in the vicinity), he decides to focus on more or less objective issues. For example, he uses the following indicators, among other criteria, to observe the variables:

- *Collegiality*: How do people treat each other? Do they laugh? Are there more or less permanent sub-groups, or does everyone associate with everyone else? Do people also socialize outside of work?

Does everyone leave immediately after the official workday ends, or do people stay for a while and talk? Do people help each other?

- *Management style*: Is there a separate canteen for the managers? How do employees speak to the manager (formally or informally)? Does the manager have a separate office where the door is usually closed? Do employees disagree with the manager? What is on the agenda for the department meetings (do people discuss work procedures, for example)? When the manager gives instructions, does he also provide an explanation? Does the manager consult with the staff? Is the manager friendly and accessible? What kind of schedule does the manager have (a great deal of planning and organization, or are there many personnel tasks)? Does the manager have 'favourite' employees? How does the manager talk about his department and the company in general?

11.5.4 Interviews

The researcher uses interviews for the following purposes:

- *Asking for information*: In many cases existing material about the organization is unavailable or unclear. To acquire complete information, the researcher will therefore ask specific, substantive questions to individuals from the company who should be reasonably well informed (such as the Head of the Personnel Office, the Controller or the Chair of the Employees' Council). This concerns more or less objective company information where the individuals being interviewed are approached purely as a source of information.
- *Questions concerning opinions and attitudes*: The researcher is very interested in the opinions, observations and attitudes of both staff and managers. This concerns not only their opinions about the cause of the decreasing production and increasing absenteeism, but also how they experience these situations. To achieve these aims, the researcher decides to talk with selected members of staff and management. The interviews are structured in the sense that the researcher has drawn up an outline beforehand that contains the topics that he definitely wants to discuss. He also provides an opportunity for the interviewees to share their own opinions, feelings and observations. But this is certainly not an informal chat! A discussion that only satisfies the need for conversation does not deserve to be called a discussion, but is referred to as a 'chat' (for

Table 11.1 The difference between an interview and a chat

Interview	Chat
Has an aim	Is coincidental
Has a time limit	A way to pass time
Requires preparation	Can take place at any time
Involves active listening and speaking	Participation can be passive
Involves two-way communication	Communication can be one-sided
Content is important	Often full of clichés
Silence is an essential element	Silence is a disturbing element

example, the brief contact conversation you might have with a hair stylist while getting your hair cut).

Table 11.1 illustrates the difference between an interview and a chat.

For these reasons the researcher provides the following information when inviting individuals for an interview – the aim of the interview, how long the interview will last and what he expects from the interviewee.

To encourage people to speak freely, the researcher decides not to record the interview; instead, he guides the interview and takes notes using a previously established scheme. This scheme has the following general form:

- Preliminaries: introductions, discuss aim of the interview, explain what happens with the results, assure anonymity, preview structure of the interview.
- List discussion themes proposed by the interviewee and the researcher. Make a list of crucial themes that must be discussed in any case.
- Introduce first theme (for example, possible causes of declining production):
  - Opening question: what do you think?
  - Researcher presents his own impressions (acquired from previous observations).
  - Summarize what has been said and make sure the summary is correct.
  Introduce second and following themes.
- Closing: any other issues.
- Brief summary, what will come next, how will we proceed?

Before beginning the actual interview process, the researcher decides to hold a few pilot interviews to determine whether or not the crucial themes indeed come up for discussion and whether he must limit the interview to a few topics and distribute more material in advance.

▋ 11.6 PRACTICAL IMPLEMENTATION

11.6.1 Scaling and items

The construct 'collegiality' emerged from open discussions with employees. By questioning further, the researcher got the idea that collegiality actually comprises two aspects. The first aspect is mutual understanding. This mutual understanding has characteristics such as: there are no serious conflicts, both individuals take responsibility to make sure the floor is clean at the end of the day and they do things for each other without complaining too much. The second aspect of collegiality is an active willingness to help each other when necessary, trade shifts when one individual has something important to do, help the colleague if he has too many goods, but don't keep too many goods to yourself to attain a higher score.

The researcher processed these collegiality themes (understanding and willingness) into an initial version of the questionnaire by including the following propositions (partly derived from his observations):

- I get along very well with my colleagues.
- If we agree to something, we keep to the agreement.
- I can trust my colleagues.
- My colleagues stand up for each other when necessary.
- There are only a few colleagues at work I can really count on.
- The atmosphere in the department is often very tense.

These are closed questions that the respondent can answer by indicating to what extent he agrees or disagree with the proposition. The researcher chose the following five-point scale for this purpose:

1. Disagree completely
2. Disagree
3. Neither disagree nor agree
4. Agree
5. Agree completely

The experiences with pilots of this initial collegiality questionnaire and interviews given at the same time led to several changes in the propositions. First of all, the propositions were reformulated so they focused more on collegiality as an aspect of the department and less on the individual's experience of collegiality. As a result, the 'I' form was eliminated. The statements were rephrased in terms of colleagues.

For these reasons, new answer categories were also chosen:

1. Totally inapplicable
2. Only partly applicable
3. Average/partly applicable
4. Quite applicable
5. Completely applicable

Secondly, the trial interviews provided new themes, i.e. possible sources of irritation resulting from a lack of collegiality: (1) colleagues who cut corners and (2) colleagues who do not inform each other about changes in the work. Apparently the construct of collegiality was insufficiently present in the first version of the questionnaire. There appeared to be 'construct under-representation'.

Comments on (1). The theme 'cutting corners' came up regularly in the interviews as a clear expression of a lack of collegiality. However, when the proposition *There are too many colleagues who cut corners* was included in the questionnaire, analysis showed that this did not contribute to the factor of 'collegiality'. It was therefore not part of what was intended to be measured. This item was therefore eliminated. The employees believe that whether colleagues 'cut corners' or not was an important aspect of working together, but it had no relationship with the theoretical construct of collegiality.

Comments on (2). The theme 'keeping each other informed about changes in the work' was referred to by employees during the interviews as a sign of collegiality. When included in the questionnaire, this proposition turned out to indeed contribute to this factor. 'Keeping each other informed about changes in the work' is therefore part of the collegiality construct. The remarkable part of this theme is that the accompanying proposition initially appears to concern mutual communication, but further analysis shows that it does not contribute to this factor.

The researcher ultimately included six questions in the next *Social Climate* survey concerning 'collegiality':

- Colleagues are generally prepared to help each other when necessary.
- If colleagues agree to something, they keep to the agreements.
- My colleagues at work cooperate well.
- The understanding between colleagues is good.
- Colleagues take account of each other.
- Colleagues keep each other informed about changes in the work.

11.6.2 Construction of the of questionnaire

Beginning with the testing phase of the research instrument, the researcher established a database to store data about every time the *Social Climate* survey was used. In this way the researcher hoped to be able to develop norms for the various dimensions of the *Social Climate* survey. This would make it possible, after a climate measurement at a department, to indicate how strong the collegiality at that department is when compared to other departments (or related departments). In addition, based on a comparison with previous results of measurements at the same department, it is possible to indicate whether the collegiality has increased or decreased.

From the description above, it appears that there were six separate phases or steps in the process of developing the collegiality questionnaire from the *Social Climate* survey.

During the **first phase**, it was investigated which themes play a role in cooperation in the work situation. The topic of 'collegiality' emerged from the initial discussions as an important theme. During further probing it turned out that this concept was repeatedly brought up in connection with three continually recurring problems: lack of interest, poor communication and mutual accusations. Note that this was an inventory of the 'domain' and that for the time being the aim was sample validity. But the suspicion also rose that there may be a single construct underlying the incidents that emerged during the discussions, which requires construct validity.

During the **second phase**, the researcher began to suspect (based on further probes and tests of the initial ideas) that the tentative construct 'collegiality' is in fact constructed of two aspects: good mutual understanding (behavioural examples are the lack of serious conflicts and working together to make sure the floor is clean at the end of the day), and actively helping each other (behavioural examples are trading shifts and helping a colleague if he has too many goods). Consequently, there has been construct clarification.

The researcher begins to glimpse the answer to the question, 'To which situations does "collegiality" apply?'

During the **third phase**, the researcher used these themes for an initial version of a questionnaire for determining the construct of collegiality. The items or propositions were operationalizations of the construct conceived during the second phase. Examples of these items are: *'I get along well with my colleagues'*, and *'There are only a few colleagues whom I really can count on'*.

During the **fourth phase**, these items were presented to individuals from the target population. Moreover, interviews were used to determine how the items were understood and which items were unclear. Based on these interviews, the researcher decided to no longer use present items in the first person ('I ...'), but in terms of 'My colleagues ...'. In addition, the items were more closely adapted to aspects or forms of collegiality instead of the personal experience of collegiality. Consequently, the construct to be measured was refined to 'expressions of collegiality'. Finally, it turned out that collegiality contained new sub-themes such as 'cutting corners' and 'informing each other about changes in the work'.

During the **fifth phase**, a second version of the questionnaire for collegiality was drawn up. This sub-questionnaire from the *Social Climate* survey was composed of six items. The answer categories were also modified.

During the **sixth phase**, this questionnaire was again presented to samples from the target population. Based on factor analysis, it turned out that the item 'cutting corners' was not related to the other items. It was therefore removed from the third version of the list. In addition, the collection of norm data began, i.e. score files of individuals from various target populations were collected.

Further consideration shows that these six steps amount to a 'ping pong' game of conceptual reflection and practical testing, i.e. jumping back and forth between theory and empiry. The guiding principle for this 'ping pong' approach is to achieve more extensive construct clarification: the researcher is becoming increasingly clear about the concept of collegiality, both theoretically (from the literature) and in empirical terms concerning the practical experience with the relevant population. When the questionnaire is ready, we will therefore have completely answered the question, 'What is the definition of collegiality?'. Construct clarification, (i.e. theoretical reflection) and the construction of a practical measurement instrument go hand in hand. However, during further application, the questionnaire will be refined even more and will therefore be modified. But the researcher can now expect that there will be no more drastic modifications.

The final Social Climate survey consisted of 15 items: five for 'collegiality'; five for 'Communication' and five for 'Management style'.

11.6.3 Data collection from research

The data must be collected as efficiently as possible. In this respect, there was a choice between filling out questionnaires on the work floor and sending the questionnaires to the home addresses of the relevant individuals.

Sending the questionnaires by post to the home addresses had the advantage that it allowed employees to fill it out whenever they wanted to. Unfortunately, postal surveys in the past often had low response rates. People often forgot to return the questionnaire or to take it with them to work. The alternative, completing the questionnaire at work, would prevent people from forgetting to return the document.

The disadvantages of this method are that the time required to answer the questions takes time away from work and that people may lack privacy when completing the questionnaire. The latter problem was prevented by reserving a separate room for completing the questionnaires. It was decided to complete the questionnaires at work. This process takes about 15 minutes for each individual. A number of days were reserved for completing the questionnaires. On these days, someone was present in the room to answer any questions that may have arisen.

Employees were sent a personally addressed letter in which the management briefly explained the research and asked for their cooperation. The letter also discussed the procedure to be followed (the designated room and time) and explained what would happen with the data. The letter also stated the date on which a report about the study would appear in the employees' newsletter.

Preceding the letter, the study was announced in the employees' newsletter. In addition, the Employees' Work Council focused attention in its own media on the study and the role that the Council would play in the remainder of the research process.

■ 11.7 DATA ANALYSIS

The data analysis was composed of a number of steps. Firstly, it was necessary to determine whether the *Social Climate* survey was satisfactory as a research instrument. In other words, did the survey measure what it was supposed to measure and was the assumed coherence actually present? After this it was necessary to study whether the data about absenteeism and duration of goods in transit satisfied statistical demands. Only after this could the relationship between social climate, absenteeism and duration of goods in transit be investigated. Finally it was determined whether there was a possible curvilinear relationship between collegiality and absenteeism.

11.7.1 Response

Data was collected from 104 departments in total. On average, 15 individuals in each department completed the questionnaire concerning social aspects of work. This resulted in a sample size at the individual level of 1530.

11.7.2 The Social Climate survey

The first step was to study whether the *Social Climate* survey satisfied the expectations. Three elements were expected to play a role. To test these expectations, factor analysis was used.

An exploratory factor analysis was conducted on the 15 questions from the questionnaire. A maximum likelihood (ML) extraction with an oblique rotation was used. Based on the 'elbow' criterion, there are three factors: the factor loadings are shown in Table 11.2. The eigen values of the first three components are 4.73, 2.13 and 1.86: together this is 58 per cent explained variance.

The predicted structure can be seen clearly in the matrix. Factor 1 corresponds with collegiality, Factor 2 with communication and Factor 3 with a people-oriented management style. Moreover, the loading from Q12 on the factor communication is understandable.

The next step was compiling the scales based on factor analysis. But first it had to be determined whether the results of these scales satisfied the statistical requirements. Is there a reasonably normal distribution? Are the scales independent? Is there enough variance? The compiling of the scores on the three scales takes place by calculating the average of the relevant questions.

Figure 11.1 shows the frequency distribution of the three scales.

The distributions of the three scales are reasonably normal with the 'centre of gravity' on the right. It is difficult to say if a ranking according to the strength of the three scales can be made from the

Table 11.2 Pattern matrix of the questions concerning work aspects (ML factor analysis with oblique rotation)

Variable	Factor 1	Factor 2	Factor 3
Q06: Helping each other	**0.76**	0.31	0.13
Q11: Good cooperation	**0.73**	0.20	0.06
Q15: Good understanding	**0.69**	−0.10	0.15
Q01:Taking account of others	**0.65**	0.09	−0.08
Q12: Keeping each other informed	**0.59**	*0.43*	−0.12
Q03: Keeping to agreements	**0.57**	0.24	0.01
Q14: Information about changes	−0.12	**0.82**	0.13
Q04: Information from work discussions	0.03	**0.74**	−0.06
Q07: Informal contacts	0.21	**0.63**	−0.23
Q10: Picking up signals	0.14	**0.57**	0.21
Q05: Support for problems	0.10	0.21	**0.79**
Q09: Appreciate performances	−0.05	0.28	**0.74**
Q02: Insure a good atmosphere	0.23	−0.15	**0.70**
Q13: Accessible	0.12	−0.24	**0.66**
Q08: Consultation about tasks	−0.01	0.18	**0.54**

Note: Bold figures refer to large loadings on the predicted factor; italic figures refer to large loadings on other factors.

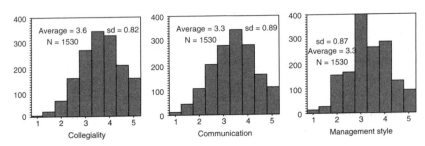

Figure 11.1 Frequency distribution of the three scales.

averages. Although an absolute answer scale (totally inapplicable to completely applicable) was used, the scales are composed of multiple questions which each have their own content: these may be easier or more difficult to answer positively. The researcher decided it was safer to limit the analysis to statements within each scale concerning the differences between individuals and the resulting differences between departments.

The correlations between the three scales are shown in Table 11.3. The three correlations differ in terms of statistical significance from 0

Table 11.3 Correlations between the three scales

	Collegiality	Communication	Management style
Collegiality	1.00	0.34	0.21
Communication		1.00	0.28
Management style			1.00

(N=1530, all $p < 0.001$). The scales are therefore certainly not independent, but the correlations are sufficiently low to be able to assume that the scales cover separate constructs.

Figure 11.2 illustrates the scale of 'Management style' on an individual department basis. This figure shows that there are significant differences between departments regarding evaluation of management style. Analogous figures can be constructed for the scales of collegiality and communication and show a comparable picture. There is therefore sufficient variation between departments to study the correlations with other data.

11.7.3 Data from existing material

Up to now, the results have been at the individual level. Absenteeism and duration of goods in transit are data that are only available at the department level. Figure 11.3 shows the distributions of these variables.

Both figures show a skewed distribution with more upward extremes than downward ones. This does not have to be a problem because the most commonly used techniques are reasonably robust against violations of normality.

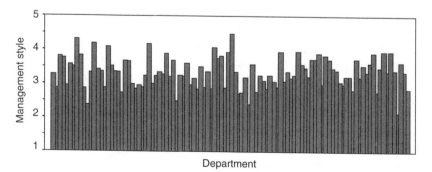

Figure 11.2 Average evaluation of management style for individual departments.

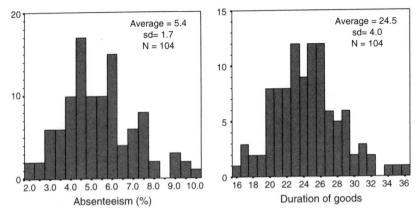

Figure 11.3 Frequency distributions of absenteeism and duration of goods in transit.

11.7.4 The relationship between social climate, absenteeism and duration of goods in transit

To be able to answer the main research questions – what is the relationship between the three scales for social work aspects and the dependent variables of absenteeism and duration of goods in transit – the data from individual employees have been aggregated on the climate scales to obtain figures for each department. Although there are other ways to obtain aggregate figures, the researcher decided to take the average. The measurement level of these variables – the interval – allows this and the average appears to be the most appropriate figure to provide a representative image of how employees view a department.

Because management style was included as a moderator variable in the final model, a hierarchical regression analysis was conducted. To this end, the three scales of collegiality, communication and management style were included as the first step as predictors of absenteeism and duration of goods in transit. The second step will test whether adding the product terms collegiality × management style and communication × management style leads to a statistically demonstrable improvement of the prediction. After all, the research model uses management style as a moderator variable. To make interpretation easier, the general average of the constituent variables was deducted from the two products.

Table 11.4 includes descriptive data from the relevant variables. The standard deviations of the three climate scales are lower now that departments have been analysed; this is because all individual variation has been filtered out.

First, the results for the dependent variable *absenteeism* will be discussed. Step 1 delivers a multiple correlation of 0.26 (7 per cent explained variance; $F (3, 100) = 2.45$; $p = 0.068$). Table 11.5 shows the results for the individual predictors.

The degree of perceived collegiality, in contrast to communication and management style, turns out to be a significant predictor of absenteeism; as collegiality is experienced as stronger, absenteeism becomes lower.

Adding the interaction terms (Step 2) insures that R goes to $0.37 (\Delta R^2 = 0.072$; $F (2, 98) = 4.08$; $p = 0.020)$. The combination of moderator effects therefore provides a significant improvement in prediction. Table 11.6 shows that collegiality × management style is responsible for this significance.

This interaction is illustrated in Figure 11.4. Realistic values have been chosen for management style: the average and two standard

Table 11.4 Descriptive data of the variables used (Mstyle = Management style)

Variable	$N=104$ M	sd	Abs.	Correlation Time in transit	Coll. Com.	Mstyle	Coll. × Msty	Com. × Msty
Absenteeism	5.4	1.7	1.00	0.16	−0.25 −0.08	−0.14	−0.20	0.02
Time in transit	24.5	4.0		1.00	0.16 −0.14	−0.18	−0.10	0.03
Collegiality	3.6	0.4			1.00 0.27	0.25	−0.25	−0.05
Communication	3.3	0.5			1.00	0.26	−0.07	0.00
Management style	3.3	0.5				1.00	0.07	0.10
Coll. × Mstyle	0.0	0.2					1.00	0.17
Comm. × Mstyle	0.1	0.2						1.00

Table 11.5 Results of the regression analysis on absenteeism: Model 1

Variable	Non-standardized coefficients		Standardized coefficient	Significance	
	B	SE	Beta	t	p
(Constant)	9.89	1.81		5.45	0.000
Collegiality	−0.97	0.43	−0.23	−2.26	0.026
Communication	0.11	0.36	0.00	0.03	0.975
Management style	−0.31	0.38	−0.08	−0.79	0.429

Table 11.6 Results of the regression analysis on absenteeism: Model 2

Variable	Non-standardized coefficients		Standardized coefficient	Significance	
	B	SE	Beta	t	p
(Constant)	10.78	1.79		6.03	0.000
Collegiality	−1.29	0.43	−0.30	−2.96	0.004
Communication	−0.02	0.35	−0.01	0.05	0.957
Management style	−0.18	0.38	−0.05	−0.47	0.642
Coll. × Mstyle	−2.62	0.92	−0.28	−2.85	0.005
Comm. × Mstyle	0.49	0.84	0.06	0.58	0.565

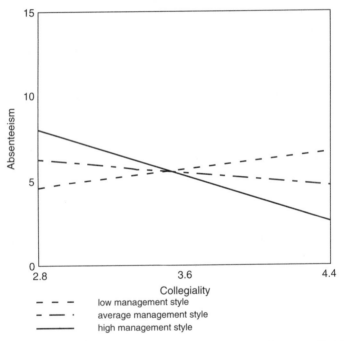

Figure 11.4 Management style as a moderator of the relationship between collegiality and absenteeism.

deviations below and above. From the figure it can be concluded that in case of a management style with little personal orientation, increasing collegiality correlates with increasing absenteeism, while with a management style that has a strong personal orientation, the expected link between collegiality and absenteeism occurs.

For the variable *duration of goods in transit,* a multiple correlation of 0.23 is obtained in Step 1 (5 per cent explained variance; $F(3, 100) = 1.83$; $p = 0.147$). From Table 11.7 it can be concluded that none of the scales provide a significant contribution to the prediction of this dependent variable. However, all coefficients do have the expected sign.

Adding the interaction terms (Step 2) insures that R goes to $0.27(\Delta R^2 = 0.02$; $F (2, 98) = 1.02$; $p = 0.364$). The combination of moderator effects therefore does not provide a significant improvement in prediction. Table 11.8 also shows that the individual terms are not statistically significant. Collegiality × management style does not have the predicted sign, but communication × management style does.

Finally it was determined whether there was a possible curvilinear relationship between collegiality and absenteeism. To this end, three groups of approximately the same size were put together based on their score for collegiality. Using analysis of variance, the relationship with absenteeism was then studied. Table 11.9 contains the descriptive

Table 11.7 Results of the regression analysis on duration of goods in transit: Model 1

Variable	Non-standardized coefficients		Standardized coefficient	Significance	
	B	SE	Beta	t	p
(Constant)	34.22	4.24		8.07	0.000
Collegiality	−1.05	1.01	−0.11	−1.04	0.300
Communication	−0.67	0.85	−0.08	−0.79	0.429
Management style	−1.13	0.90	−0.13	−1.26	0.212

Table 11.8 Result of the regression analysis on duration of goods in transit: Model 2

Variable	Non-standardized coefficients		Standardized coefficient	Significance	
	B	SE	Beta	t	p
(Constant)	35.24	4.31		8.18	0.000
Collegiality	−1.39	1.05	−0.14	−1.33	0.188
Communication	−0.71	0.85	−0.09	−0.83	0.407
Management style	−1.02	0.91	−0.12	−1.11	0.268
Coll. × Mstyle	−3.02	2.21	−0.14	−1.37	0.175
Comm. × Mstyle	1.25	2.03	0.06	0.61	0.541

Table 11.9 Descriptive data for absenteeism divided into three levels of collegiality

Collegiality	Mean	Standard deviation	N
Low	5.7	1.6	34
Middle	5.3	1.5	35
High	5.2	2.0	35
Total	**5.4**	**1.7**	**104**

Table 11.10 Results of the variance analysis on absenteeism (Collgrp = group variable for collegiality)

Source	SS	Df	MS	F	p
CollGrp	6.043	2	3.021	1.038	.358
Residue	294.120	101	2.912		
Total	300.162	103			

statistics of the three groups and Table 11.10 the results of the variance analysis.

Although the averages show a somewhat flattening decline, it turns out that the three groups do not differ from each other significantly. The fact that the relationship between collegiality and absenteeism is not demonstrated here, but does emerge from the regression analysis, probably has to do with the coarseness of the information and the possible non-inclusion of other relevant variables in the variance analysis.

In summary it can be stated that:

- The *Social Climate* survey is a valid instrument that provides insight into three factors.
- Duration of goods in transit is independent from both management style and the social climate of the department.
- There was a link between collegiality and absenteeism.
- Management style and collegiality together do have an effect on absenteeism; management style with little personal orientation and an increasing collegiality correlate with increasing absenteeism, while if there is a strongly people-oriented management style, the expected link between collegiality and absenteeism occurs; as collegiality is experienced as being stronger, there is less absenteeism.

▌ 11.8 REPORTING

11.8.1 Target group

Earlier it was argued that there are more parties who are interested in this study than just the management. These interested parties are the employees, the Employees' Work Council, the Trade Union, science and commerce.

Every target group is interested in different parts of the research.

- Management: what is the cause of the complaints about the duration of goods in transit and absenteeism, and what can we do about it?
- The Employees' Council and the Trade Union have a comparable interest, but are primarily interested in the policy recommendations to reduce absenteeism and improve management style.
- Science: can we indeed measure the social climate of an organization and use this together with management style as a predictor for absenteeism and the quality of service?
- Commerce: how does the instrument work and where else can we use it?

11.8.2 Structure of the report

Since every target group has different interests in the research, in each report the emphasis was placed on different aspects of the research. To limit the quantity of work, it was agreed that a management report would be drawn up for the Transpost management and sent in unmodified form to the Employees' Council. In addition, a more extensive report was drawn up that contained all other information relevant to the organization. Finally a scientific article was written.

The management report emphasized the conclusions and the recommendations. The management report consisted of three parts:

1. The management report: a summary of the research, conclusions and recommendations.

2. A more extensive introduction with the process leading up to the research and the aims of the research, a summary of the research and the conclusions.
3. Recommendations.

The more extensive report emphasized the results for each research question. These results were discussed as much as possible in the text and illustrated with graphs. Tables were used only to support the text. The results were illustrated with well-chosen quotes from the respondents. The extensive report contained:

1. An introduction to the process leading up to the research and the aims of the research.
2. The design of the research.
3. The response.
4. A description of the respondent group.
5. The research results for each research question.
6. Conclusions.

In the scientific article that was published about this research, three elements were emphasized: the position of the research in the scientific framework, the construction of the *Social Climate* survey and the scientific value of this survey.

The article had the following structure:

1. A short summary of the research question, the method of research, analysis and results.
2. Theoretical framework.
3. Derived hypotheses.
4. Method of research.
5. Description of the response and the respondents.
6. Analysis technique used and the results of the various steps.
7. Conclusions and recommendations for further research.

▮ 11.9 PRESENTATION

11.9.1 What is the target group?

For the presentation, the various target groups should still be taken account of and the presentations made accordingly.

Two presentations were given within Transpost: one for the management and a short presentation for the Central Employees' Council. A brief article was also published in the employees' newsletter. Finally, a scientific presentation was given by means of a poster presentation at a congress.

11.9.2 Which means are appropriate to the form of presentation?

The presentation for management took place during a management meeting and lasted 30 minutes. Ten minutes were reserved for questions and discussion. A handout was used (the management report) in combination with an overhead sheet presentation. The presentation primarily emphasized the results and the reasons behind the recommendations.

The presentation for the employee participation bodies was held during a meeting of the Central Employees' Council. The presentation lasted 45 minutes and primarily emphasized the conclusions of the research and the consequences of the recommendations. The members of the Employees' Council were given both the management report and the extensive report. Because there are many members in the Central Employees' Council, overhead sheets were used for visual support. The most important points were shown on the overhead sheets by means of keywords or short sentences. Numerical information was shown by means of drawings and diagrams. The actual presentation lasted 20 minutes; the remaining time was reserved for questions and discussion.

The article in the employees' newsletter focused on the research as part of a special issue. This issue included not only the short report of the researcher, but also interviews with the chair of the Central Employees' Council, the company director, a department head and an employee. In addition, the Central Employees' Council discussed its further role in the research in its own column. The report of the researcher primarily dealt with the operational method of the research, the response, the results and the conclusions. A reply coupon was also included which could be used to order a copy of the complete report.

A poster presentation during a conference is characterized by the fact that the audience must be able to read the text and understand the intention of the poster without the researcher providing an explanation. The researcher decided to use a layout with blocks of text in a large font, alternating with models and tables. The title and headings had to be readable from a distance of two metres in order to attract attention. The text had to be readable from one metre. Colour was used to attract the attention of conference participants. The poster primarily dealt with the construction of the *Social Climate* survey and the analyses and results. The poster ended with recommendations for follow-up research. For interested readers, a handout was available (the material on the poster in a normal sized font).

FURTHER READING

Literature about the research question

Campbell, J.P., Daft, R.L. and Hulin, C.L. (1982). *What to Study: Generating and Developing Research Questions*. Beverly Hills, CA: Sage.

Literature about literature research

Cook, T.D. and Leviton, L.C. (1980). Reviewing the literature: a comparison of traditional methods with meta-analysis. *Journal of Personality*, **48**, 449–72.
Cooper, H.M. (1982). Scientific guidelines for conducting integrative research review. *Review of Educational Research*, **5**, 3–8.

Literature about research strategies

Runkel, P.J. and McGrath, J.E. (1972). *Research on Human Behavior*: A systematic Guide to Method New York: Holt, Rinehart & Winston.

General literature about case studies

Andrieu, M. (1977). Benefit cost evaluation. In L. Rutman (ed.), *Evaluation Research Methods: A Basic Guide* London: Sage, pp. 219–32.
Easton, G. (1992). *Learning from Case Studies*, 2nd edn. London: Prentice Hall.
Yin, R.K. (1984). *Case Study Research. Design and Methods*, 2nd edn. London: Sage.

Practical suggestions for case studies

Buchanan, D., Boddy, D. and McCalman, J. (1988). Getting in, getting on, getting out, and getting back. In Bryman (ed.), *Doing Research in Organizations*. London: Routledge, pp. 53–67.

Experiments

Cook, T.D. and Campbell, D.T. (1979). *Quasi-experimentation. Design and Analysis Issues for Field Settings*. Boston: Houghton Mifflin.

Literature about interviewing

Dillman, D.A. (1978). *Mail and Telephone Surveys*. New York: Wiley.

Literature about data analysis/statistics

Hair, J.F., Anderson, R.E., Tatham, R.L. and Black, W.C. (1996). *Multivariate Data Analysis, with Readings*. New York: Macmillan.

Appendix

CHECKLIST FOR EVALUATING RESEARCH REPORTS

▌▌ AIM AND RESEARCH QUESTION

- Have you clearly described the aim of the research and the reason for choosing this research topic?
- Have you made it clear whether the research question is descriptive, explorative or analytical?
- Have you described the research question clearly and completely and is it precisely delineated?
- Do the sub-questions emerge logically from the main research question?
- Are the concepts well defined and used consistently throughout the report?

▌▌ CONTENT

- Is the research report scientifically and socially relevant?
- Does the report have depth/originality? Does it provide additional knowledge?
- Does the research report have a solid scientific and theoretical foundation? (For example, a complete overview of the relevant theory, the current state of knowledge in books and especially in international journals and a correct choice of adequate models.)
- Have interesting hypotheses been formulated (if applicable)?
- Are the data collection methods adequate for the research topic? (For example a sample from a research population that is representative for the research topic; a fully explained methodology; the level of non-response and the reasons for this; a detailed description of the measurement instrument in terms of reliability, validity,

re-coding and composition; and a good explanation about why the relevant statistical analysis techniques were chosen.)

- Have the results been presented correctly and objectively on the basis of the sequence of hypotheses where your own opinion is clearly distinguished from the facts?
- Based on the research question, are the conclusions adequately attuned to the results and derived from them in a completely logical fashion?
- Does the research report have a complete and adequate discussion? (For example, a discussion of the results with a reference to the theoretical framework, alternative explanations for the results and the shortcomings of the research.)
- Are good recommendations made in the report? (For example, recommendations for theory, the relevance of the research for practice and recommendations for future research.)
- Is the abstract short, complete, readable independently from the report, and does it contain no new information?

STRUCTURE

- Is the report clearly structured? (For example, a unifying theme, a consistent and logical line of reasoning, a clear distinction between primary and secondary issues, a step-by-step treatment of the material and a clear structure shown by the division into appropriate chapters and sections.)

WRITING STYLE AND APPEARANCE

- Is the title of the report brief, attractive and does it reflect the actual content of the report?
- Does the report specify the research framework, the date, and the names of the author, thesis supervisor and clients (if applicable)?
- Are references to literature given correctly in the text and in the reference list?
- Is the discussion of the literature research clearly distinguished from your own opinion?
- Are standpoints clearly argued and supported?
- Is the research report carefully prepared? (For example, the writing style, cross references and layout.)

INDEX